# PLANNING FOR CHANGE IN TURBULENT TIMES

## The case of multiracial primary schools

Mike Wallace and Agnes McMahon

CASSELL

Cassell
Villiers House            387 Park Avenue South
41/47 Strand             New York
London WC2N 5JE          NY 10016-8810

First published 1994

**British Library Cataloguing-in-Publication Data**
A catalogue record for this book is available from the British Library.

ISBN  0-304-32674-7 (hardback)
       0-304-32676-3 (paperback)

Typeset by Colset Private Limited, Singapore
Printed and bound in Great Britain by
Redwood Books, Trowbridge, Wiltshire

# Contents

# Series Editors' Foreword

Development planning has recently become an increasingly popular strategy for school improvement. Building on the experience of schemes for school self-evaluation or school-based review in the 1980s, development planning in the UK has, in the 1990s, become a more inclusive and sophisticated school-based strategy for managing change.

Development planning, like school self-evaluation in the previous decade, however, suffers from a contradiction in purpose. To some it is a strategy for development, for others it is a bureaucratic device to ensure uniformity and control. This contradiction inevitably results in a confusion of method and often a cynicism on the part of those responsible for and subject to the plan.

There is another, more profound problem with development plans. It is that the planning process, most often in its bureaucratic form, distorts the reality of change in schools. Plans often assume a degree of rationality that is seldom reflected in the daily life of teachers and students. The aspirations of many plans are not reflected in the hearts and minds of those responsible for implementing the plan.

In *Planning for Change in Turbulent Times* Mike Wallace and Agnes McMahon, through their incisive case studies, confront in an authentic and resonant way the practicalities of planning in today's primary schools. They expose the fallacies and limitations of the 'development plan as a blueprint for change' approach and present a more realistic and dialectical view of how planning supports the management of change in schools. This study, by linking a wide-ranging review of theoretical perspectives to the practicalities of change in primary schools, increases and enriches our understanding not only of planning as a school improvement strategy, but also of the broader process of development in primary schools during an era of change.

David Hopkins
David Reynolds

# Acknowledgements

This study was made possible through a substantial grant from the Leverhulme Trust, and we are most grateful to the Trustees for their confidence in supporting our work. The foundation for the research was laid in an earlier exploratory project on the management of multiple innovations funded by the Economic and Social Research Council. The present research constitutes an outcome of that investment. We would like to acknowledge the help of the headteachers, staff and the chairs of governors of the case-study schools, the headteachers of the survey schools and LEA staff who were so willing to make time for our interviews under the often extremely difficult circumstances portrayed in this book. We have been ably supported by Ray Bolam, Valerie Hall, Eric Hoyle and David Oldroyd, our present or past colleagues at the National Development Centre for Educational Management and Policy, and by June Collins, Angela Allen, Norma Meechem and Joan Moore, the secretarial staff. Mike Wallace would like to express his thanks to Sue Sheridan and Max Brittain for their hospitality. He appreciates enormously the loyalty and forbearance of Liz Lindsay in both creating the conditions for writing and putting up with the consequences.

# Abbreviations

DES       Department of Education and Science
DFE       Department for Education
ESL        English as a second language
HMI       Her Majesty's Inspectors
LEA       Local Education Authority
LMS       Local management of schools
NCC       National Curriculum Council
QTS        Qualified-teacher status
SACRE    Standing Advisory Council on Religious Education
SATs       Standard Assessment Tasks
SEAC      School Examinations and Assessment Council
Section 11 Mechanism for funding posts for specialist minority ethnic group support staff

# Chapter 1

# Introduction

Social life is riddled with contradictions, and school management is no exception. A central theme of this book is that planning for change must address a tension between two contradictory influences: planning based on annual cycles for long-term coherence versus more or less continual, incremental planning for short-term flexibility. On the one hand, a planning process based on annual cycles enables priorities to be established and a coherent direction for medium- and long-term development to be sustained. Yet in frequently and often unpredictably changing circumstances, cyclic planning can lead to rigidity, with plans becoming increasingly irrelevant to current concerns. On the other hand, incremental or step-by-step planning gives the flexibility rapidly to modify existing plans and to create new ones whenever changing circumstances dictate the need. Yet loss of coherence and duplication of effort may result from plans which are not connected to long-term aims. In extreme cases such an approach may amount to little more than day-to-day crisis management. There appears to be no simple middle ground between long- and medium-term planning and short-term flexibility.

We will argue that the origin of this contradiction lies in the shifting balance between environmental turbulence, favouring an approach to planning which protects short-term flexibility, and environmental stability, which makes possible planning for long-term coherence. *Turbulence* refers to changes in information and practice relating to the internal environment of an organization, and to changes in information about demands coming from the external environment. Conversely, *stability* means the continuance of existing practice within the organization, uninfluenced by internal changes or changes in external demands. Schools are organizations where there may be turbulence in some areas while others are stable. While it is unlikely that every aspect of a school will be turbulent, this study is concerned with schools where the balance of turbulence and stability is weighted heavily towards the former.

In this first chapter we explain our reasoning behind the research focus to which our overarching theme relates; examine the context of national and local policies which have in large part forced planning for change in schools to balance coherence with flexibility; look in detail at development planning, widely heralded as a solution to the problem of planning in such an environment; provide a rationale for the theoretical orientation of our work; summarize our research methods; and introduce the rest of the book.

# RATIONALE FOR THE RESEARCH

This was an investigation of how planning for change, which entails finding some working resolution of the tension between seeking coherence and retaining flexibility, was managed in schools operating within a turbulent environment. Arguably, in comparison with other schools in England during the early 1990s, staff in multiracial schools in the primary sector faced the maximum range of changes in challenging and culturally diverse contexts. The aims of our research were twofold: to explore how planning to implement a multiplicity of innovations, and to respond to other changes, was carried out in circumstances of environmental turbulence; and to identify planning structures, procedures and processes that appeared to be effective. The study therefore had a management (as opposed to a multicultural and antiracist education) focus. Multiracial schools were chosen because of our hunch that the context of cultural diversity gave rise to additional changes with which staff and governors of culturally homogeneous schools would not have to cope. Planning in multiracial primary schools was influenced by changes connected with multicultural and antiracist education, together with other changes linked with their community.

We were aware that an unprecedented array of largely externally imposed changes associated with the central government reform agenda placed an equally unprecedented and externally imposed demand upon planning in schools if their staff were to cope effectively. Not all school staff faced the same innovation overload, although it is unlikely that any teacher enjoyed a quiet life in the early 1990s. Primary-sector schools (including middle schools for pupils up to the age of 12) appeared to be disadvantaged in three ways.

First, most primary-school staff in England, as generalist class teachers, were required by legislation to implement changes of varying magnitude in nine of the ten subjects within the National Curriculum, along with religious education; by contrast, as subject specialists, most secondary-school colleagues could concentrate on one or two. Second, primary staff generally had less experience with planning for large-scale, externally initiated innovations than their secondary counterparts. The Technical and Vocational Education Initiative and its extension and the General Certificate of Secondary Education examination had affected virtually all secondary schools in the late 1980s. Third, little or no non-contact time during the teaching day was available in primary schools compared with a substantial allowance in secondary schools because of a historical inequality in staffing ratios between the two phases (Alexander *et al.*, 1992). Much work of planning for change in primary schools had to take place outside the teaching day.

Those primary schools serving a multiracial community seemed to face the greatest challenge in coping with the new planning task. According to Tansley and Croft (1984), approximately 10 per cent of primary schools have at least 10 per cent of pupils whose first language is other than English. On this definition, and if we include pupils from a minority ethnic background whose first language is English, over one-tenth of primary schools serve multiracial communities. Pupils from minority ethnic groups have distinctive educational needs if they are to gain full access to their entitlement to a state education, in addition to needs shared with the majority ethnic group. For example, those pupils whose first language is not English need support as bilingual learners with gaining fluency in English, which will be their main medium of instruction and so a gateway to the rest of the curriculum. Some changes affecting multiracial primary schools are designed to address certain of these needs.

Such schools are to be found mainly in urban and inner-city areas, since most minority ethnic communities are concentrated in towns and major conurbations. The 1991 census figures on people from minority ethnic groups show that they tend to live in the largest cities, while there has been a shift within the white population into the surrounding suburban and more rural areas. Overall, whites have moved to areas of greater prosperity (Owen, 1992). In many inner-city areas both minority and majority ethnic groups endure economic and social deprivation, although the social and economic circumstances of black pupils and parents from minority ethnic groups are uniquely affected by racism (House of Commons, 1985). Her Majesty's Inspectors (HMI) recently highlighted how, in the primary phase, 'two thirds of the inner city schools (as compared with one third nationally) had significant proportions of disadvantaged pupils' (Alexander et al., 1992). We were concerned that central government reforms might impose the greatest innovation load upon schools whose pupils had the most pressing educational needs, so threatening their education and hence potential for social mobility. This concern rendered all the more pressing our search for ways of planning for change that might work in such an environment.

## Earlier exploratory research: the multiple-innovations project

Our focus grew out of earlier exploratory work with a broader remit: to examine how school staff managed the implementation of multiple innovations, with a view to developing theory on the management of planned change (Wallace, 1991a). Four schools in the same local education authority (LEA), regarded by LEA staff as effective in coping with change, were studied. A significant finding was that the compulsory development planning initiative (which LEA staff had recently introduced) was little used to guide planning in the schools. Yet it had been designed to support planning to implement the variety of other innovations originating within the schools, the LEA and central government. While the relevant document had been completed and a copy sent to the LEA as required, staff subsequently modified some existing plans that had been contained within the document and created new plans without reference to it. Paradoxically, the 'top-down' compulsory innovation of development planning was intended to increase the 'bottom-up' capacity for self-determination in the schools. Staff in these institutions appeared to have used their capacity for self-determination by superficially implementing this innovation while relying upon different, more flexible and largely undocumented means of managing the implementation of other innovations.

The assumption within the LEA's development planning initiative that plans could be laid for a year at a time seemed not to allow for the incremental strategy - often unpredictable at school and LEA levels - adopted by central government ministers for introducing national reforms. The schools were forced to respond as each new requirement was announced, whether or not it was included in the priorities in the development plan. The question arose whether the approach to planning for change must in some way be contingent upon the context. Significant factors included:

- the range of innovations to be introduced;
- their origin, since staff were reliant on sources at other levels in the education service for the information necessary to implement external innovations;
- their focus, as some innovations like the development planning initiative were designed to influence how the implementation of multiple innovations was managed;
- the ways in which central and local government introduced reforms;
- the degree of control at school level over the choice of innovations, their content, and when they were introduced.

The present study was intended to enable hypotheses emerging from the multiple innovations project to be refined by focusing more narrowly upon the process of planning for change in schools coping with a highly turbulent environment.

## THE POLICY CONTEXT

Environmental turbulence for multiracial primary schools originates at three levels within the education system. The internal school environment is one source. Headteachers, in particular, have the authority to instigate school-wide change according to their educational and managerial beliefs and values, and governors have increasing powers under the local management of schools initiative (LMS) to set a direction for development. The multiple innovations project indicated that headteachers were the prime movers of change, especially in the early years of their headship. This finding is in line with other research in the United Kingdom (Weindling and Earley, 1987; Nias *et al.*, 1989) and the United States (Hall and Hord, 1987) where many principals of elementary schools adopted the role of 'initiator'.

Governors of the multiple innovations project schools generally supported the professional staff, rather than pushing for change themselves, although they had the powers to do so. It is probable that the national picture is more varied, with much greater intervention by some governing bodies. Teachers have considerable control over initiatives at the level of their own classroom and the area of management responsibility that many hold. Other factors giving rise to turbulence may not be directly related to innovations, yet require a planned response. They may include occasional short-term crises, such as widespread illness among staff; and longer-term issues, like high staff turnover.

A second source of turbulence, in the external environment of schools, lies in the activities of LEA staff and members of the local council. LEA staff have developed policies to be implemented in schools in accordance with the wishes of councillors, such as promoting equal opportunities or formation of primary-school clusters (e.g. Galton *et al.*, 1991), which are unconnected or only distantly linked with central government interests. A few LEAs have engaged in large-scale interventions into primary schooling (e.g. Alexander, 1992). Increasingly within recent years, LEA initiatives concerning schools have been taken in response to central government concerns, whether directly, as in local LMS schemes, or indirectly, as in reorganization of the schooling system to remove surplus pupil places. LEAs are being restructured as their role is being forced by central government legislation to shift towards providing those services that staff and governors within increasingly autonomous schools are willing to purchase (Brown and Baker, 1991).

When our present study began, a major innovation for LEAs was to develop new structures and procedures for school inspection and for provision of advice and training support to school staff. Governors and staff in schools were having to familiarize themselves with the emerging arrangements, while many LEA staff with whom they normally dealt were being transferred to new roles or were facing redundancy.

## Increasing central government influence

The dominant source of environmental turbulence for English schools in recent years is massive central government intervention, building up from the mid-1980s. Policies for education reform affecting primary schools include:

- a National Curriculum, divided into separate subjects (in contrast with the integrated approach widespread in primary schools), and phased in year by year;
- assessment of the National Curriculum, whose results are published;
- tighter regulation of religious education and a daily collective act of worship;
- an increasing proportion of parents and local community representatives on governing bodies;
- responsibility for financial management and the appointment and dismissal of staff falling to headteachers and governors under LMS;
- nationally imposed salaries, conditions of service and promotion structure;
- a budget for staff development with an annual entitlement of school closure days - 'training days' - available for in-service training;
- biennial appraisal of all teaching staff;
- open enrolment of pupils to promote competition between neighbouring schools within the same phase;
- the possibility of individual schools opting out of LEA control and becoming funded directly by central government;
- the duty imposed upon LEAs of developing local schemes within certain central government reforms such as LMS and appraisal,

supporting schools with the implementation of reforms, and monitoring and inspection. (More recent legislation has largely removed the latter LEA duty by privatizing inspections.)

These policies represent 'statements of prescriptive intent' (Kogan, 1975) that are translated into narrower innovations which, in turn, may be defined as planned changes representing a significant shift in the practice of those who implement them (Rogers and Shoemaker, 1971). Central government policies generally lead to innovations that are initiated by people at a higher level in the education service than the schools where they are to be implemented, whether they are within central government agencies like the National Curriculum Council (NCC) and the School Examinations and Assessment Council (SEAC), or belong to an LEA group such as an LMS unit. The multiple innovations project findings suggested that, as policymakers outside schools do not normally spend much time in them, they are likely to be relatively unaware how an innovation for schools arising from a new policy fits in with what staff there are already doing (Wallace, 1991b). One reason may lie in policymakers' focus upon a policy or its associated innovation in isolation from the setting where it will be implemented. Innovations are never introduced into a vacuum: they are addressed by those who have to implement them within the framework of existing practice which includes other innovations and the rest of ongoing work.

Certain central government policies are particularly significant for multiracial primary schools. Changes demanded by parts of the ethnocentric National Curriculum, for example, do not closely match the multicultural approach adopted in many of these schools. Stipulation within the 1988 Education Reform Act that the daily collective act of worship must be 'predominantly Christian', unless schools apply to the local Standing Advisory Council on Religious Education (SACRE) set up in each LEA for 'determination', does not square with the hitherto widespread multifaith approach to assemblies; nor does the demand in the Act that religious education 'shall reflect the fact that the religious traditions in Great Britain are in the main Christian whilst taking account of the teaching and practices of the other principal religions represented in Great Britain'. However, vagueness of the wording within the 1988 Education Reform Act has led one legal expert to suggest that it will be possible for the new provisions to be reinterpreted or even disregarded (Poulter, 1990).

The policies outlined above are the responsibility of the Department for Education (DFE), until 1992 called the Department of Education and Science (DES). An additional policy change with unique significance for multiracial schools originates with another department.

## Section 11

The Home Office has been the main source of additional funding for the provision of specialist support for pupils from minority ethnic groups in schools since it was introduced through Section 11 of the Local Government Act 1966 (Bagley, 1992). Local authorities are reimbursed at the rate of 75 per cent of expenditure for 'special provision in the exercise of any of their functions in consequence of the presence within their areas of substantial numbers of people from the

Commonwealth whose language and customs differ from those of the rest of the community' (Home Office, 1990a). It is intended to 'tackle issues particular to ethnic minority groups that prevent them from entering fully into mainstream activities'. This funding source is restricted to the salaries of staff engaged in meeting needs of people with origins in New Commonwealth countries other than Britain. The legislation therefore prohibits support via Section 11 posts for pupils from minority ethnic groups who have recently come from countries elsewhere, such as refugees from Vietnam, Somalia or Iraq.

The way in which Section 11 funding was administered at central government and LEA levels over many years resulted in what Young and Connelly (1981) referred to as 'something of a lottery for schools'. A Home Office 'scrutiny' was undertaken towards the end of the last decade which entailed visits to local authorities and schools and consultation with interested groups. The scrutineers found that 'there is no clear view of what the Section 11 grant is intended to achieve, what more detailed objectives should be pursued, or the mechanism for assessing performance' (Home Office, 1989). Examples of good practice were reported where provision was targeted upon the needs of minority ethnic groups, but there was also abuse of the system:

> At its best we saw Section 11 funding additional provision to meet extreme need in ways which might not have been possible without additional targeted financing. Standing in schools in some areas with 80% or 90% of the children from non-English speaking backgrounds it was difficult to comprehend how a school would succeed in teaching English, without additional people and the opportunity to employ members of the community with bilingual skills. Yet unless such schools are successful the children will be deprived of the basic skills necessary to play a full part in society.
>
> ... At worst we saw Section 11 used to fund token ethnic minority posts within institutions which were making no effort to adjust to ethnic minority needs. The creation of posts could lead to an assumption that all ethnic minority problems were to be pushed in the direction of Section 11 postholders, with no thought of all staff having a responsibility towards all clients. There were arguments that some local authorities continued to use Section 11 to subsidise what should have been mainstream provision ... the objective of maintaining revenue had become a more important motivation for some local authorities than judging the effectiveness of provision made.
>
> (pp. 19-20)

The scrutiny recommended measures within existing legislation to specify objectives and introduce procedures for monitoring and demonstrating to the Home Office the effectiveness of provision in meeting identified needs of minority ethnic groups. It also recommended new legislation to remove a serious inequity linked with the concept of 'Commonwealth immigrant' built into the Act. This notion was reported to be offensive to individuals from a minority ethnic background who were British citizens born in this country. The restriction of provision to people from the New Commonwealth should be removed and a wider definition of eligible groups should be adopted. Those black groups who suffer similar racial disadvantage to New Commonwealth groups should be included, but whites, such as Poles and Ukrainians (who were less likely to suffer racial discrimination), should not.

The Home Office response was radically to tighten the procedure for allocation of grants within the parameters of existing legislation (Home Office, 1990b). Local authorities are now required to bid competitively each year for grant support. All provision is required to meet new criteria and specific Home Office objectives. For schools, these objectives cover language and learning skills of pre-school-age children; support with learning English as a second language; promoting achievement in all areas of the curriculum; strengthening links between schools and parents; and provision of pastoral support. Work must take place in mainstream classrooms whenever possible.

The objectives exclude initiatives undertaken previously in a number of LEAs to provide broader cultural support, to develop multicultural and anti-racist education and to promote equal opportunities in schools. The Home Office (1990c) policy statement for the administration of Section 11 grant claims that:

> The Government fully recognises the benefits that derive from the maintenance of religious, artistic, cultural and linguistic traditions among ethnic minority communities. It does not, however, consider Section 11 grant to be an appropriate use for initiatives aimed at such purposes.

> (p. 3)

A recent survey of LEAs (Taylor, 1992) indicates that central government reforms designed to restrict their powers, coupled with a lack of awareness among some elected members and school governors and pressure on schools to implement the National Curriculum, have led to multicultural and antiracist education generally being accorded a lower priority.

Rather than base support on the number of posts required to meet the special needs of all pupils from minority ethnic groups which mainstream funding does not cover, the Home Office now gives grants for focused and time-limited 'projects'. While staff posts might constitute a project, Section 11 funding for such posts will be guaranteed only for its duration, normally limited to three years but possibly extended up to five. Extension of projects beyond the original termination date is subject to the acceptance of a new bid in a subsequent year. Local authorities have to accept the possible financial implications if contracts for staff funded through Section 11 are to be offered on a longer-term basis than the ending of the current project. An allowance is made for teachers who held a mainstream post hitherto and are now taking on work funded through Section 11 to receive in-service training related to the needs of pupils from minority ethnic groups. Grants under the new system started in April 1992, although the Home Office notified some LEAs considerably earlier where their projects were approved in principle.

This policy shift was interpreted locally in different ways. In some LEAs, school staff had to complete a bid which was collated by the LEA; in others the bidding procedure was carried out by a central team and minority ethnic group support staff were subsequently allocated to schools. The competitive bidding procedure is increasingly a feature of central government policies in which LEAs bid for financial support to a ceiling dictated by central government. Where schools contribute to bids, staff have to plan to introduce an innovation with no guarantee that the resources for implementation will be secured.

Other central government policies not directly connected with education have also made an impact on local services to schools. A notable example is the community charge or poll tax, a locally collected tax which contributed to funding of education. Elected members in many LEAs sought cuts in spending on education to avoid being 'charge-capped' by central government (which imposed a limit on the amount of tax that could be gathered locally), or to influence the local electorate by keeping down the size of the community charge.

## DEVELOPMENT PLANNING

A central government policy with critical importance for the process of planning for change in schools is the DES requirement, since 1989, that the central government grant to enable LEAs to fulfil their duty to support schools with the implementation of national reforms is conditional upon LEAs ensuring that schools have an annual 'national curriculum development plan' (DES, 1988a). Virtually all LEAs have responded to this demand by introducing, with central government approval, the more comprehensive innovation for schools of completing school development plans. Most are compulsory, as in the case of the LEA investigated in the multiple innovations project. They generally prescribe both a consultative planning process and a document in which priorities and implementation plans are recorded, but compulsion in practice tends to be restricted to the document. Formal planning and review processes were developed throughout the last decade, influenced by central government demands that schools should be externally accountable. Some LEA staff have worked on development planning for schools since the mid-1980s (e.g. Enfield, 1985), and the former Chief HMI, Norman Thomas, advocated development plans to coordinate in-service training in primary schools (ILEA, 1985; House of Commons, 1986).

A major development project, funded by the DES and directed by Hargreaves and Hopkins, drew together experience in fourteen LEAs and a sample of their schools. A key outcome was two advice documents (DES, 1989a, 1991a). The first of these documents, sent to all English LEAs and schools, advocates school development planning as a key to integrating the various demands upon planning for change:

> The distinctive feature of a development plan is that it brings together, *in an overall plan*, national and LEA policies and initiatives, the school's aims and values, its existing achievements and its needs for development. By coordinating aspects of planning which are otherwise separate, the school acquires a shared sense of direction and is able to

control and manage the tasks of development and change. Priorities for development are planned in detail for one year and are supported by action plans or working documents for staff. The priorities for later years are sketched in outline to provide the longer term programme.

(DES, 1989a, p. 4)

The planning process is based on annual cycles, each consisting of four sequential processes or stages:

*audit*: a school reviews its strengths and weaknesses;

*plan construction*: priorities for development are selected and then turned into specific targets;

*implementation*: of the planned priorities and targets;

*evaluation*: the success of implementation is checked.

(p. 5)

Detailed plans are made for the year ahead, and for the next two in outline. At the end of the initial cycle, detailed plans for the following year are made with reference to the outline plans made previously. In this way the development plan rolls forward at the beginning of each year, 'leaving room in the plan to meet future demands arising from national or local initiatives and the school's changing needs'. Environmental turbulence is taken into account through the annual renewal and updating of the plan. Agreement on priorities and targets at the plan-construction stage is to be followed by the development of detailed action plans which include the identification of 'success criteria' by which progress with implementation may be monitored.

It is recognized that implementation of plans might not be straightforward. The implementation and evaluation stages are regarded as 'interlaced, not as a period of implementation followed by a "big bang" evaluation at the end. If implementation and evaluation are linked, evaluation can help to shape and guide the action plan rather than being a *post mortem* upon it'. Through regular progress checks, formative evaluation enables adjustments to be made within the plan for any priority, in addition to the summative evaluation at the end of the cycle. This component of the model also allows for environmental turbulence (which might cause, say, delay in implementing a priority) but only within priorities agreed during the annual plan construction process.

This approach influenced a report by the Audit Commission (1991) on LMS and budgetary planning within the primary-school planning process, covering both maintenance and development activities. Resource considerations should be integrated within a cyclic process similar to the one described above. It is argued that the 'process of school planning is a continuous one, all stages of which can and should take place all the time. Schools should draw together their thinking about needs and resources in a development plan which serves educational purposes and pupils' interests.' Yet the cycle advocated in the report belies such a continuous process, since it does not cover the possibility of ongoing adjustment of plans in response to changes in circumstances connected with maintenance activities or developments with budgetary implications.

Governors are viewed as taking final decisions on the development plan, the preparation of which is to be led by the headteacher.

## LEA development planning initiatives

The advice from both these quarters does not extend to any recommended documentation. However, not only was it distilled from LEA practice, but it also appears formatively to have influenced many LEA staff, some of whom have published their development planning documents and advice, making them widely available to school staff throughout the country (e.g. Sheffield Education Department, 1991; Warwickshire County Council, 1991; Bradford Education, 1992). The DES advice document has had a significant impact on schools. According to a national survey of governing bodies carried out in the 1990 spring term, 60 per cent of headteachers who had elected to be governors had used it and, of these, 90 per cent had found it helpful (Keys and Fernandes, 1990).

Research currently under way on development planning in primary schools (Mortimore *et al.*, forthcoming), which began with a survey in 1992 of LEAs throughout the United Kingdom, indicates the spread of LEA initiatives. A policy that all primary schools should have a development plan existed in 90 per cent of LEAs. About 75 per cent of respondents reported that all, or almost all, schools had development plans in 1991/2.

Many LEA development planning initiatives for schools were designed to serve three purposes for which, under recent policy shifts, LEAs were held accountable to central government: helping to guide development activity in schools (in covering the requirement that they have a National Curriculum development plan); collecting information needed annually by LEAs for supporting development through, for example, provision of in-service training programmes; and collecting information which LEA staff may use in monitoring and formal inspections. Mortimore and his colleagues found that 80 per cent of LEAs referred to school development plans in their monitoring role and 60 per cent used them in supporting development work in schools. Over half required school staff to submit a completed document while one-third required a summary of priorities.

Preparatory training, especially for headteachers, commonly emphasized a consultative approach to annual review, decision-making and planning. Written guidance was frequently issued to schools on the process to be followed in drawing up, implementing and evaluating the plan each year. A completed document provided LEA staff with information needed for whichever purposes the initiative was designed to fulfil, accounting for the length and sophistication of some documents, running to twenty pages or more. In some cases an LEA inspector linked with the school was to be involved in drawing up the plan, a copy of which was retained by LEA staff.

Published handbooks (e.g. Skelton *et al.*, 1991; Davies and Ellison, 1992; Hargreaves and Hopkins, 1991) represent an additional resource promoting development planning. The various models put forward have a common form: sequential cycles of review, planning, implementation and evaluation lasting between one and three years. Most of these cyclic models have been trialled in schools in some way, and therefore have proven to be of value in guiding planning, at least when they were developed. Yet environmental turbulence following from central government reforms has certainly increased since the fieldwork connected with some of these models.

Some adopt the financial year as the basis for the cycle; others use the academic year. Whichever cycle is chosen for a development planning model, schools actually have to deal with both. A variety of influences could account for the widespread adoption of cyclic models. Factors may include a long tradition in schools of planning for the academic year; familiarity within many LEAs with models for school self-review (e.g. ILEA, 1977; McMahon et al., 1984) based on occasional cycles and developed at a time when the context of schooling was reasonably stable; central government imposition upon LEAs of a planning cycle for in-service training grants and LMS, based upon the financial year; the associated requirement that schools complete a financial management plan for each financial year (DES, 1988b); the central government timetable for introducing the National Curriculum based on the academic year; and, in some LEAs, the popularity of a handbook advocating a yearly 'collaborative planning cycle' (Caldwell and Spinks, 1988), based upon the experience of cyclic planning in a Tasmanian school.

Development planning represents an innovation for LEAs as well as schools, and in some cases has undergone modifications as central government policies have unfolded. LEA initiatives vary in the comprehensiveness of what is included within development plans. Some focus solely upon the curriculum and associated staff development; others include the possibility of identifying additional priorities, like appraisal, as innovations to be implemented; and, with increasing experience of LMS in the early 1990s, financial management has frequently been integrated within the development plan process and documentation. Some LEAs introduced development planning earlier than others, so LEAs and schools across the country vary in their length of experience with the process. Our study spans some of these developments.

## RATIONALE FOR THE THEORETICAL ORIENTATION

The conceptual framing of the study was quite eclectic. First, the design was influenced by the findings of the multiple innovations project. A model of 'flexible planning' was developed as an outcome of this work (Wallace, 1991c), combining the contradictory influences of cyclic planning for long-term coherence with incremental planning for short-term flexibility. The research raised the question whether models based on sequential annual cycles are flexible enough to guide planning for change where school staff experience great environmental turbulence. An opportunity was sought in the present study to check the application of the model and to consider how it relates to existing planning and decision-making theories as applied to schools.

Second, the hypothesis that flexibility in planning for change is needed in turbulent environments suggested the corollary that pressure for flexibility is less significant under more stable conditions. Contingency theory of management, applied to schools in the United States by Hanson (1979), offered a conceptual framework for considering how planning for change at school level may be affected by changes in the balance of stability and turbulence in the external and internal environment.

Third, interpreting school development planning as an innovation for both schools and LEAs, together with a focus on the innovations which formed much of the content of planning for change, required the conceptual tools of theory on the management of planned educational change developed mainly in North America on the basis of extensive research (Fullan, 1991). However, this work has focused primarily on single innovations, neglecting the surrounding context (Bolam, 1982), which in English schools includes a range of other innovations.

Fourth, a complementary focus on multiple innovations was needed to grasp how planning for change must address at any time several innovations that may interact with each other in various ways. Consequently, categories developed inductively in the multiple innovations project were employed for analysing the evolution of the profile of innovations and other changes forming the content of plans. Another important component of the context of planning for change is routine planning for the maintenance of existing practice, such as the annual allocation of staff and classes. The multiple innovations project indicated that planning for change can encroach into planning for maintenance where innovations, like LMS, have direct implications for routine planning.

Fifth, cultural diversity was likely to be a key factor affecting participation in planning and the content of plans. Parents from minority ethnic groups, and all pupils, staff and governors, have some contact with aspects of both minority and majority ethnic cultures, including beliefs and values about education, schooling and religion. In addition, other research in primary schools (e.g. Nias *et al.*, 1989) has demonstrated the significance of the professional staff subculture in planning and decision-making. Accordingly, some reference was made to cultural concepts. Individuals and groups at school level and elsewhere would probably differ in the ability to take action to realize their beliefs and values depending, for example, on their legal status with respect to the determination of changes in schools. Access to and the use of power was also reflected in the analysis.

## DESIGN AND METHODS

The research was funded by the Leverhulme Trust for two years from September 1990. The aims of exploring planning for change in turbulent environments and identifying processes that appeared to be effective were reflected in the decision to work in three LEAs with contrasting approaches to development planning and different levels of experience with this innovation. These LEAs were a shire county with several large towns; a small metropolitan borough within a major conurbation; and a large city containing an extensive inner-city area.

When fieldwork began in September 1990 the county had a compulsory plan based upon the financial year, in its second year of formal operation; the city's compulsory plan, based upon the academic-year cycle, was also in its second year; and borough staff encouraged schools to participate in its voluntary development planning initiative where participants could choose from a range of ideas. Initial enquiries revealed plans in the borough and the city to reorganize schooling in order to remove surplus capacity by closing some schools, a likely source of additional turbulence. It turned out that, in seeking turbulent environments, we had chosen well. By the time fieldwork finished in July 1992, county staff were reviewing their development planning procedure for schools; reorganization in the borough had been postponed for a year; and the city schools were about to reorganize and were not expected by LEA staff to compile a development plan for an interregnum of two terms.

The project design consisted of two phases. The first, during the 1990 autumn term, consisted of interviews with twenty-two LEA staff and twenty-four headteachers in the three LEAs. This sample was intended to provide us with a diversity of contexts in order that we could determine the likely range of factors affecting planning. Criteria for selecting schools included the age range of pupils, the proportion of children from minority ethnic groups, and the location. Documents were collected, including development plans.

In the second phase, two schools from each LEA were selected in the light of the initial findings. As before, they were chosen to reflect a range of factors that the research hitherto suggested would be significant, including the approach to planning for change, the commitment of heads to development planning, their reported success in coping with multiple innovations, and cultural diversity among the pupils. Focused, interpretative case studies (Merriam, 1988) were carried out between May 1991 and July 1992, entailing six one-day visits spread over the four terms. Interviews focused on headteachers, staff with substantial management responsibility, minority ethnic group support staff and chairs of governors. Some 187 interviews were conducted with ninety-one informants, each lasting between half an hour and two hours. Documents relevant to planning were collected, including development plans and bids to participate in various initiatives. Follow-up interviews were also conducted with nine LEA staff concerned with development planning and Section 11 bids.

We received comments on our interpretation of the findings at feedback sessions from those who participated in the initial interviews and from the staff in the case-study schools. The headteachers at these schools and an inspector or adviser in each LEA were invited to comment on the draft of this book.

## Integrating data collection and analysis

Our theoretical orientation provided a focus for data collection. We also worked inductively, gaining insights which fed into subsequent rounds of fieldwork. All interviews were semi-structured, enabling us to seek answers to our questions and interviewees to bring their own perspective and experience to bear. Our methods were informed by the approach to qualitative data analysis advocated by Miles and Huberman (1984), who argue that analysis should begin before and continue throughout data collection. Research questions were derived from an initial conceptual framework and literature review, using the multiple innovations project as a starting point. Interviews in the first phase were structured around topics that appeared likely to be significant in planning for change. In the second phase, a more tightly structured round of interviews was conducted in the case-study schools, based on questions that the first phase suggested were salient. Subsequent interviews followed up progress with planning, especially in relation to development plans and changes that formed the content of plans.

A criticism of much qualitative research is that the process of analysis lacks the rigour, according to explicit rules, of quantitative methods. Miles and Huberman point out that conclusions may be impressionistic, and what appears significant to researchers may relate to their implicit assumptions: pure induction is impossible since any researcher must start somewhere in focusing data collection. Our guiding principles were, first, to make our assumptions explicit; second, to build in rigour through cumulative summarizing of the data, linked to our research questions, so that we could justify our interpretations and conclusions by referring back to their source; and third, to adopt a procedure that was manageable within our resources. Even so, each day's interviews required several days for analysis.

Every interview was taped and notes were taken. We wished to avoid accumulating unedited tape transcripts, since the interviews inevitably contained redundant information and the time required for transcribing would delay the opportunity for analysis. Each tape was played back and, with reference to the interview schedule and our notes, a summary tape prepared which included our interpretations and quotations to substantiate them. This summary was transcribed and later categorized within an interview summary form. The data contained in the forms were then collated. One set of forms and matrices was used to display the data from the twenty-four initial interviews with headteachers, much of which were quantified. A site summary, in a similar format, was prepared for each case-study school and a final list of variables was generated.

## Limitations of the research

We relied on interviews and document survey, meaning that our interpretation of what our informants said is not backed by observation of, say, staff meetings. The sample of LEAs and schools was opportunistic, and we considered ourselves fortunate that respondents were so willing to make time to support our work. We did not attempt to build up a picture of a typical process of planning for change in primary schools; and as it was a largely qualitative study our findings cannot be taken as representative of schools across the country. On the other hand, they are likely to have implications for other LEAs and schools, since all have been dominated by central government reforms. Within our focus on planning for change we concentrated on informants with management responsibility in the school and minority ethnic group support staff. The views of parents and most governors were relayed through informants such as teacher governors and minority ethnic group support staff responsible for home-school links. Repeated interviewing in the case-study schools produced a 'halo effect' in that, by asking questions, we drew respondents' attention to our concerns such as progress with development planning. However, headteachers implied that our occasional presence made little difference to practice in the schools.

We followed the causal chain only part way from the management of planning to pupil learning, not seeking measures of changes in classroom practice or their impact on pupils. We looked for evidence of the outcomes of the process of planning for change itself as a basis for considering the effectiveness of different approaches, recognizing that there might be intervening variables which could affect whether effective planning led to pupil learning. Despite the methodological limitations of the research, we think our findings raise important practical and theoretical issues.

## TOPICS COVERED IN THE REMAINING CHAPTERS

The next couple of chapters extend our overview of the field of enquiry. Chapter 2 discusses our theoretical orientation, including the flexible planning model; Chapter 3 introduces the LEAs and summarizes the approaches to planning and associated issues at LEA and school levels highlighted by the initial interviews. We identify a range of factors which promoted environmental turbulence or stability and note their impact on the planning process.

The subsequent chapters present the findings from the six case-study schools. Chapter 4 introduces each school in turn, to give the reader a feel for each site. We then develop four cross-site themes. Chapter 5 addresses how planning was managed; Chapter 6 focuses on development planning as both a strategy for managing planning for change and an innovation in itself; Chapter 7 explores how planning was affected by factors promoting environmental turbulence or stability (extending the list developed in Chapter 3); and Chapter 8 analyses the flow of plans and examines the fit between the flexible planning model and activity in the schools.

Finally, Chapter 9 considers the effectiveness of approaches to planning in the schools, identifying performance indicators that we developed as the research proceeded. We summarize what we have learned about planning for change and raise issues for researchers, school staff, governors, and LEA and national policymakers.

# Chapter 2

# Theoretical Orientation of the Study

This chapter introduces concepts and models which informed the research questions we asked and our interpretation of the answers. We begin by defining planning, locating development planning as conceptualized in many LEA initiatives and handbooks within a range of planning and decision-making models, and putting forward the model of flexible planning. We then consider how the form taken by planning efforts may be contingent upon balance of stability and turbulence in the internal and external environment of schools.

Factors connected with the implementation of single innovations are discussed and development planning is considered as an innovation. The distinctiveness of planning to implement multiple innovations is asserted and concepts are highlighted that assist analysis of planning in such a context. Finally, ideas related to culture and power are outlined.

## WHAT IS PLANNING?

There are many definitions of planning, mostly linked to particular models. Ours is simple: planning is the process of identifying a purpose and deciding upon the steps that must be taken to accomplish it. Planning for change - like change itself - is a process which focuses upon modifying present ways of working and implementing new practices. Within this definition a variety of activities may be included within the planning process, such as evaluating present work; gathering information; identifying priorities, targets and success criteria; decision-making; making detailed action plans; and devising means of monitoring progress.

Planning relates to action at different levels within schools or between school and LEA or district levels. Our concern is mainly with the level of plans affecting most or all teaching staff within each school. Much activity here links with school policies which provide a framework for more detailed planning of associated innovations or adjustments to present procedures. Decisions on the adoption of policies and the management of their implementation are the subject of planning, rather than detailed drafting of policies. Plans made at this strategic level may be more or less closely linked to LEA or district plans. For example, Bradford LEA has attempted to dovetail cycles of school and LEA development planning so that the latter is informed by identified school priorities and needs for LEA services (Bradford Education, 1992). Many school development plans introduced by LEAs are supposed to take into account LEA policies and initiatives.

The comprehensiveness of planning may vary. Depending on the existing state of affairs, planning for change may include the curriculum, pedagogy, pastoral care, management, and the internal and external environment within the boundaries of a school. Equally, the focus of planning may differ, encompassing three overlapping areas:

- *planning for change* - covering all planned developments (whether or not they are implemented), responses to unplanned crises, issues or other events not directly connected with innovations but entailing new practices, and changes to routine procedures;

- *development planning* - a delineated process entailing a procedure and documentation intended as a means of managing some or all planned developments (which may or may not lead to a sustained effort at implementation);

- *planning for maintenance* - routine planning required for continuation of existing practices, such as devising the timetable.

Planning is a process that has to be managed. It is generally organized through individuals and groups occupying particular roles (headteachers, for example, taking responsibility for managing planning); structures, including regular meetings for different groups; and procedures, such as a formal review involving a questionnaire for staff. An investigation of planning for change must ascertain how planning is managed, including making plans for the adjustment of existing arrangements for managing planning or for introducing new arrangements!

An important purpose of planning structures and procedures is to enable individuals and groups occupying various roles to participate. Different individuals and groups are commonly involved at particular times. At one extreme a head may make a unilateral decision on whether, say, to consult teachers about a curriculum initiative; at the other, all staff and parents may be invited to complete a questionnaire on their preferences for the direction of development in the school, and the head accepts the majority view. Participation in planning procedures also varies along a dimension from shared decision-making, through consultation on ideas and preferences, to being informed about decisions made by others. The actions of headteachers are a key influence on the degree of participation which they, as leaders, allow others to have in decision-making, since they are in a position to set many parameters for participation.

Within the realm of consultation, boundaries may be more or less tightly drawn. We have adopted the term 'open consultation' for occasions when opinions are sought without boundaries being stipulated, for example when a review begins with staff being invited to state their preferences for future development. 'Bounded consultation' covers occasions when boundaries are specified, as when staff are asked to give their opinions on proposals for development put forward by the head.

## Planning and rationality

Models of planning within organizations have been developed which emphasize different factors. Some are an idealized prescription of how planning should take place while others describe patterns of practice. Some address the whole planning process, others focus on decision-making within it. Arguably, each has something to say about what may be observed on the ground, yet their assumptions are divergent.

A key variable is the degree of rationality attributed to the planning process: how far a logical procedure can or should be employed in reality. Some models are designed to rationalize planning, implying that planners should adopt a more logical approach than many currently do. Wise (1983) notes that the term 'rationalization' has two meanings: the first refers to the logical process of identifying goals and organizing activities to achieve them, as reflected in such models. The second meaning is negative: 'to employ explanations that seem superficially reasonable but are actually unrelated to the true explanation'. Models developed in part as a reaction against those prescribing a high degree of rationality assert that they are rationalistic in this pejorative sense because the preferred planning steps appear to be logical but fail to connect adequately with the reality of planning in organizations. It is questioned how far such rational approaches are possible, never mind desirable. Wise suggests that efforts by policymakers in the United States to introduce comprehensive logical planning procedures as part of a wider series of reforms rest on an overly rational view of management, amounting to an attempt at the 'hyper-rationalization' of education which is bound to come to a sticky end:

> Educational policies fail because they are premised on the idea that the
> school is a rational organization - like a factory - which can be managed
> and improved by rational procedure. Indeed, much of the collective
> effort of policy makers, researchers, and administrators is aimed at
> making school reality conform to the rational model. We then bemoan
> the fact that the schools fail to conform to the model. It just may be
> that we need a new paradigm.
>
> (p. 113)

A question arises over the degree to which the reality of a turbulent environment can conform to the assumptions underpinning development planning based on annual cycles, or whether the assumptions and procedures flowing from them need to be changed.

One significant trend has been increasing recognition of individuals' cognitive limitations which constrain the use of a very logical and comprehensive approach to planning. The social world is simply too complex for anyone to grasp and predict the effect of every possible factor that may affect plans. In parallel with this trend, there has been acknowledgement of the limited control staff in management positions hold over development within their organization where they have no jurisdiction over changes in the internal and external environment. Such a constraint may apply most strongly to public-sector organizations (including schools) because of the high level of external political control over their work (Johnson and Scholes, 1988).

We have contrasted five of the main models of planning and decision-making, all from the United States, in Table 2.1. The assumptions of the approach to development planning outlined in Chapter 1 will be compared with

**Table 2.1** Comparison between planning and decision-making models

| Model<br>Criterion | Long-range planning<br>(Simon, 1947) | Incremental decision-making<br>(Lindblom, 1959) | Garbage-can decision-making<br>(March and Olsen, 1976) |
|---|---|---|---|
| 1 Rationality of actors and planning activity | Highly rational | Rational within cognitive limits, complex problems cannot be fully analysed | Irrational |
| 2 Predictability of future | Predictable | Relatively unpredictable | Unpredictable |
| 3 Timescale | Five years or more | Implicitly short or medium term | Implicitly short term |
| 4 Consistency of goals | Single set of consistent, enduring goals | Inconsistent as values, goals and means interrelate | Inconsistent and ambiguous goals |
| 5 Adequacy of information | Sufficient for exhaustive, qualitative analysis | Sufficient to inform judgements on incremental change | Inadequate – variable participation by individuals with limited understanding of organization |
| 6 Environmental turbulence | Low, little concern with external environment | Implicitly low, incremental change is the norm | High internal turbulence because of variable participation, pursuit of competing goals |
| 7 Control by senior managers | High, top-down management | Implicitly high, administrators in position to make decisions | Low, legitimate participation by many individuals |
| 8 Logic of process | Single, long-term cycle, sequential steps | Repeated cycles, sequential steps | Illogical interaction between components, more or less continual |
| 9 Main components | Optimizing: agree values, clarify goals, identify range of means, analyse all relevant factors, determine on best means | Satisficing: focus on few alternatives, limited analysis, choice of means offering marginal improvement | Streams of problems, solutions, participants, choice, opportunities, all interact |
| 10 Origins and application to schooling | Origin in economic model of decision-making | Origin in government policymaking | Origin in universities and schools |

these models as a backdrop to introducing the notion of flexible planning (included as a sixth model in the table) which informed our research. Since the models have different emphases we are not comparing like with like. The table indicates where a model does not cover a point of comparison. For example, not all accounts make the timescale for planning clear but, from the assumptions that are made explicit, a reasonable guess can be made. There are ten points of comparison, of which the first seven are assumptions about planners and the nature and context of planning. The assumptions for each model are interlinked; in long-range planning an extensive timescale is merited on the assumptions that the future is highly predictable, organizational goals are consistent and enduring, and managers control the content and process of planning. This set of assumptions links with the next two points of comparison: the chosen process

| Strategic planning (e.g. Steiner, 1979) | Evolutionary planning (Louis and Miles, 1990) | Flexible planning (Wallace, 1991c) |
| --- | --- | --- |
| Rational within cognitive limits, includes use of intuition | Rational within cognitive limits, includes emphasis on developing shared values and use of intuition | Rational within severe cognitive limits |
| Relatively unpredictable because of changing external environment | Relatively unpredictable because of changing internal and external environments | Combination of predictable and unpredictable |
| Three to five years | Implicitly short or medium term | Short and medium term, adjusted continually, spasmodically, annually |
| Multiple, competing changing goals | Changing broad themes including short-term goals from which vision often emerges | Multiple, competing, changing, often ambiguous goals |
| Sufficient to inform judgements on change | Implicitly sufficient to inform judgements on themes and associated experimental action | Combination of inadequate (mainly for externally initiated changes) and adequate for implementation |
| Medium, external environment influences decisions | High internal and external turbulence | High turbulence, low stability but variable over time |
| Medium, bounded by legitimate pressure from groups in the external environment | Medium, including participation by staff representatives | Low to medium, including participation by staff and strong external pressure |
| Medium-term cycle of broad goal-setting, more frequent detailed operational planning for each goal, sequential steps | Combined search for consensus on themes and goals, with experimental, opportunistic action, more or less continual | Combination of continual, spasmodic and cyclic planning, rolling forward more or less continually |
| Agree mission, clarifying educational goals, analyse internal and external environments, make planning assumptions, identify targets, identify means, do detailed operational planning | Analyse external environment, clarify mission gradually, scan internally for opportunities, encourage experimental action, highlight success | Continual creation, monitoring and adjustment of plans, spasmodic response to new information, cyclic planning within conflicting annual cycles |
| Origin in reactions against rationalistic economic model used by school district administrators | Origin in secondary schools | Origin in primary and secondary schools |

and the components that constitute the model. Finally, a note is made of its origin and application to schools.

## Long-range planning

This 'blueprint' model was the first approach offered in texts on organizations, and derived from economic and statistical theories of decision-making during the 1940s (see Simon, 1947). It is a highly rational process controlled by senior managers, where a logical sequence of steps entailing the exhaustive analysis of different courses of action leads to the selection of the optimal way forward.

The model has been heavily criticized as unrealistic or, following Wise, hyperrational. March and Simon (1958) discussed extensively the cognitive limits to rationality: planners are unlikely to have full information on all possible alternatives, let alone the ability to predict the consequences of following one or other of them. Rather than 'optimizing' - selecting the one best alternative - they generally 'satisfice' - generate one alternative that seems good enough. The assumption of a high level of control by senior managers suggests that implementation automatically follows planning. Yet extensive evidence from studies of schools in both the policy implementation (e.g. Boyd, 1988; Odden, 1991) and local educational change process traditions (e.g. Berman and McLaughlin, 1978; Fullan, 1991) suggests that planned change generally undergoes 'mutual adaptation', meaning that the change as originally designed becomes altered during implementation.

## Incremental decision-making

The other models partially or wholly reject the hyperrational conception of decision-making on which long-range planning is based, and most were derived inductively from analysis of planning in different organizational contexts. In the light of his observations of how government policy evolved, Lindblom (1959) extended the notion of satisficing by putting forward an incremental model dubbed 'the science of muddling through'. He argued that decision-making tends to proceed by 'successive limited comparisons', concerned with the marginal differences between a few alternatives. He claimed that for complex social problems comprehensive analysis is impossible. Values, goals and means cannot be analysed and selected separately. Rather than begin by agreeing upon values prior to identifying goals then means, leading to evaluation of these means, one or more policy alternatives are selected for consideration where values are implicit in the choice of goals and means within each alternative. The analysis is more or less limited, aiming for a small improvement in the present situation. Therefore, potential radical alternatives are ruled out and some possible but unpredictable consequences of the alternatives under consideration are ignored. Decision-making proceeds through cycles of trial and error, implying a short- to medium-term timescale.

Subsequently Lindblom (1979) refined the model, allowing for the rationality of the process to be increased. The approach already described, which he called 'disjointed incrementalism', is common in practice. He advocated 'systematic analysis', where successive limited comparisons are made rigorously so as to be as thorough as possible without aspiring to comprehensiveness.

## Garbage-can decision-making

Neither of the first two models paid much attention to the environment in which decision-making occurs. The model that March and Olsen (1976) developed from research in universities and schools highlights turbulence in the internal environment of an organization resulting from the behaviour of different individuals and groups. This anarchic model denies rationality in decision-making and consequently has no place for cyclic activity.

Certain features of organizations lead to ambiguity for their members: the poorly defined and inconsistent goals held by individuals, their limited understanding about how aspects of the organization work, and their variable participation in decision-making. Far from emerging out of a logical sequence of analysis of goals and means, decisions are conceived as the outcome of idio-syncratic and illogical interaction in a 'garbage can' between four variables or 'streams' that flow into it: problems, whether part of official business or connected with personal concerns; solutions, consisting of individuals' ideas and preferences which they seek opportunities to realize - in other words solutions looking for a problem; participants, whose involvement in decision-making depends upon its priority relative to other demands on their time; and choice opportunities, viewed as occasions when decisions are expected to be made.

Despite the irrational nature of decision-making such organizations are sustained over time. Weiner (1976) labelled them 'organized anarchies'. The model fails to explain why organizations endure when the decision-making process at their heart is apparently incoherent and disjointed.

## Strategic planning

By contrast, strategic planning is a comprehensive model with many variants which has been much more influential in guiding practice in commerce and industry than in education. It has been elaborated through extensive work in American business schools (Cope, 1981). The model has been applied to the education sphere at individual organization level (Kaufman and Herman, 1991; Caldwell and Spinks, 1992) and in the articulation of coordinated plans between district and school levels (Cunningham, 1982). Most advocates lean towards the rational long-range planning model from which strategic planning was derived in offering a similar cyclic sequence of activities, but with more attention to articulating an organizational mission from which goals are derived, specifying targets and making detailed operational plans. Relatively few accounts of strategic planning, such as Johnson and Scholes (1988), distinguish between the *logic* of a sequence of core activities - where reviewing leads to identifying priorities, then to planning implementation of changes - and the way in which *in practice* these activities may both interpenetrate and occur in varying order.

Strategic planning parts company with long-range planning in emphasizing the influence of the external environment. The future is assumed to be rela-tively unpredictable because of changes in environmental factors which cannot be controlled at school or district level. Such factors are not merely acknowl-edged: steps are advocated to deal with them. Strategic plans tend to cover up to five years and are regularly (often annually) updated in response to environmental changes affecting existing goals or leading to the formulation of new ones. Detailed operational plans are made within the strategic plan, often yearly, for each goal.

As in incremental decision-making, analysis of alternatives is limited and qualitative, including a role for intuition (Simon, 1989) - the informed hunch - in making judgements about action. Large amounts of subconsciously held infor-mation and associated value judgements are assimilated within a consciously created 'big idea' or judgement. However, intuition operates inside a formal set of procedures. Steiner (1979), for example, accepts that organizational leaders are capable of creating strategic plans using an 'intuitive-anticipatory' approach, but questions the wisdom of this practice:

> Generally it is done in the brain of one person. It may or may not, but often does not, result in a written set of plans. It generally has a comparatively short time horizon and reaction time. It is based upon the past experience, the 'gut' feel, the judgement, and the reflective thinking of a manager. It is very important and must not be underestimated. . . . If an organization is managed by intuitive geniuses there is no need for formal strategic planning. But how many organizations are so blessed? And, if they are, how many times are intuitives correct in their judgements?
>
> (pp. 8-9)

For Steiner, intuition is most effective within a formal planning system, drawing on the ideas and judgements of a wider group which is kept informed about the content of plans. Strategic planning comes closer than long-range planning to accepting the value of a short-term intuitive-anticipatory approach in offering a rapid response and hence flexibility. In so far as the tension we have noted between retaining flexibility and building coherence is addressed, strategic planning appears to opt for coherence through a systematic procedure bounding the use of intuition.

The influence of different interest groups within the environment implies that there will be multiple, evolving and sometimes competing goals, probably agreed by negotiation and compromise rather than as the optimal outcome of logical analysis (Patterson et al., 1986). These advocates of strategic planning give a nod towards the garbage-can model by acknowledging the ambiguity that surrounds decision-making in organizations. Goals are frequently general and unclear because of the variety of interest groups involved in their identification. Membership of these groups, from both inside and outside organizations, often changes over time. Moreover, issues which receive attention in the occasional formulation of goals tend to include the most pressing ones, whether or not managers wish to address them, because they have limited control over the choice of goals.

A significant question for our study is: how much environmental turbulence is the strategic planning model designed to cope with? The answer seems to be not much. Some texts on strategic planning based on private-sector organizations contain exhortations about retaining flexibility to respond to changing environmental circumstances (e.g. Luffman et al., 1987) yet fail to show how flexibility may be integrated within the logical sequence of activities they so exhaustively describe. The practical guidance offered belies the exhortation. Such texts frequently deal with large, even multinational, companies which are not so subject to pervasive intervention by governments as are schools. Private-sector organizations may be less prone to this source of turbulence which, for so many schools, has increasingly dictated responses which often fly in the face of existing plans. Where these texts allow for modification of operational plans towards enduring strategic goals, they offer little guidance on how to adjust existing plans and create new ones in response to externally imposed changes in these goals.

Texts focusing on schools give more attention to strategies for retaining flexibility but do not place them centre stage. Lewis (1983) implies that they are for emergency use only. He suggests that a short-term strategy, termed 'problem-solving planning', may be used to deal with problems that arise but should not become the norm, claiming that 'administrators who permit a problem to last for more than two months have outlived their usefulness within the organization'. On this assumption pretty well all headteachers struggling with multiple government reforms should be put out to grass! Cunningham (1982) allows for a temporary switch to a more incremental approach in turbulent times:

> Under conditions of extreme instability, it is possible to make adjustments in how planning is conceived. That is, instead of proceeding in a rationalistic fashion, with the future conceptualized and laid out, it may be necessary to proceed piecemeal, planning what can be planned, ready to retreat when it is necessary, and taking advantage of opportunities as they arise.
>
> (p. 52)

Kaufman and Herman (1991) allow for formative evaluation to lead to a shift in detailed plans or within a strategic goal itself, yet do not show how such a shift is to be effected within the context of other plans. Strategic planning appears to share some of the rationalistic assumptions of long-range planning, despite attempting to address turbulence arising from the external environment. Responsiveness is normally obtained through updating of strategic plans at the same point in each cycle and the reformulation of operational plans. Only exceptionally is it deemed appropriate to employ a more flexible short-term strategy. While accepting the possibility of tension between strategies for obtaining long-term coherence and those for retaining short-term flexibility, strategic planning actually puts the main emphasis on promoting coherence.

The cyclic process of development planning widely prescribed for schools shares many assumptions of strategic planning variants. First, development planning follows a logical sequence: review takes into account the external and internal environments and stated aims of the school; priorities, targets and success criteria are set within these aims; action plans make targets operational; and subsequent review leads to annual updating and rolling forward plans for change envisaged for the next few years. Second, response to environmental change is made by modifying detailed plans within a priority following formative evaluation and, annually, by reconsidering priorities and rolling forward outline plans for change covering future years.

## Evolutionary planning

A contrasting model designed to address planning for change in schools facing high environmental turbulence is 'evolutionary planning', developed inductively by Louis and Miles (1990) in a study of reform efforts in urban high (secondary) schools in the United States, many of which are multiracial. Evolutionary planning follows strategic planning in centring upon a mission and analysing the external environment but gives much greater prominence to intuition, opportunism and living with ambiguity, and eschews the sequence of planning steps required by more rationalistic models. Flexibility must be retained within a broad sense of direction because

> the environment both inside and outside organisations is often chaotic. No specific plan can last very long, because it will become outmoded either due to changing external pressures, or because disagreement over priorities arises within the organization. Yet, there is no reason to assume that the best response is to plan passively, relying upon incremental decisions. Instead, the organization can cycle back and forth between efforts to gain normative consensus about what it may become, to plan strategies for getting there, and to carry out decentralized, incremental experimentation that harnesses the creativity of all members to the change effort.
>
> This approach is evolutionary in the sense that, although the mission and image of the organization's ideal future may be based on a top level analysis of the environment and its demands, strategies for achieving the mission are frequently reviewed and refined based on internal scanning for opportunities and successes. Strategy is viewed as a flexible tool, rather than as a semi-permanent extension of the mission: if rational planning is like blueprinting, evolutionary planning is more like taking a journey. There is a general destination, but many twists and turns as unexpected events occur along the way.
>
> (p. 193)

In contrast to strategic planning, it is argued that a vision (which may be formalized as a mission statement) may emerge later from less comprehensive themes identified at the beginning of a reform effort which encompass a range of innovations, and plans for change may evolve as a consequence of experimental action for improvement within these themes. School staff are cautioned against spending too much time on consultation exercises, collecting large amounts of data and extensive planning at the outset of a school improvement project. Excessive planning early on inhibits action, although it is important to consult more widely once the initiative is under way.

The logic of planning for change within a turbulent environment is very different from the hyperrational version of long-range planning. It is both radical in terms of a broad vision and incremental in terms of opportunism, experimentation and an emphasis on developing shared ownership of the reform effort. The latter focus tallies with the consultative review and planning process within development planning. Hopkins (1992) argues that development planning is a 'paradigmatic illustration of a school improvement strategy' since it addresses both teaching and learning and school management, and offers a means of changing staff culture by engaging staff in setting a direction for development and implementing changes.

Evolutionary planning is unique among these models in suggesting a way of developing some degree of coherence through a flexible, emergent strategy which is responsive to changing internal and external environmental factors. Yet rationality is not abandoned (unlike in the garbage-can model). It is sympathetic with strategies for 'whole school curriculum development' that Nias *et al.* (1992) found in primary schools in England as the current wave of reforms began, and it contrasts with systematic approaches like development planning:

> Often it was neither sequential nor 'rational' in a linear sense. Particular curriculum developments were sometimes spontaneous, at others they seemed opportunistic, as heads and members of staff capitalised on the curricular interest or classroom interests of an individual. Curriculum review too was fluid and, sometimes, improvised. Neither development nor review were pre-arranged and pre-programmed except on a minority of occasions.
>
> (p. 245)

Evidently there was scope for less systematic approaches to planning for change in primary schools than development planning, at least in a context where the opportunity remained for innovations to arise within the school.

Similarly, evolutionary planning rests on the notion of a reform effort where there is reasonable control over the content and timing of changes at school level. The pervasiveness of central government intervention since the time of the study by Nias and her colleagues has imposed many elements of a mission upon schools in this country, though leaving some leeway for local interpretation, along with an externally imposed timetable for implementing a range of external innovations. The variety of changing circumstances to which school staff must respond militates against a simple linkage between an enduring mission or set of themes and incremental activity connected with innovations. The model implies more choice over the adoption, timing and implementation of innovations than school staff in this country have recently been afforded.

Since it is centrally concerned with change, evolutionary planning does not cover the planning entailed in maintaining existing practice while implementing multiple innovations. The model does not address the annual cycles within which planning for change in English schools must take place. Consequently, a model seems to be needed which is both cyclic and evolutionary.

## FLEXIBLE PLANNING

The flexible planning model assumes that rationality holds good in part. There is both a place for logic and an acceptance that there are heavy constraints on its use. Intuition plays a significant role; it is a form of rationality if the attempt is made to inform and share judgements, even if its logic is obscure. Flexible planning reconciles elements of both the evolutionary and strategic planning models in addressing the tension between flexibility offered by an evolutionary strategy and coherence offered by a cyclic approach consisting of sequential steps. Its starting points are, first, that both cycles and continual elements are necessary within the national and local policy context of schooling; second, that the internal and external school environment consists of a mixture of environmental stability and turbulence whose balance varies over time; and third, that activities promoting short-term flexibility and those promoting long-term coherence coexist in tension with each other.

'Flexible planning' is an oxymoron: flexibility implies the capacity for rapid response to changing circumstances while planning suggests the formulation of a design which leads to a sequence of prespecified changes over time. We speculate that the tension between these contradictory influences is more helpfully conceived as a dialectic than as a fixed proportion of each influence. Planning activity may vary at times between major planning exercises specifying action well into the future and rapid, often informal activity in response to unanticipated events. The idea of a dialectical relationship captures the way the contradiction between the two modes affects the actions of planners.

The philosopher Hegel used the term 'dialectic' to describe how a process of argument proceeds by resolution of contradictions, starting with an initial proposition, the thesis. This proves to be inadequate and generates its opposite, the antithesis, which in turn proves inadequate, and the opposites are taken up into a synthesis, retaining what was rational in the thesis and antithesis (see Flew, 1979). By loose analogy, our use of the term allows for the possibility that, where the balance of stability and change is continually in flux, action according to one of the two opposing influences will tend to bring consequences that lead to the ascendance of the other. Major planning exercises are soon likely to be supplemented by the requirement for flexibility, existing plans having to be modified as the situation changes. Day-to-day crisis management alone, while very flexible, is unlikely to prove cost-effective where the timetable of many external innovations does allow phasing of their implementation to reduce overload. The model allows for oscillations within planning activity to match the shifting balance between stability and change in the environment and points to the self-negating tendency of sustained action according to either one of the two contradictory influences alone.

This dialectic is played out through the three components of the model portrayed in the concentric circles in Figure 2.1:

- response to spasmodic shifts in information about external innovations and unrelated crises and issues, affecting
- the continual creation, monitoring and adjustment of plans for the short and medium term within a long-term vision, linked to
- cyclic planning for the academic and financial years.

## Reconciling coherence with flexibility

The basis of planning for coherent development is a multiplicity of decisions about the future which may be divided into three levels, although in reality they lie along a continuum (see the middle circle in Figure 2.1). First, there are 'broad-sweep' plans for the long term within a vision of a desirable future, which may be shared through the articulation of a mission. Medium- to long-term plans may

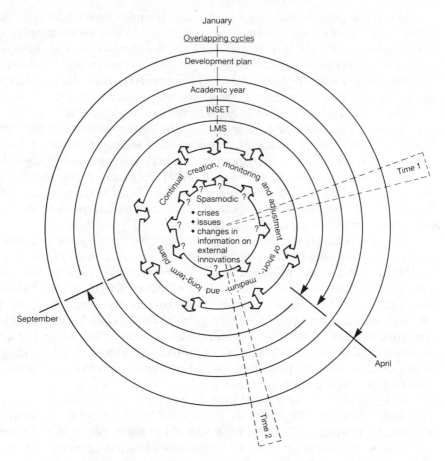

Figure 2.1 *The flexible planning model*

cover a period from, say, one to five years hence (thus a shorter period than long-range planning). Second, there are slightly more specific short- to medium-term plans, spanning perhaps a month to a year ahead. Third, there are very short-term, detailed plans covering the immediate future, from the present to about a month ahead.

These three levels of plan nest together, short-term and medium-term plans lying within more general long-term plans. As time passes they roll forward, at some points in major leaps as a result, perhaps, of an occasional review, at others incrementally in response to changing circumstances. What were long-term plans are developed into medium- and short-term plans, short-term plans are enacted and new long-term plans are created. The timetable of periodic events and activities within the overlapping cycles is addressed through these rolling plans. Within flexible planning they are updated frequently, dictated in part by the rate of environmental changes; in development planning they are updated yearly during the consultative review and planning exercise.

29

Structures and procedures for planning include those for regular consultation, decision-making, disseminating information and monitoring progress with implementation, which may include cyclic exercises such as whole-school reviews and a structure of meetings for groups in various roles. The form taken by these structures and procedures may vary widely, one option being a major review each year with a less extensive review each term or so.

The basis of flexibility is a process of more or less continual creation, monitoring and adjustment of rolling plans. Monitoring covers largely informal means of gathering information internally and seeking information from outside - whether from the local community, neighbouring schools, the LEA or central government and its agencies. Keeping informed in this way facilitates response to the many spasmodic and often unpredictable short-term crises and longer-term issues that arise, together with changing information about external innovations (as depicted in the inner circle in Figure 2.1).

Continual monitoring, frequent adjustment of existing plans and occasional creation of new ones require structures and procedures. Monitoring entails establishing individual roles and tasks connected with seeking internal and external information. The need for communication of findings and adjustment and creation of plans implies a structure of regular meetings, together with a procedure for arranging *ad hoc* meetings to make decisions in response to unanticipated changes. A routine procedure may be established for calling a rapid-response review whenever information about a change in the environment suggests that present priorities and development activity may have to be modified or a new priority addressed.

Adjustment and creation of plans is not necessarily confined to concrete proposals. Potential flexibility is maintained by contingency planning (see Hanson, 1979; Steiner, 1979), but the cost of the effort required to devise such plans must be balanced against the benefit of being prepared for possible changes. Through a modicum of contingency planning it is possible to reduce uncertainty to some extent. Contingencies vary in their predictability. With more predictable contingencies, uncertainty lies in when rather than whether, say, staff illness is likely to occur or the Secretary of State will modify a demonstrably unworkable policy. A common decision in the multiple innovations project schools was to refrain from altering existing practice with some external innovations on the assumption that a change in policy was bound to arise sooner or later.

While the various overlapping cycles (illustrated in the outer circle of Figure 2.1) give rise to a regular sequence of planning events, all either constitute or are affected by external innovations, and are subject to change as relevant policies evolve. The inconsistency between the timing of the cycles means that it may not be easy to dovetail the plans for each. Both these factors imply that an element of flexibility in planning is needed to cope with the annual cycles in addition to regular planning events for each one.

The flexible planning model covers a combination of linked continual, cyclic and spasmodic factors that the multiple innovations project suggested must be addressed by the planning process in schools within a highly turbulent environment. Any time is represented by a narrow segment (for example Time

1 in Figure 2.1), and the progress of plans, their connection with points in each cycle, and the influence of spasmodic factors may be traced - say, from Time 1 to Time 2. We attempted to track the flow of plans in the present study (see Chapter 8).

Table 2.1 indicates how, like development planning, flexible planning has affinities with both strategic and evolutionary planning models, but it emphasizes flexibility in responding to the environment. The idea of tension between opposites built into the model is also reflected in the assumption that some aspects of the environment are predictable while others are unpredictable. Information needed for decision-making is a combination of inadequate (mainly related to some external innovations) and adequate for planning implementation of changes. Critically, the balance of stability and turbulence in the internal and external environments is viewed as variable over time but weighted towards turbulence. The applicability of the model rests on this contingency; other models may match more closely a relatively stable environment.

## CONTINGENCY THEORY AND PLANNING FOR CHANGE

Contingency theory offers a way of thinking about the relationship between planning activity in organizations and their environment. The contingency theory of management asserts that both the form taken by organizational structures and procedures and their effectiveness are contingent upon variations in the internal and external environments (Hanson, 1979). It is assumed that there is no one best way of managing, but that similar environmental factors affect organizations and their management in similar ways. The conceptual origins of contingency theory lie in the notion of organizations as open systems which interact with their environment (Katz and Kahn, 1978). One of the major dimensions of variation of environmental factors (such as cultural diversity, public representation in decision-making or financial constraints) affecting organizations is the continuum between stability and turbulence. As any environmental factor becomes more turbulent the problems it creates become perceived as more urgent. The overall balance of environmental stability and turbulence is a result of the degree of turbulence in respect of each environmental factor at any time.

Hanson argues that an increase in environmental turbulence brings the need for greater coordination among individuals and groups within an organization: 'Integration refers to the quality or the state of collaboration essential for achieving a unity of effort. This collaboration comes in the form of flexibility of procedures, open communication, shared information, and the presence of special integrating personnel.' Advocates of development planning appear to have set out to achieve such coordination, but we question whether exclusive emphasis upon a cyclic approach fails to address the need to sustain coordination to respond to further environmental changes.

A pioneering study of British companies by Burns and Stalker (1961) revealed that they tended to have a mixture of two management structures, depending upon the degree to which there was stability and turbulence in their environment. 'Mechanistic' structures, with tight hierarchical specification of roles, were found in stable situations but could prove rigid in the face of environmental changes. 'Organic' structures, on the other hand, tended to be developed in companies facing greater turbulence. Roles were more fluid and less hierarchical, allowing more lateral communication and quicker response to changing tasks. Some companies responded to increasing turbulence by both retaining a mechanistic structure and parcelling off an organic structure, such as a research and development unit, to address particular changes. Kast and Rosenzweig (1973) claimed that a mechanistic form of organizational structure was appropriate for a stable environment but an organic form was more suitable for a turbulent environment with a high proportion of non-routine situations where innovative responses were required.

A broadly parallel contingency assumption underpins the flexible planning model. In so far as structures and procedures based upon an occasional planning cycle may be viewed as 'mechanistic', they may be retained in turbulent environments while a more 'organic' and flexible approach to planning for change coexists with them. The two approaches may be compartmented off from each other, as when new priorities are addressed outside a development plan. The compulsory (mechanistic) development planning cycle is followed while, independently, other priorities are dealt with by more flexible (organic) procedures as and when they arise. We hypothesize that, to the extent that the context of schooling is turbulent, a continual process of creation, monitoring and adjustment of plans is dictated, in line with the flexible planning model. To the

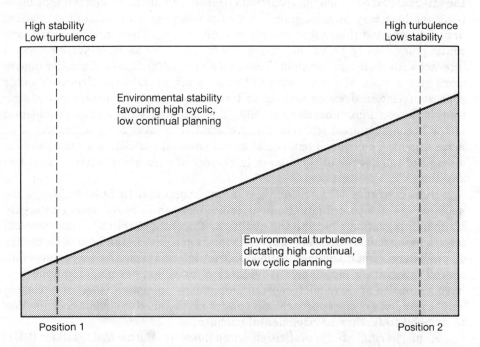

Figure 2.2 *Relationship between environmental stability and turbulence, and implications for planning*

32

degree that the context is stable, there is more scope for reliance on a systematic, cyclic approach. Figure 2.2 is an attempt to portray this hypothesis diagrammatically.

The left-hand extreme represents the most stable situation possible, where some turbulence will remain as cohorts of pupils will vary and there will be turnover of staff over time. The right-hand extreme portrays a very turbulent context, where some stability will still exist because not everything will be changing (except, perhaps, when a school is closed or a new school opened). The diagram indicates the variable relationship between stability and turbulence. For example, as the range of innovations addressed within a school grows, planning for change increasingly affects planning for maintenance, so leading to uncertainty over what otherwise would remain routine. In other words, the environment becomes more turbulent as stability is reduced. As this balance shifts towards turbulence, the balance of cyclic and continual planning must shift towards the continual, although even at the most extreme position annual cycles must still be addressed. Conversely, as the balance shifts towards stability, school-level planners will have greater choice over employing a single planning cycle. While all the case-study schools faced a high degree of turbulence, the balance varied both between schools and within any school over time.

## DEVELOPMENT PLANNING AS AN INNOVATION

Research in North America suggests that requiring schools to develop an implementation plan for innovations is itself a managerial innovation (Fullan, 1991). Development planning is unlikely to be exempt from problems associated with any other planned change. Levine and Liebert (1987) demonstrated that, where the assumptions which such an innovation reflects ill match the context for implementation, the well-intentioned attempt to improve elementary (primary) schools' implementation plans may inhibit the implementation of the other innovations which the plan was designed to facilitate. A compulsory annual school improvement plan initiated by district administrators could even give principals an excuse for failing to make improvements because they could claim that the prescribed planning steps had been followed, the plan had been approved at district level and an effort had been made to carry it out. This problem was particularly prevalent where overly ambitious plans were encouraged.

Implementation of development planning at school level appears to have been widespread but variable. A recent large-scale survey of primary and secondary school headteachers in England and Wales (Arnott et al., 1992) suggests the good news. The researchers found that 99 per cent of respondents were expected under LEA policy to prepare school development plans and two-thirds found LEA guidelines on implementing the innovation helpful. Only about 10 per cent did not value development planning in some way, and over half acknowledged its value in planning, prioritizing and evaluating.

More detailed case studies of the review stage in fourteen schools from five LEAs suggest the bad news that, as the thesis of 'mutual adaptation' would predict, both the form and depth of implementation varied with the existing approach to management (Constable *et al.*, 1991). Staff from nine schools were little involved in the review, in two cases because of the unwillingness of heads, who controlled implementation. There was also evidence of staff not necessarily wishing to be involved, which the researchers related back to the approach to management: 'If staff have come to accept that their own involvement in whole-school development is not wanted, or has little impact, they may not wish to become involved in, what for them is, an unrewarding exercise.' These findings are supported by a study in three LEAs which showed that both LEAs and schools were at very different stages in the implementation of the innovation of school development planning (Weston *et al.*, 1992).

Completion of a development plan document indicates little about the process of compiling or using it. Weston and her colleagues found that their twelve case-study primary schools all had a document but 'in a number of cases it was in the drawer rather than being in active use on the head's desk - one piece of accountability fulfilled rather than an essential planning tool'. Lack of staff engagement may also relate to focusing on the document while failing to help the staff to change how they habitually reflect on their practice (Hutchinson, 1993); they may be unable to find meaning in the new approach. It seems possible that development planning as an innovation could be less a means of changing the staff culture in the direction of collaboration and improvement, as Hopkins (1992) implies, than requiring a favourable culture as a precondition for full staff participation.

Evidence from the United States on participative decision-making suggests that involvement by members of an organization may foster commitment to change but is not essential (Conway, 1984). More important is clarity and specificity of goals, whether set participatively or by managers alone. Too much participation detracts from individuals' satisfaction with their involvement in the organization. It therefore seems likely that some teachers may not wish to be involved in a major consultative development planning exercise and will act accordingly.

## The change process

Fullan (1991) emphasizes how 'users' draw on their previous experience in trying to make sense of an innovation they are implementing. They may not fully understand the new practice until it has been implemented. Development planning is an innovation for groups at different levels in the education system who must each make sense of it. Drawing on the work of Bolam (1975), Table 2.2 indicates how the central government arrangements for funding LEA in-service training to implement the National Curriculum, including the responsibility placed upon LEAs to ensure that schools have a National Curriculum development plan, represented an innovation for which LEA staff were the users. Staff in many LEAs were also 'change agents' in launching development planning for schools. Similarly, headteachers were users of LEA development planning initiatives while being change agents of the version of the process that they introduced into their schools. As 'gatekeepers' for their organization (Havelock, 1969), heads often received the bulk of LEA preparatory training support and promoted a process that accorded with their managerial beliefs and values, including how far different constituencies participated. Arnott and her co-researchers found that governors took part in preparing the development plan in only 23 per cent of cases and staff other than heads and deputies were reported as being principally involved in just 51 per cent of schools.

The change process is widely conceived as a sequence of interacting phases:

- adoption - the period from the first intimation of a change to the decision to proceed with implementation;
- implementation - the attempt to put the change into practice, lasting up to three years or so;
- institutionalization - the change becomes an integral part of current practice; or alternatively
- rejection or postponement - where a decision is taken to call a halt to implementation.

Where LEA staff made development planning compulsory, staff in schools did not have the opportunity to decide whether to adopt this innovation. Yet instigators at LEA level had the choice of whether and when to go further than insisting upon a National Curriculum development plan.

Factors connected with the characteristics of an innovation which, according to Fullan (1991), act in combination to affect implementation are:

- need - how far users of an innovation perceive a need for it relative to other competing needs;
- clarity - about the goals of an innovation and the strategy for its implementation. The more complex the innovation, the less clarity users are likely to experience during early implementation. There is also a danger of false clarity when a change is interpreted in an over-simplified way;
- complexity - the difficulty and extent of change in practice required of users of an innovation;
- quality - for an innovation to succeed it must be implementable, yet many inadequately thought through and resourced innovations are

**Table 2.2** Development planning as an innovation

| Change agent | Innovation | User |
| --- | --- | --- |
| Central government ministers and civil servants | Bidding for in-service training grant and ensuring schools have a National Curriculum development plan | LEA staff |
| LEA staff | School development planning procedure and document | Headteachers, other staff (to a varying extent governors) |
| Headteachers | Approach to development planning procedure and completing document | Other staff in school (to a varying extent governors) |

adopted on the grounds of political expediency or where a need is perceived but there is insufficient preparation time;

- practicality - the extent to which potential users of an innovation perceive it to offer concrete possibilities for action that are feasible within their context.

The multiple innovations project findings indicated that, in the LEA concerned, the development planning initiative was introduced at very short notice; its quality and practicality may have been compromised by the rapidity of its development and introduction with little opportunity to trial the model or prepare school staff. A consequence was lack of clarity about the process being advocated over and above the completion of the development plan document.

Fullan, drawing upon the research of Louis and Miles (1990), identifies themes associated with successful implementation. Headteachers are in a unique position to foster action according to these themes, which are:

- vision building - leaders have a vision of what the institution should become (addressing the content of an innovation) and how to achieve the desired state (addressing the implementation process). It is important that support for this vision is gained from those in the organization involved in implementation;

- evolutionary planning - as discussed above, plans for implementation are adapted as the process proceeds;

- initiative-taking and empowerment - leaders share power within the institution and encourage others to take initiatives within the vision;

- staff development and resource assistance - preparatory and ongoing training and other resources are needed for users to learn new practices;

- monitoring/problem-coping - formative evaluation of implementation provides feedback to users about ideas and practices that do or do not work. Problems with implementation are to be expected and routine strategies help users to cope effectively;

- restructuring - the development of management structures and roles that facilitate implementation of innovations.

Development planning is a managerial innovation intended as a form of restructuring to aid implementation of other innovations. Research evidence suggests that headteachers may have varied widely in how far they shared their vision with others, attempted to gain the support of staff and governors, and empowered them in making decisions over future developments. Similarly LEA staff appear to have varied in their involvement of representatives from schools in developing a shared vision, the preparation time made available, and the in-service training support offered to users at school level and to LEA staff responsible for working with a set of schools on their development plans.

# PLANNING FOR MULTIPLE INNOVATIONS

The multiple innovations project was designed to identify factors that are salient in managing, alongside other work, the implementation of a continually evolving profile of innovations, each of which is going through the interacting phases described above. The origin of innovations within central government, LEAs and schools has significance for planning implementation. Most of the planning for change at school level during the present period of external intervention is to implement other people's innovations, with all the potential for reinterpretation and misperception between levels that we highlighted in relation to development planning.

Innovations were found to vary along four dimensions which, in combination, appear to have a strong impact on planning for a range of changes. They are defined in Table 2.3. The initial configuration of an innovation may change along one or more of these dimensions if it is adapted during implementation. Factors associated with each dimension, which affect planning at school level for a particular innovation within the context of other innovations, include:

- size - major innovations like assessment tend to require more extensive planning, involving more staff than minor innovations. Each major innovation puts a squeeze on the time and other resources available to cope with other innovations;

- complexity - an innovation split up into sub-innovations, such as the National Curriculum with its subjects and levels, is likely to require considerable planning effort which limits the attention that may be given to other innovations;

- relationship with other innovations - many of the central government reforms are designed to interrelate. Planning for, say, assessment of the National Curriculum means taking into account plans for other innovations, especially the National Curriculum itself. An integral part of implementing development planning is planning the implementation of other innovations. Problems with one innovation may imply hold-ups with another, as where uncertainty over an LMS budget may inhibit spending on resources connected with the National Curriculum;

- degree of compulsion - most central government and associated LEA innovations for schools are either fully compulsory or constitute an 'offer you dare not refuse' because they are technically optional but carry desired resources. A compulsory innovation must be addressed, so competing with other innovations.

In Chapter 7 we examine aspects of our case-study schools' innovation profiles, showing not only the planning headache of dealing with a large number of innovations at different phases, but also portraying how many of these innovations were heavyweights - major, complex, interrelated and compulsory - contributing to a planning migraine.

The multiple innovations project showed how factors connected with the

**Table 2.3** Dimensions of variation between innovations

| minor ←—————————————————————————————→ major | |
|---|---|
| (minor significance for the school) One or more individuals, and/or occupying small proportion of time | (major significance for the school) One or more functional groups (e.g. heads of faculty, infant department) and/or occupying a large proportion of time |
| simple ←—————————————————————————————→ complex | |
| No sub-innovations representing discrete sets of tasks for same or different staff | Contains sub-innovations representing discrete task areas for same or different staff |
| discrete ←—————————————————————————————→ interrelated | |
| Planned or implemented without a deliberate link with other innovations | Planned or implemented with deliberate link with other innovations |
| optional ←—————————————————————————————→ compulsory | |
| Users free to choose whether and how to implement | Users required by others to implement without flexibility |

From Wallace (1991a).

headteachers, with information about externally initiated innovations, and with other changes that necessitated a coordinated response, all intruded into the planning process. These factors included:

- the way heads continually sought 'room to manoeuvre', reflected in the plans they fostered, to assimilate external innovations in accordance with their largely unchanging beliefs and values, including those concerning the protection of colleagues from innovation overload;
- the unique overview heads sustained because they were often the first at school level to receive information about external innovations on which so much planning for change depended;
- the frequency of staff being unable to plan implementation of an external innovation while they waited for information to arrive from central government or its agencies;
- contradictory messages about an external innovation where new information conflicted with earlier announcements;
- the short notice with which an external innovation was sometimes launched;
- conflict between external innovations, where the implementation requirements of one cut across those of another;
- the capacity of staff for implementing innovations being to a greater or lesser extent overreached;
- occasional crises and longer-term issues.

The outcome of these factors was an opportunistic coping strategy led by heads who attempted to continue to express their beliefs and values as far as possible, at times by fending off external demands. Responses were made through the existing management structures, roles and procedures and, where deemed necessary, new ones were created. We shall see in Chapter 5 how heads in the present study orchestrated the management of planning within their wider strategy for coping with multiple innovations.

## THE CONTEXT OF CULTURAL DIVERSITY

Cultural diversity may affect planning for change in multiracial primary schools in so far as the content of planning could take into account the beliefs and values of one culture or ignore those of another. Different cultural groups may be offered greater or lesser access to the planning process and may vary in how far they make use of whatever opportunities they are given.

Culture refers to the way in which a group of people shares a set of beliefs and values about aspects of social life, including schooling and religion. Different groups may hold allegiance to contradictory sets of beliefs and values, possibly leading to cultural conflict. Equally, the same group may include subgroups with partially overlapping and partially distinctive beliefs and values. Increasing attention has been paid to the culture of the teaching staff within their role as professionals (e.g. Sarason, 1971; Deal, 1985; Nias *et al.*, 1989), and how its content may be influenced so that staff come to value collaboration and continuous improvement (Fullan, 1991; Hargreaves and Hopkins, 1991). Less attention has been paid to the beliefs and values that one group involved in schooling has about another, especially the views of parents about teaching staff as educators and vice versa.

Cultural diversity implies that there are two or more groups, each with its own culture, interacting within a larger community. Multiracial schools serve communities of at least two ethnic groups, one or more of which will often be black (mainly from Asian or Afro-Caribbean backgrounds), while another is white (possibly containing different groups of European origin). Even schools where all pupils are black are likely to have a significant proportion of white teaching staff. Each culture may include beliefs and values about the other cultures and the validity of their beliefs and values. Complicating factors are, first, that the beliefs and values of individuals and groups exposed to those of another culture may change; and second, that over time an increasing proportion of children and parents will be of mixed race and their beliefs and values may include elements of both cultures.

Arguably teachers, support staff, parents and children from a minority ethnic background tend to experience the dual influence of their heritage culture and the white majority culture to which they are exposed more strongly than whites in a multiracial community will feel the influence of the minority ethnic group culture, since the white culture dominates in the society at large. We sought to determine how far beliefs and values of groups among staff and parents (whether from a minority ethnic background or not), including their concerns about religious education and collective worship, affected planning for change according to their level of participation in the process (see Chapter 5).

An associated factor which reflects cultural assumptions is the possibility of racism - whether direct prejudice as, for example, may be expressed among pupils in the playground, or institutional racism, defined in the Swann report as practices which:

> whilst clearly well-intentioned and in no way racist in *intent*, can now be seen as racist in *effect*, in depriving members of ethnic minority groups equality of access to the full range of opportunities which the majority community can take for granted.
>
> (House of Commons, 1985, p. 28)

We examined how far planning for change included considerations linked to perceptions of racism or a concern to guard against it, for example through the development of an antiracist policy for a school.

Culture may be conceived as integrally linked with power (Wallace and Hall, 1994) if we take the latter to mean the use of resources of whatever kind, according to the beliefs and values of individuals or groups, to achieve their desired outcomes. Resources may vary widely, including sanctions, rewards, reference to norms of behaviour and knowledge of various kinds. Bacharach and Lawler (1980) distinguish between two forms of power. Authority implies the use of resources to achieve ends where that use is perceived by an individual or group as legitimated by beliefs and values associated with formal status and is potentially backed by sanctions. Influence is the informal use of resources to achieve desired ends where individuals and groups perceive that there is no recourse to sanctions.

Planning for change may be affected by the actions of different individuals and groups among staff, parents and governors according to the beliefs and values they share with others. Conversely, planning may be influenced by individuals and groups failing to participate, whether through inhibition, indifference, incomprehension or ignorance (see Gronn, 1986). An issue in the present study was the desire expressed by some parents that the staff used more formal teaching methods. Staff resisted this pressure by referring to their authority as professionals to continue working in line with their beliefs and values about informal teaching methods, a stance which parents did not challenge further. We will examine the degree to which different individuals and groups used power to affect the planning process. Having elaborated at length on our perspective, let us now turn to what we learned from the initial survey of LEA staff and heads about the range of factors likely to affect planning for change.

# Chapter 3

# Approaches to Planning

Here we set the scene for the case studies by focusing progressively on planning for change at school level, beginning by introducing the three LEAs. We concentrate on contextual features and strategies for managing innovations which affected multiracial primary schools at the time of our initial interviews with headteachers, and summarize progress with the LEA development planning initiatives for schools. We then report the findings of the headteacher survey, examining first who was centrally involved in planning. Our account of how planning for change was managed indicates how LEA activities influenced planning at school level and reveals the significance of innovations which constituted part of the planning process. The implications of other innovations for planning are discussed. Finally, we summarize the range of factors which make for environmental turbulence or stability at school level and consider which models of planning most closely match our findings.

## THE WIDER LOCAL CONTEXT

Interviews with LEA staff during the 1990 autumn term suggested that the factors summarized in Table 3.1 formed part of the local external environment of schools which would impinge on the content of their plans. Most factors were interrelated and were affected by the political allegiance of the local council and its education committee. The council had a major hand in interpreting central government policies and in determining priorities for managing the LEA and its expenditure. Planning in the schools, as public-sector organizations, was subject to political influence from their external environment which stemmed from both local and national government.

### The county

A combination of demographic factors affected teacher supply in one corner of the county. House prices were high throughout the region, deterring young teachers from settling locally. The teacher shortage was most acute in that part of the LEA which bordered a large conurbation. Teaching staff in the adjacent urban boroughs were entitled to an extra allowance for working in a high-cost area, resulting in these boroughs attracting teachers who lived within the county border. The neighbouring LEAs also paid supply teachers at a higher rate than the county.

Since 1984 the majority of members of the county council had been loyal to the Conservative Party. These councillors were less concerned to promote multicultural initiatives than the previous council but were committed to

**Table 3.1** The local context for planning in multiracial primary schools (autumn 1990)

| Factor | LEA | | |
| --- | --- | --- | --- |
| | County | Borough | City |
| Demography | Large towns, ribbon development, rural areas | Urban sprawl | Large inner-city area, surrounding suburbs, outlying rural area |
| Teacher supply | Severe shortage in some areas, adequate in others | Widespread moderate shortage | Adequate |
| Political allegiance of local council | Conservative since 1984 | Pendulum authority, Labour replaced by Conservative in 1990 | Labour since 1980 |
| Devolution of LEA services | Extensive devolution in progress | Devolution under consideration | Some devolution, retaining many centralized services |
| Spending on education | Cuts proposed | Cuts proposed | Major primary schools initiative late 1980s, maintaining existing level of spending, expanding nursery provision |
| Priority to promote equal opportunities | Was high in early 1980s, now lower priority | Was high in late 1980s, now very low priority | High, several new initiatives |
| Organization of primary schooling | Varied: primary, first and middle (transfer at 8 and 12), first (transfer at 9) | First and middle (transfer at 8 and 12) | Varied: primary in suburbs and rural areas, first (transfer at 9) in inner city |
| Reorganization to remove surplus pupil places | Under consideration in one town | Proposed for September 1992, revert to primary, involving amalgamations | Proposed for September 1992, revert to primary, involving amalgamations, closures and new schools |
| LEA restructuring | Recently restructured to create separate inspection and support services | Recently restructured inspectorate and advisory teacher service | Recently restructured advisory service, proposal to increase it |

extensive devolution of finance to schools, reflected in the LEA development planning initiative. Currently, county councillors were considering making cuts in the education budget.

Partly as a result of past redefinition of county boundaries, the system of schooling varied between areas, with a two-tier primary and secondary system and two three-tier systems with transfer at either age 8 and 12 or 9 and 13. The LEA had recently been restructured and separate inspection and support services had been created within the 'quality assurance' division, although in practice the roles of adviser and inspector were almost interchangeable. Confusion among school staff and governors over which LEA staff to contact about particular issues had arisen because of a massive reallocation of posts throughout the education department, including the deployment of some staff to new liaison responsibilities in different areas of the LEA.

# The borough

The borough was one of many small LEAs within a very large conurbation where there was a widespread problem over recruitment of teaching staff, from beginning teachers to heads. LEA staff reported difficulty in obtaining sufficient supply teacher cover to release staff during the school day for in-service training linked to the introduction of the national reforms.

A factor resulting over the long term in a climate of repeated change in the LEA was the pendulum effect of the voting pattern in borough council elections, held every four years. Throughout the previous two decades the majority political party in the council had alternated between Conservative and Labour, the policies of one administration often being countermanded by those of the next. In the late 1980s a Labour-controlled council had taken initiatives to promote equal opportunities in schools and within the LEA. The existence of surplus capacity in secondary schools had led to consideration being given to reorganizing schooling from a three-tier system of first, middle and secondary schools with transfer of pupils at ages 8 and 12 to a primary and secondary system with transfer at 11.

During the local council elections in May 1990 the successful campaign of Conservative Party candidates included a promise to reduce the poll tax, which would cut the then-current income of the borough council. The largest item of expenditure of all such councils was education, so the return of a Conservative-controlled council heralded a policy shift towards the reduction of expenditure on education. The new council immediately curtailed the existing LEA equal opportunities initiatives for schools and engaged in a voluntary charge-capping exercise to fulfil the promise of a tax cut. Councillors announced a proposal to reorganize schooling which entailed amalgamations between first and middle schools sharing the same site, to take place in September 1992. All amalgamating schools would have a temporary governing body to deal with reorganization which would exist alongside the present governing body until the new schools were created.

Consideration began to be given to reviewing LEA services to schools, including the inspection and support structure. The local context in which schools had to plan changes was becoming increasingly turbulent because of uncertainty over innovations such as equal opportunities initiatives; the likelihood of cuts in school budgets; the possibility of reorganization leading to compulsory redeployment or even redundancies; and the prospect of further changes in the LEA structure which had just been redesigned with separate inspection and advisory teaching teams.

# The city

The city council had been controlled by the Labour Party throughout the 1980s. Spending on primary-sector schools, especially in the inner city where most multiracial schools were located, had been dramatically increased through a major initiative in the second half of the decade. This project had included provision of additional school and external support staff, a primary teachers' centre, enhanced capitation, extensive refurbishment of buildings, and the

43

development of comprehensive provision of centralized in-service training courses. Most of the expenditure came from the city council, with some support from a central government grant. Allied initiatives included the building of several new schools.

Parameters imposed by central government for the development of an LMS funding formula within each LEA meant that the weighting of resources given to inner-city schools under this project could not be sustained, leading to removal of many extra resources that had been enjoyed in these schools and their redistribution to other schools outside the inner-city area. This is a clear example of a central government policy whose implementation at LEA level cut across an existing local initiative, with knock-on effects for school-level planning. The response required of inner-city schools was to plan how to manage with fewer resources, including lower staffing levels.

Nevertheless, overall provision of staffing remained high in the city compared to the other LEAs. The city council was committed to expanding nursery education and inner-city schools had been identified as a priority for expenditure. Promotion of equal opportunities was a local priority of long standing, and recent initiatives included the appointment of advisers with an equal opportunities brief and the launch of an LEA-backed support group for black governors. There was a regular LEA equal opportunities strategies group meeting with wide representation to ensure that relevant issues were addressed within initiatives such as LMS, and central provision of in-service training also dealt with these issues. Since promotion of equal opportunities was not a policy with strong Conservative central government support, initiatives at local level were more likely to be sustained in the face of national reforms - and therefore reflected in planning in schools - where the local council was controlled by other political parties.

Reorganization of schooling had been under way for several years, Roman Catholic schools and those in an outlying area having already switched to a primary and secondary system with transfer at age 11. The DES had approved the LEA proposal for inner-city schools to revert from the existing three-tier system of first, middle and secondary schools with transfer at 9 and 13. Reorganization was scheduled for September 1992, the same date as had been chosen more recently in the borough. Planning in the city had taken place over a much longer period and agreement had been reached with DES officials to give all inner-city schools LMS in April 1993 so as to retain control over the appointment of staff until after reorganization was completed. First schools in the city would take two additional year groups of pupils and middle schools would close or be converted into primary schools. In the borough most first or middle schools would merely lose their oldest year group of pupils, a less radical change. However, amalgamations in both LEAs represented a complex innovation for staff in the schools affected.

The LEA advisory service had been restructured and expanded during the time of the primary schools initiative and further expansion was being considered in the light of extra work required to implement the national reforms. The city council had decided to retain both inspection and support activities within the advisory service. This policy was developed in the face of central government pressure on LEAs to delegate the costs of the support function to schools within LMS so that staff could buy in support from a range of sources according to needs identified at school level. Support activity had been a major plank of the LEA efforts to improve primary schools during the recent initiative and advisory work continued to be viewed as a significant means of influencing school development. Of the three LEAs, the city retained the most centralized approach to managing its schools, continuing the tradition established over the past decade by the Labour council but at odds with Conservative central government policy. (By the end of our fieldwork pressure from schools for the city LEA to devolve more money to schools led to a reversal of the policy of centralized provision and expansion of support services.)

While planning in schools was likely to be affected by different combinations of local contextual factors, all three LEAs included some giving rise to environmental turbulence. School reorganization promised a massive upheaval for staff in the borough and the city; education cuts in the county and the borough implied implementing the current wave of innovations with fewer resources; reduction in LEA support for equal opportunities initiatives in the borough would make them more difficult to sustain.

## LEA MANAGEMENT OF CHANGE

Let us move closer to the school level by examining the approach adopted in each LEA to the management of innovations with implications for multiracial primary-sector schools. Table 3.2 shows how relevant factors included the LEA-level innovation of restructuring to manage LEA support and monitoring responsibilities as defined by central government; innovations concerning the management of planning in schools; and strategies for dealing with the central government innovation of bidding for Section 11 funds. The Home Office had recently sent detailed guidance and LEA staff were in the early stages of preparing their submission.

### The county

The LEA 'quality assurance' structure consisted of advisers and inspectors, backed by a cadre of advisory teachers. Schools had been divided into clusters with a liaison officer - an adviser, inspector or advisory teacher - attached to several of these groups who could give support over development planning issues. Inspections covered only a small proportion of schools in any year. Centralized provision of in-service training courses was complemented by the devolution of a substantial sum for school-led training.

LMS for primary-sector schools was currently to be phased in over several years, but county councillors keen to speed up devolution were considering how to bring forward implementation. The LEA-level innovation of introducing LMS to schools was also subject to some change at the early implementation stage. The component of the LEA's formula covering provision for pupils with special educational needs was accepted by central government officials on the condition that this component was reviewed. (No more acceptable measure was found after consultation, so this part of the formula remained in the event.)

**Table 3.2** LEA management of innovations affecting multiracial primary schools (autumn 1990)

| | LEA | | |
|---|---|---|---|
| Factor | County | Borough | City |
| Support structure | Advisers, subject-based advisory teachers, liaison officer for each school, clusters of schools | Advisory teachers working in 'teaching and learning strategies' teams, link inspector for each school, clusters of schools | Advisers, phase-based advisory teachers, adviser liaises with each school, a few clusters of schools |
| Monitoring structure | Inspectorate, formal inspections | Inspectorate, formal inspections, 'substantial visit' to every school over a year | Advisers, formal inspections, negotiated reviews, 'paired visits' |
| Management of in-service training | School staff consulted, centralized provision of courses, extensive devolution to schools | School staff consulted, centralized provision of courses, training for clusters of schools, moderate devolution to schools | School staff consulted, centralized provision of extensive range of courses, moderate devolution to schools |
| Development planning initiative | Annual development plans completed by all schools | Annual development plans completed by schools in voluntary project, National Curriculum development plan completed by all schools | Annual development plans completed by all schools |
| LMS scheme | To be phased in 1990–93, but consideration of delegation being completed in 1992, DES required funding formula to be modified | To be phased in 1990–93 but proposal to accelerate implementation | All inner-city schools to receive LMS in 1993 after reorganization |
| Section 11 bidding procedure | Each school staff wrote bid, collated by LEA staff into large projects | Each school staff wrote bid, collated by LEA staff into large projects | Central LEA team gathered information from schools, submitted own bid for a few very large projects |
| Existing structure of Section 11 funded support | Teaching posts in schools, language and administrative assistants, central peripatetic team of ESL and bilingual teaching staff | Teaching posts in schools, language and administrative assistants, central peripatetic team of bilingual and ESL teaching staff | Central peripatetic ESL teachers, bilingual and cultural assistants |
| Anticipated content of Section 11 bids | Teaching posts appointed direct to schools within each school's project | Teaching posts, language and support staff centrally allocated to schools as support teams | Expansion of central allocation of assistants, absorption of home–school liaison officers previously funded by LEA, ESL teachers to be absorbed into mainstream post |
| Stance on collective worship | Left to schools to consider applying for determination | Left to schools to consider applying for determination | Liaison with community groups, liberal interpretation by SACRE, no schools applied for determination |
| Governor training | Extensive training and information service | Limited training | Moderate amount of training |

School staff and governors had already experienced problems over the first budget, despite the best efforts of the team responsible for introducing LMS to schools, because of difficulties over a few months in setting up the LEA's computerized system for providing budgetary information. As one member of the LEA staff commented:

> Coming into April when every school had a formula derived budget there were the most terrible problems, and schools were being charged for people who had left or who had died, or supply teachers who worked there for a week and then moved on. But they were still set up on the payroll. The budget was late, it was inaccurate in all sorts of

ways - when they [governors] needed to know about insurance or building problems they couldn't find the person they wanted. . . . We had all changed our jobs and our titles . . . it suddenly became a very cold, hard world and familiar faces weren't there.

Section 11-funded support comprised a centrally administered team of ESL and bilingual teaching staff and teaching posts and language and administrative assistants based in particular schools. Each school's staff was required to prepare a project bid and send it to the central LEA team for collation into the LEA submission to the Home Office. Training had been provided for heads to help them with this new task. It was expected that in future the centrally administered posts would be terminated and all teaching posts would be appointed directly to schools, in line with the wider LEA policy of devolution.

Another consequence of this policy was the development by LEA staff of a wide-ranging support service for governors which was not matched by the level of support in the other two LEAs. Provision included a rolling programme of training for new and inexperienced governors and distance learning materials on particular innovations, located at a growing number of resource centres. Other initiatives included a recruitment drive, provision of area coordinators, a twenty-four hour helpline, a termly governors' newsletter and an information pack for new governors.

## The borough

The LEA structure for supporting schools had been reorganized and was based on advisory teachers who facilitated the introduction of National Curriculum subjects. Pastoral support was provided by an inspector linked to each school. Much of the training was organized on an area basis within designated school clusters. Monitoring was the exclusive role of inspectors, who carried out a few large-scale formal inspections coupled with less comprehensive 'substantial visits' intended to cover every school during the first year of the new arrangement. Each school's staff in this LEA could expect to be monitored by LEA inspectors as well as being able to call upon the support of the link inspector. The coverage of this strategy was not matched by the inspections of varying degrees of formality and scale in the other LEAs (see Table 5.2 in Chapter 5).

In common with the other LEAs, the approach to managing in-service training for schools was affected by the new central government arrangements for allocation of grants which confined expenditure to 'national priorities' connected with the national reforms and other central government concerns such as teacher recruitment and improving pupil discipline (DES, 1990). In the past, LEAs had also received a central contribution to locally identified priorities. However, the new borough council was not allocating additional money for in-service training to meet locally identified needs, so planning for change at school level would now have to take into account the lack of LEA funds to support initiatives that were unrelated to central government concerns. This strategy formed an extra constraint on equal opportunities work begun prior to the election of the present council. While school staff were consulted about their in-service training needs, a procedure required by central government as a condition of the grant, LEA staff perceived that central government had predetermined the major areas of need for all LEAs. A moderate sum of in-service training money was devolved to schools for activities connected with the national priorities.

LMS was originally to be phased in over four years, all schools having partially delegated budgets from April 1990. LEA staff and councillors were currently considering bringing implementation forward so that all primary-sector schools would have full delegation by April 1992. Appointments entailed in reorganization of schooling would be controlled by the governors of each school, giving rise to the possibility of redundancies among present staff if governors chose to appoint heads and teachers from other LEAs.

The LEA response to the new Section 11 grants system was to require each school to submit its own bid to the LEA based upon an assessment of needs. Bids would be collated into several large projects within the overall LEA submission. The LEA inspector responsible for the education component was keen that headteachers should engage directly in the process which included consulting parents. Training had been provided to brief school staff. It was planned to expand the existing system of teaching, language and assistant posts by creating a centrally administered team for each school.

## The city

Advisers were responsible for managing the support structure, leading teams of advisory teachers and providing some in-service training, and they also had pastoral responsibility for several schools. Their work included monitoring, the range of inspection activities comprising full school reviews, negotiated reviews covering an aspect of work agreed with school staff, and consultative 'paired visits' where advisers worked jointly with staff to review agreed areas.

There was a strong tradition of centralized provision of in-service training, expanded during the LEA primary schools project. Release of teachers for in-service courses had been made possible by enhanced staffing of many schools, a legacy of which remained. Money for school-based in-service training had been devolved but its use had been confined to activities which lay within the national priorities. Less money was now available to support school-led equal opportunities and multicultural initiatives through this means. All schools were at the same stage with the introduction of LMS. Preparatory training had been given to heads before and after the beginning of formula funding in April 1990.

The Section 11 bidding procedure in the city was centralized, in contrast with the other LEAs, an LEA team preparing its bid on the basis of statistics collected from schools. Consequently school staff had little involvement in formulating the few large projects in the submission to the Home Office. The existing central ESL team of teachers was to be disbanded and assistants' brief for cultural support to be removed in line with the new Home Office restriction on the use of funding. They would in future be responsible for liaison with parents in addition to giving language support in the classroom. Home-school support staff, presently allocated to some multiracial schools and funded by the LEA, would be absorbed into the Section 11 structure with the same brief as their colleagues. The system would be expanded through the appointment of more assistants.

## LEA DEVELOPMENT PLANNING INITIATIVES

We noted in Chapter 1 how each LEA had a different approach to development planning. The initiative in the county predated the DES requirement that schools have a National Curriculum development plan, while the others were launched largely in response to it. Table 3.3 compares the LEA development

**Table 3.3** LEA development planning initiatives (autumn 1990)

| | LEA | | |
| --- | --- | --- | --- |
| Factor | County | Borough | City |
| Origin | To support LEA management of in-service training from 1988 (after DES training grants scheme introduced) | LEA project to synthesize existing separate plans: development plan, in-service training, equal opportunities | Response to DES requirements for National Curriculum development plan and for LEAs to identify schools' in-service training needs |
| Compulsion for schools | Compulsory to complete document and submit to LEA | Voluntary participation in LEA project | Compulsory to complete document and submit to LEA |
| Link with LEA management of in-service training | Subsumed within development plan | Recommended that it be covered within development plan | Subsumed within development plan |
| Link with school's management plan | Incorporated within development plan for schools with LMS | No link | No link |
| Planning cycle | Financial year – coming year in detail, next two years in outline | Not specified but considering financial year – coming year in detail, next two years in outline | Academic year: coming year only |
| Focus of plan | Curriculum, management structures and procedures, staff development | No focus specified | Mainly curriculum |
| Number of areas for development in any year | Up to six areas | Not specified but recommended that number be limited | Up to four areas advised |
| Recommended procedure | Annual consultation with staff, governors (approval required) and liaison officer; review, identify areas, action planning, implement, evaluate | Annual consultation with staff and governors (approval required); audit, construct plan, implement, evaluate | Annual consultation with staff (governors to be informed); review, identify areas, action planning, implement, evaluate |
| Documentation | Eleven pages of forms, extensive guidance notes: two copies sent to LEA, one copy to liaison officer | (No forms for plan), extensive draft guidance notes, to be adapted to fit school context | Eighteen pages of forms, brief guidance notes for compiling, reference to DES (1989a) for guidance on procedures; one copy to LEA via pastoral adviser |
| LEA implementation strategy | Introduced to all schools in 1988, preparatory training given; present version under review | Three phases 1989–92, covering all schools; expected to produce guidelines; training for heads and chairs of governors | Introduced to all schools in 1989; training for heads; implementation rushed; present version modified in light of feedback |
| LEA use of development plan | Inform LEA in-service training provision, inform inspectors | (Not used for managing in-service training); inform inspectors where plan available | Inform LEA in-service training provision, inform inspectors |

planning initiatives and progress with their implementation at the time of the headteacher survey. Here we focus on development planning for schools as an innovation at the LEA level.

## The county

The introduction of development planning in the county was a major, carefully planned and implemented innovation. Some schools had been experimenting with development planning since the late 1980s, so the ground had been prepared for this initiative. Nevertheless, LEA staff provided considerable support in the initial phase. Preliminary design work was led by the LEA senior inspector for in-service training as one of her first tasks after joining the county staff in September 1988. At that time, an LEA concern to clarify and improve procedures for identifying teachers' in-service training needs and for costing training provision coincided with discussions about whether and how funds should increasingly be devolved to schools.

The first guidance document on school development planning was drafted by this inspector, circulated to individuals and groups for comment and trialled in a few schools before going to the education committee for approval. The inspector stated that by the time the document was finalized and distributed to schools in February 1989 it had been widely discussed in draft form and had gained considerable support from headteachers. Briefing was thorough: the inspector organized day conferences with all the primary and secondary headteachers to discuss the document; advisory teachers organized conferences for school coordinators responsible for in-service training; and evening meetings were organized for governors. LEA staff also introduced a longer training course on planning for school and staff development which was designed for the headteacher and one or two other staff from a school. All headteachers would have the opportunity to attend over several years.

The guidelines for school development planning were widely distributed: each primary school received three or four copies and could obtain more on request, and a copy was sent to the chair of governors in each school. School staff were strongly encouraged, rather than compelled, to produce a development plan and by the end of the 1989 summer term a plan had been received by LEA staff for each of the schools. Since the plans covered a financial year, they were drawn up in the spring term and submitted to the LEA early in the summer. In the first year each school staff received written feedback about the plan. The senior inspector for in-service training read each document and within ten days wrote a letter to the headteacher commenting on the school's submission. Typically she would comment on content, possibly suggesting how the plan might be improved and drawing the head's attention to relevant training courses or literature that might be helpful. Where possible, she would encourage networking by identifying other schools who were working on similiar priorities and suggesting that the head might find it useful to contact them.

Information about priorities identified at school level was put onto a central database and the advisers and advisory teachers were notified about schools which had chosen their subject area as a priority. In turn, they telephoned the schools offering advice and support. The inspector perceived that the personal feedback that each school had received on its plan and the offers of help from advisory staff had demonstrated to school staff that the LEA took development planning seriously. This strategy had helped the innovation to take root.

The development plan was based on the financial-year cycle, with up to six development areas being addressed in any year. Plans were to be made in detail for the coming year and for the next two in outline. Recently, the initiative had been made more comprehensive by integrating the LMS management plan with the development plan document.

The recommended procedure, consistent with the DES guidance, entailed an annual consultation exercise with staff and governors (whose approval was required for the final plan, incorporating the LMS management plan), and preferably also the liaison officer for the school. The development plan contained eleven pages of forms and substantial guidance notes on the procedure. Copies of the completed document were to be submitted to the LEA and to the liaison officer who was expected to follow it up informally with the school, although in practice there was seldom time to do so. Information about in-service training needs and the proposed use of training days contained within the plan was used in planning LEA provision, and the document informed school inspections.

## The borough

The borough's initiative was in its second of three phases and had reached about half of its schools. The purpose of the project was to synthesize existing separate plans which school staff were required to complete: the National Curriculum development plan; an in-service training plan required by the LEA to fulfil the central government requirement that schools must be consulted over their needs; and an equal opportunities plan, the legacy of an LEA initiative under the previous Labour council. The project was intended to support school staff and governors with developing their own approach to coordinating planning, in contrast with the other LEAs. As one inspector stated: 'The whole idea of the IDP project was how to best ... put it together from the school perspective, rather than the LEA again giving them sheets that they just had to fill in.'

Since participation was voluntary, all schools were still required to complete a National Curriculum development plan and an in-service training plan, and those with LMS had to have a management plan. Staff in schools within the project were encouraged to incorporate these plans within their development plan. The design of the development plan was less sophisticated than the county approach, having yet to deal with the implications of LMS. The attempt to enable school staff to create a version of development planning that suited their context meant, first, that no particular annual cycle was specified, although consideration was being given to recommending the financial year; second, that guidance did not delimit the kind of development areas to include; and third, that the number of areas to be tackled in any year was left open. There was room

51

for considerable variation over the form the development plan would take in different schools.

The recommended procedure followed the DES guidance which had influenced the project leaders, most of whom were seconded from schools. The draft guidance document emphasized consultation, though it was recognized that headteachers would control its extent in practice:

> The approach recommended in these guidelines involves a high degree
> of staff participation in the planning process. This is an essential part
> of obtaining ownership of, and commitment to, the plans by the
> people who will have to implement them. The extent to which this
> participation is legislative and executive as opposed to being
> consultative is a matter for individual heads. However these guidelines
> recommend full consultation with staff. The crucial thing to remember
> is that the process towards the plan is as important as having a plan.

The LEA strategy for implementing the innovation of development planning, encouraging participants to adapt the guidance, was consistent with the concern for developing ownership within the recommended process at school level. The guidance notes stated: 'It is important that each school should use the guidelines in a way that makes them specific to their own establishment.' The approval of governors was to be sought for an outline plan once priority areas for development had been identified. The development planning process was viewed as a matter for professionals, but subject to the oversight and support of governing bodies. The guidance notes (used in training for project participants), like the DES document, did not run to forms for completing the development plan.

LEA project staff anticipated offering training by 1992 for heads and chairs of governors in any school who wished to participate, and making available to all schools the final version of the guidance notes which would by then have been extensively trialled. The project schools' current development plans were not used to inform LEA staff except where they could be made available for inspections. However, consideration was being given to using the consultative development planning process as a means of supporting schools with reorganization.

## The city

The development planning initiative in this LEA was a hurried response to central government requirements for a National Curriculum development plan. It was also influenced by the earlier requirement that LEA staff must identify in-service training needs in schools. The city development plan focused primarily on the curriculum, emphasizing National Curriculum requirements, although school staff were free to identify other priorities (such as increasing parental involvement). School staff were already required to complete a form outlining their in-service training needs which was used by LEA staff in preparing their bid for the DES grant.

The DES timetable imposed upon LEAs, as we implied in Chapter 1, provided the advisers responsible for the initiative with a planning headache (see

Figure 3.1). This information was required from schools in the summer preceding the next financial year for which the grant was to be allocated. LEA staff opted for a single academic year as the basis for the development plan cycle, in parallel with the timetable for introducing the National Curriculum on the basis of academic years. It was suggested that school staff work out their in-service training requirements, already submitted to the LEA, in more detail for the coming academic year. The next financial year, to which the DES grant applied, overlapped with only the final term covered by the development plan since the first two terms of the academic year in hand related to the present financial year. School staff had been consulted over their in-service training needs for these two terms the previous summer. In any summer term school staff had to provide the LEA with an outline of their in-service training needs for a financial year beginning in ten months' time, then at the beginning of the following autumn term work out details within the development plan for the academic year, the first two-thirds of which related to needs identified the previous summer and the final third to the needs identified in the current summer.

LEA staff recommended that up to four development areas were identified in any year. Budgeting within LMS was excluded from the plan. The recommended consultative process was similar to the other LEAs, school staff being referred to the DES (1989a) document for advice. It was expected that governors would not have an input but would be informed about the plan. The document consisted of eighteen pages of forms, requiring information on the school context and progress with development. The final three forms covered the plan itself. One copy of the document was to be submitted to the adviser with pastoral responsibility for the school, who was expected to scan it, where possible follow up in school, and pass it on to the adviser managing the initiative in primary schools. Information about priorities for development was collated and made available to the LEA support team, who gave priority on in-service training courses to staff from schools where a relevant area had been identified as a priority. Development plans were also used to inform inspections.

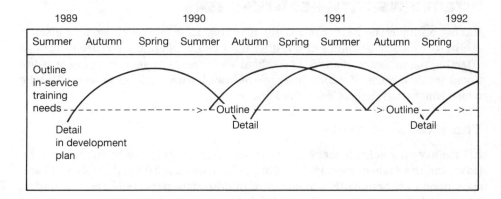

Figure 3.1 *Overlapping planning cycles for city schools*

## LEA development planning initiatives as an innovation

The perception among LEA staff, as both designers and users of the innovation at LEA level, of the need for development planning in schools was strongly influenced by central government innovations, including the National Curriculum. The diversity of LEA approaches reflected different solutions to dilemmas of design and implementation, none of which was likely to be without problems.

The *complexity* of the development planning initiative was difficult to keep within bounds, first because of the variety of central government innovations and their timetables for implementation which planning for change at school level would have to take into account; and secondly because of the need imposed by central government for LEA staff to gather information from schools. Restricting the focus - as encouraged within the city initiative - made for a reasonably simple innovation for schools which, however, lacked the comprehensiveness and range of components (such as the LMS budget) that the county initiative had addressed. The acceptability of the innovation to school staff would be enhanced in the borough, where participants were encouraged to take ownership, yet it would not influence any school staff who neither decided to participate nor chose to use the guidance document. Greatest impact was likely upon county school staff who, as users of the innovation at their level, both had most experience with implementing development planning and had the most comprehensive plan.

*Clarity* for all users was likely to be constrained by the way the innovation itself evolved as LEA staff became more familiar with it and responded to feedback from schools and changes in central government policy. During the 1990 autumn term staff in all three LEAs were grappling with the new restriction on categories of in-service training eligible for DES grant to prespecified national priorities. County staff, for example, were planning how to continue the policy of devolving a substantial proportion of the grant to schools. Areas within development plans would have to be presented in such a way that they lay within the national priorities.

## INTERVIEWS WITH HEADTEACHERS

Having outlined the LEA context for planning at school level, we now discuss the headteachers' accounts in building up a complementary picture of factors affecting planning for change. The school-level context generated several additional factors, most of which interrelated both with each other and with the wider contextual factors described above.

## The site-level context

All twenty-four schools were in urban areas, including two in suburban locations, and the socio-economic status of parents was almost exclusively working-class in half of them, with a minority of middle-class parents in the remainder. There were no 'leafy lane' schools. A few heads implied that there were limited possibilities for raising money from parents and the local community to support school initiatives. One, in a school within an area of high unemployment, mentioned that a constraint upon routine planning for educational journeys was the difficulty many parents experienced with paying any charge. An HMI survey of fundraising (DES, 1987), carried out prior to LMS, found that while 38 per cent of primary schools raised a sum equivalent to over 30 per cent of their capitation allowance, 28 per cent were able to raise the equivalent of less than 10 per cent of the allowance.

The age of school buildings ranged from Victorian to brand new. Planning problems could arise with buildings of any age. They could be connected with maintenance: one head in a new building was spending considerable time negotiating with the builders and LEA staff to sort out defects and omissions. Exceptionally, such problems could give rise to major planning exercises. The head of a newly built school in the city reminisced on the crisis which led to the closing of the original Victorian building. Early one morning, before pupils arrived, there was a major fall of plaster in the hall and the head had promptly to arrange for the pupils to be bussed to other sites. The building was demolished and two new schools built to replace it. In all, three city headteachers reported moving to temporary sites while the original building was refurbished or a new school built under the modernization programme launched by the city council.

Problems with building maintenance seem increasingly likely to affect planning nationally because of the legacy of deteriorating poor-quality post-war buildings and the failure of local authorities to sustain adequate programmes of routine maintenance, a higher priority having been given to emergency repairs (National Audit Office, 1991; *Times Educational Supplement*, 1991a). The central government curb on local government expenditure through community charge-capping has exacerbated the problem. For, although decisions on the maintenance of school buildings rest with local government, this area competes with other local services for the allocation of available funds, over which central government has imposed increasingly tight limits.

A related issue is the vandalizing of buildings and equipment, dictating planned prevention and response measures. Vandalism is more prevalent in metropolitan than county authorities, and arson is on the increase (National Audit Office, 1991). Damage to school buildings caused by vandals prompted a planned response in a few of the survey schools. With the advent of LMS, a complicating factor may lie in who pays for the damage. One head in a school prone to vandalism with a partially delegated budget reported how the annual maintenance sum had been used up within the first half of the financial year, largely on replacing windows. After about twenty windows were smashed over a half term, the head put in an order to the LEA for repairs. She was informed that the windows could not be fixed until the next financial year, five months away. The head consulted the chair of governors and went to see the LEA official responsible for the LMS initiative. She stated that the chair had approved her plan to close the school until the following April, whereupon arrangements were made to repair the windows the next day. This example indicates how an innovation may interact negatively with planning for maintenance, and how a head may have to drop other work to respond to a high-priority problem unrelated to education.

The survey schools catered for seven different age ranges of pupils (see Table 3.4), and two-thirds had a nursery. One-third took pupils up to the age of 12, with the consequence that staff had to plan for the first year of Key Stage 3 within the National Curriculum, including a modern foreign language. Anticipated reorganization in the borough posed a planning problem over how much to spend on new resources for Key Stage 3 when the school would lose this year group within less than two years. The 8-12 middle schools, on the other hand, did not have second-year pupils and so staff did not have to plan for the first round of National Curriculum assessment, an innovation which was beginning to dominate planning elsewhere.

The schools were of medium to large size with a median of 263 children, the national median being under 200 pupils (DES, 1992). The smallest had 125 pupils in a building designed in the mid-1980s for over 200 on the expectation that new houses would be built nearby. Owing to a collapse in the housing market, development had not started. The largest school had 450 pupils. Large size was linked to a higher proportion and greater range of levels of promoted posts, which heads used for delegation of management responsibilities among staff. All the schools had coordinators for different subjects within the curriculum and about one-third also had year or department leaders. The task of detailed planning for the implementation of many innovations connected with the curriculum, pedagogy and pastoral care was generally delegated to the member of staff concerned. Another factor connected with size was the complexity of communication about changes, including consultation procedures such as the development plan review and ensuring that staff were made aware of new information about external innovations.

Most teaching staff were women: seventeen of the heads and three-quarters or more of the teachers in any school. Recent or current planning connected with staffing in a minority of schools included making arrangements to cover individuals who were taking maternity leave. Only two of the heads, both in the borough, were from minority ethnic groups. A substantial proportion of minority ethnic group support staff funded under Section 11 were black. There were few mainstream teachers from minority ethnic groups, reflecting the national situation (Commission for Racial Equality, 1988) and linked in parts of the county and the borough to the general teacher shortage. Several heads

**Table 3.4** Pupil age ranges in the survey schools

| Pupil age range | Type of school | Number of schools |
| --- | --- | --- |
| 3–8 | First school | 4 |
| 5–8 | First school | 1 |
| 3–9 | First school | 8 |
| 3–11 | Primary school | 3 |
| 3–12 | Combined first and middle school | 2 |
| 5–12 | Combined first and middle school | 2 |
| 8–12 | Middle school | 4 |

stated that they wished to appoint staff from minority ethnic backgrounds but that they had few applicants. Initiatives were under way or being planned in all three LEAs to support individuals from minority ethnic groups in gaining a teaching qualification.

The ethnic background of pupils was diverse, including black and white groups and a few of mixed race. The range of minority ethnic groups and the proportion of all the children they represented had a major impact on planning for change as Section 11 support available in any school related to the number of pupils from minority ethnic groups within the New Commonwealth and their identified needs for additional support. Survey schools catered for between 16 and 93 per cent of pupils from minority ethnic groups, with a median of 58 per cent. The content of some innovations connected with pupils from minority ethnic backgrounds reflected factors associated with particular groups. For example, developing support for pupils and parents with learning English was particularly significant in one school where 86 per cent of pupils' parents were from Pakistan and Bangladesh. Virtually all these children were bilingual learners with English as their second language. Planning for maintenance could include taking into account the wishes of parents who were concerned about aspects of the curriculum. Some Muslim parents were reported to have requested that their children should not draw pictures of people's faces and that their daughters should be allowed to wear tracksuits during physical education lessons (see also Sarwar, 1991). Special requests were not confined to parents from minority ethnic groups: white parents belonging to the Plymouth Brethren or Jehovah's Witnesses had withdrawn their children from assemblies in three schools.

Although the proportion of pupils from minority ethnic groups varied, most schools had a preponderance of children from either an Asian (maximum 86 per cent) or Afro-Caribbean background (maximum 40 per cent), reflecting the settlement pattern of the local community. Only a quarter of the schools contained 10 per cent or more of children from both backgrounds. The greatest range of ethnic backgrounds was represented in the three schools with 7 per cent or more of 'international' children, most of whose parents were students following higher education courses. In one, thirty languages were spoken.

The schools with less than 10 per cent of pupils from Asian backgrounds and which also had under 10 per cent from Afro-Caribbean backgrounds were the only ones not to have Section 11 funded posts. Both were voluntary-aided and the admissions policy required parents to accept the religious character of the school. In one, a Roman Catholic school, 87 per cent of pupils were Roman Catholic and the rest had to be baptized Christians and were admitted on recommendation from their minister. The other, an Anglican school, contained 16 per cent of pupils from minority ethnic groups, most of whom were from Sikh families who wished their children to be educated in a school with a religious ethos, rather than the other schools nearby which were not connected with any faith. Planning for the desired expansion of these schools was constrained by the requirement that the governing body, and therefore the diocese, must pay for 15 per cent of new building. The scale of building depended upon what the diocese could afford.

## The central role of headteachers as orchestrators

The survey suggested that headteachers were central in *orchestrating* planning for change. They did not merely manage systems but led the way in creating and using them to suit their purposes. Heads established the approach adopted in the school according to their managerial beliefs and values (for example about democratic decision-making). They created management structures like staff meetings and, in a few schools, working parties for planning tasks and a 'senior management team'. They also allocated staff roles, as mentioned above, whereby they delegated responsibility for planning implementation of particular innovations. Similarly, heads sought room to manoeuvre to express and protect their educational beliefs and values through their influence on the content of plans for individual changes. Some beliefs and values were made explicit to staff; others might remain unspoken but be reflected in the headteachers' actions. As orchestrators, heads played a very significant role, whether up front or behind the scenes, in 'doing the right things' by shaping the planning process and its content according to their lights, as well as 'doing things right' in ensuring that the planning process ran as smoothly as possible.

The heads had spent between six months and fourteen years in their present post, the median of three and a half years indicating how most had been appointed within the last five years. A large majority of the heads mentioned how they had acted as innovators in some way, especially in their early years in post. Some initiatives were connected with management, including appointing staff who shared their philosophy, reshaping staff responsibilities, and establishing a consultation procedure. Other initiatives mentioned by individuals included promoting team teaching, replacing furniture and arranging for community language teaching.

Two-thirds of the heads indicated how they had defended existing practices against external innovations or protected staff from unintended consequences of increasing external pressures. Five had held back information from staff to save them from anxiety or had persuaded them not to implement innovations before they were legally required to do so. Two encouraged staff to reduce the scale of their plans for school performances for parents because of the extra pressure they would otherwise add to an already burdensome workload.

Few heads reported consultative exercises to gather the views of parents, although all had regular contact with individuals. Where parents were consulted, heads initiated the process. In two cases consultation was restricted to parents' views on adopting a school uniform, though one head had sent a questionnaire to parents as part of the review phase of the school's development planning initiative. More commonly, attempts were made to 'educate the parents': to inform them and, where necessary, gain their acceptance of the educational beliefs and values of staff.

## A less central role for governors

Most heads claimed that governing bodies did not initiate plans for change. Governors for half the schools were reported to offer passive support for initiatives proposed by staff, one-third offered more active support, and the remainder were perceived by heads to attempt initiatives themselves. This pattern is consistent with research conducted by Baginsky *et al.* (1991) into the governing bodies of forty-three primary, secondary and special schools. Only two of the headteachers in that study thought that governors took an active part in decision-making. Two of the heads in our survey mentioned their gratitude at having governors who were professionals with expertise upon which the heads could capitalize; they included a surveyor, bank manager and lawyer.

In the least participative governing bodies it was difficult to fill vacancies, some governors did not attend meetings and were eventually struck off, and the head and staff did much of their work for them. One head stated how the staff produced the annual governors' report and presented it for governors to amend and approve. By contrast, the few heads whose governing bodies did attempt to take initiatives perceived that governors were tending to intervene in what they believed were matters for professional staff. One of these heads commented on learning how to negotiate control with governors:

> I have a governing body that would like to run the school if they could.
> I did have a very hard time as a brand new head not knowing the ropes
> when I first came in because I am extremely open about what I do.
> And I was actually told by the authority which had always preached
> openness that I was telling them [governors] too much. They were
> using it against me. But I think that is to do with a lack of political
> awareness on my part rather than anything else and I'm getting much
> better at managing the governing body. I discuss everything with them
> but I also take gambles and I get my own way.

An extreme case was a headteacher from a school where 90 per cent of the pupils were from an Asian background. He had been appointed before the implementation of new powers for governors which include control over appointments. The chair had led the governing body in taking these powers in full, removing the head from staff appointments except for his legal right to be present, and taking control of finances. Yet the chair had not shown commitment to managing the school, coming to meetings only once a year (the minimum attendance required to avoid being struck off) although he lived close by, and failing to answer any letters from the head. Room to manoeuvre had been found by the head, in regaining some control over the budget for example:

> At the next meeting I proceeded to pull out from under the table every
> catalogue I could lay my hands on and asked the governing body to
> order what the school needed. They then decided that it was a better
> idea to delegate financial responsibility back to the headteacher.

The head reported how he retained as much control as possible by filtering information: 'I let the governing body know what I think they need to know and we just carry on and do what we want to.' The heads wished to retain overall control of the direction of school development in the face of the new powers which a few governing bodies were testing.

Two-thirds of the governing bodies included one or more individuals from minority ethnic groups but, in the large majority of cases, these groups were under-represented in comparison with the proportion among pupils. This finding tallies with the results of a national survey of governing bodies carried out by Keys and Fernandes (1990). They found that, overall, fewer than 2 per cent of governors had a minority ethnic background while around 20 per cent of those schools where the relevant information was given had at least 6 per cent of pupils from minority ethnic backgrounds. The latter group of schools had more vacancies for governors and more inexperienced governors than schools with less than 6 per cent of pupils from minority ethnic backgrounds.

Heads from the schools in our survey with no governors from minority ethnic groups indicated how they had tried unsuccessfully to persuade individuals from these groups to become governors. Reasons reported for this failure included diffidence among members of minority ethnic groups about putting themselves forward, sometimes exacerbated by a lack of fluency in English, and their work pattern precluding them from attending governors' meetings. According to the headteachers' testimony, neither parents nor governors from the schools in our survey had much influence over the content of changes. More significant were the heads' beliefs and values, including those relating to minority ethnic groups such as how far they promoted multicultural education.

## DEVELOPMENT PLANNING

Development plans had been completed in all the schools in the county and the city (see also Chapter 6). Two schools in the borough had recently joined the LEA project while the remainder had declined the invitation to participate or had dropped out when they discovered that it duplicated their existing practice. All heads in the borough claimed to have procedures of their own for planning for change which included a National Curriculum development plan. Several heads had been unwilling to take on another external innovation.

Approaches to planning for change adopted by these heads are instructive because they indicate what was found useful in a context where there was no compulsory development planning initiative. Much planning for change was not committed to paper, but these heads were at different stages of introducing their own version of a development planning procedure and document. Each entailed an occasional staff consultation exercise and a document which was in all cases shorter than those launched in the other two LEAs, focusing exclusively on the implementation of changes within identified areas for development. The brevity of these documents, in one case reduced to a flowchart on one sheet of paper, related to the limited information perceived to be necessary at school level for managing the implementation of innovations. Other information that LEA staff in the county and the city had included to meet their needs was omitted. Let us examine two examples.

Four years earlier, one head had implemented an annual review based on the GRIDS scheme (see McMahon *et al.*, 1984), coupled with voluntary appraisal interviews with teaching staff to identify individual needs. The innovations had now been institutionalized as an integral part of management practice. At the end of the autumn term each year teaching and non-teaching staff completed a questionnaire. The head compiled a chart showing the collation of views on priorities for school-wide development, which she displayed in the staffroom, and the chart was discussed at a full staff meeting.

Separately, at the end of the academic year 1988/89 an action plan was drawn up for all curriculum areas including those not covered by the National Curriculum, such as equal opportunities and special needs. Each action plan covered up to three years, and was subdivided into a series of statements about the existing situation and associated activities with an indication of the proposed timing, the additional resources and staff training required, and who was responsible for implementation. The list of activities was prioritized at the outset and a year later was reviewed and updated. The head monitored progress through the year, and consulted the deputy and curriculum post-holders about any modifications needed as circumstances changed. The completion date for particular activities was recorded and priorities re-established among the remainder. While much of what was planned was implemented as originally expected, a few activities were not. For example, the science coordinator had retired, leading to a delay in some related work. Both the annual consultative exercise and the curriculum action plans had a restricted focus and were not designed to cover all changes for which plans had to be made. Development planning was based on an annual cycle but also included a routine procedure for modification of curriculum plans whenever circumstances rendered it necessary.

A second head had just launched a two-year development plan, entailing a major consultation exercise which began with a SWOT analysis (a review of strengths, weakness, opportunites and threats) completed by all teaching and non-teaching staff. The head or deputy followed up by interviewing each individual. Governors were involved in designing a questionnaire sent to parents, and the head collated all this information and highlighted the requirements of external innovations. A two-year plan was drawn up as a matrix depicting the timetable for activities in each area. The plan was discussed by the senior management team (incentive allowance holders, the deputy and the head) then the rest of the staff, and was submitted to the governing body for approval. The head had worked out the annual cycle of LEA and school management activities relevant to governors and inducted them in its use so that they were prepared for their part in supporting development work. Separate action planning sheets were to be drawn up by the coordinator for each area in the term before activity began. The two-year cycle was chosen because the head envisaged, first, that reorganization in September 1992 would necessitate another major review and planning exercise; and secondly, that the high rate of staff turnover would mean that after a couple of years it would be necessary to repeat the exercise if new staff were to have ownership of the plan.

Changing circumstances had already led to changes within priority areas. Central government ministers had just announced that history and geography within the National Curriculum were not to be subject to national testing as previously stated, reducing the perceived urgency for staff to work on this area. The head expected that a working group would review each area when activity was due to be completed and report back to governors.

Both examples show how, where heads were free to choose, formal development planning was based on cycles of a year or more, but our survey could not establish how far the initiatives guided planning for change over time. Practice in another borough school suggests that a more flexible approach could also be adopted. The headteacher kept a flipchart sheet on her office wall where senior staff had listed development activities for the term. The chart was updated at weekly meetings, forming a checklist for short- to medium-term goals which was modified repeatedly as the situation unfolded.

In all three LEAs the heads involved teaching staff in whatever formal procedure for development planning was adopted. Three heads mentioned bounded consultation where they conducted an initial review with senior staff and then presented their proposals to the rest of the teachers. LEA staff played little part in the formulation of development plans, although four of the heads in the county acknowledged that the liaison officer was available if needed. Summative evaluation of development plans in county and city schools took the form of a summary written by the head as one section of the next development plan document, usually after discussion with staff. In a few cases, staff responsible for aspects of development activity contributed to this account. Very few of the schools had recently been subject to an LEA or HMI inspection, so most heads had not experienced external evaluation of their current planning procedure or progress with priorities.

## Content of plans

Development plan documents were gathered from twenty schools. Planning for change covered by the documents in schools across the three LEAs was dominated by the National Curriculum, as would be expected since they were designed to encompass the National Curriculum development plan. Assessment, especially for schools with pupils in year two, was also prominent, linked to the central government policy to introduce testing for pupils at the end of Key Stage 1. A priority relating to pupil behaviour in several county and city schools was associated with technically optional LEA initiatives taken in response to the provision of central government funds. The government action was linked, in turn, to a national inquiry into pupil discipline commissioned by ministers, whose report had recently been published (DES, 1989b). City school development areas were limited to the curriculum, reflecting the thrust of the LEA development planning initiative. A wider range of areas, such as promoting closer community links, preparing for LMS or appraisal, improving the public image of the school, and reviewing the work of minority ethnic group support staff, was represented in documents from schools in the county and the city. Nevertheless, only about one in eight identified priorities were unrelated to national reforms, indicating that central government was much the largest source of innovations. Priorities initiated at school level included improving outdoor play areas and promoting equal opportunities.

Most of the proposed activity set out in development plan documents was progressing according to schedule, implying reasonable control at school level over the areas covered. However, all the heads in the county and the city had made some kind of adjustment to one or more aspects of their plans for change since their current development plans were completed and submitted to the LEA. There was no requirement to update LEA staff about adjustments within the range of priorities indicated in the development plan, so it seems probable that LEA staff did not take such adjustments into account when supporting and monitoring schools. Half the heads in the borough also commented on how they had recently altered aspects of their plans. Over half of all the heads mentioned that targets within one or more priority areas had not been reached or that the timing of activities had shifted.

A major stimulus for such changes was new information about implementation of central government reforms, including related LEA initiatives and, less commonly, LEA initiatives unrelated to central government interests. Four heads in the county stated how they had been led to expect that central government ministers would allow two extra training days in the current year for primary schools. No official announcement had been made before the deadline for submission of the development plan to the LEA. Soon afterwards, DES officials announced that one extra day was being made available, resulting in school staff planning additional activities within their existing priority to prepare for pupil assessment at the end of Key Stage 1.

The staff of one county school took up an opportunity to participate in a project on multicultural education at the invitation of the LEA. As the invitation came after the development plan was completed, planning for this project was carried out independently. The head, in consultation with staff, had changed the timing of activities within three priority areas in the development plan. Work on history and geography was delayed once it was known that there would be no compulsory assessment. Preparation for assessment was brought forward as staff were so worried, and an initiative on pupil behaviour was set in train because of staff concern about racist remarks made by pupils. Another of the head's priorities for change, not shared with staff and therefore outside the development plan, was to employ younger staff whenever the opportunity arose so as to bring in new ideas. The present staff had not been informed as the head did not want them to feel undervalued.

Staff in one city school had included work on pupil behaviour in their development plan, expecting they would be included in the LEA project, but later discovered that they were not. Instead of their planned activities they did extra work on preparing for assessment. The head of one borough school noted how the LEA announcement of reorganization of schooling had affected the timing of work on various priorities within the development plan. Staff in another school in the borough had altered priorities when documents on technology had arrived from the National Curriculum Council, other development areas making way once information needed for implementing technology had been received.

Not all factors leading to adjustment of planned development activity were directly connected with innovations. A few heads mentioned short-term crises or longer-term issues that took top priority for a time. One county head, in the area with a chronic teacher shortage, reflected on how planned development activity was thwarted by the inability to find supply teachers on which much of the work, such as visiting other schools, depended. The head had been forced to take full responsibility for a class over two terms because a teacher vacancy arose which it proved impossible to fill: 'I just couldn't get down to anything else really, apart from surviving in the classroom.' A combination of high staff turnover and teacher shortage hindered development work in several county schools.

These examples suggest that the statements within development plan documents reflected (and therefore could have guided) to a varying extent the development activities which actually took place. Staff could modify existing plans or create plans for new priority areas without being constrained by what they had proposed on paper. Most heads appeared to operate in a way which was congruent with the model of flexible planning put forward in Chapter 2. The cyclic component consisted of an occasional development planning exercise, culminating in a set of proposals for the coming year or more. The spasmodic and continual components seemed to be expressed through incremental planning for change, within and outside the priorities identified in the development plan, whenever the perceived need for adjustments arose.

Just two heads in schools with a compulsory development plan, both in the county, had initiated a regular staff review of the development plan during the year, where its content was updated. This arrangement rendered the annual plan more flexible than the LEA guidance required. The updated version guided subsequent development activity in school but, not being an LEA requirement, it was not forwarded to LEA staff.

## Headteachers' views of LEA development planning initiatives

Opinions in county and city schools varied about the benefits or drawbacks of the development planning initiatives. Much depended upon the past experience of heads and staff. About half the heads had previously used the GRIDS approach to school review and regarded development planning as an extension of this process. One new head took over a school where there had been little staff consultation in the past and encountered difficulties when some staff members refused to contribute to establishing priority areas for development, arguing that everything identified needed changing. The head's response was to draw up the list of priorities alone.

The main benefit, mentioned by half the county and city heads, was that the procedure helped to focus staff and gain their commitment to a limited range of priorities for development. Perceived drawbacks related to the character of each LEA initiative. Three county heads found the detailed series of forms very time-consuming to complete, and three commented that modifications had to be made during the year. Four city heads complained about duplication between information required within the development plan document and that provided to the LEA through other channels. Three remarked that subsequent changes in circumstances meant that plans had to be modified anyway. The LEA development planning initiatives appeared generally to be perceived as a mixed blessing, with questions over their congruence with a situation that was liable to change at any time.

# OTHER INNOVATIONS AFFECTING PLANNING FOR CHANGE

We have seen how LEA development planning initiatives affected the management of a very significant proportion of planning for change at school level. The introduction of LMS also influenced planning, although most schools had yet to receive full delegation. Not only did planning have to take the annual financial cycle into account, but also formula funding and transition arrangements for its implementation meant that resourcing could now and in the future be significantly higher or lower than the historical level. About half the schools were losers and a third winners under the new system but most had been buffered by the transition from the historic to the formula-based levels of funding, spread over several years. An important site-level factor concerned the age of staff and therefore the demand their salaries made upon the overall budget since central government ministers had insisted that the formula was based upon average salaries. Two heads mentioned the strain on the budget imposed by a mature staff with the maximum number of annual salary increments.

In the city, most schools in the inner-city area had been forced to shed staff because, as we noted earlier, the DES would not allow the LMS formula to reflect the generous resourcing level these schools had experienced under the LEA primary-schools project. A problem which was particularly marked in the borough, but also affected schools elsewhere, was the range of anomalies for which some schools were billed by LEA staff. A head in a school sharing a site with two others was billed for the electricity and the services of the caretaker for all three schools. The electricity bill also included the cost of street lights in the road outside the school, which were apparently on the same meter. The 'teething problems' that LEA staff responsible for LMS had reported were experienced by heads in the schools affected as undesirable but unavoidable aspects of the innovation, which could consume an inordinate amount of their time. In contrast to LMS, innovations which were not such a central part of the planning process caused fewer problems at the time of our interviews. Work on the National Curriculum was reported as being generally in hand, although staff in schools catering for Key Stage 1 pupils were more concerned about assessment than teaching the National Curriculum itself.

Section 11 bids were awaiting a Home Office decision, and heads, especially those in the county and the borough who had put in their own proposals to the LEA, felt unable to plan further until the outcome of the bids was known. The main impact of the change was to increase uncertainty over sustaining the existing level of support should their proposals be unsuccessful, and to increase the likelihood that staff funded under Section 11 in future would have a short-term contract for the life of any project. Another effect of the new regulations made an impact on almost a quarter of the schools. The existing restriction of funding to pupils from the New Commonwealth had been highlighted, yet these schools included children from elsewhere needing support with learning English. The heads were faced with a dilemma over whether to comply with the regulations or to continue with their present practice of offering specialist language support, through Section 11 funded staff, to all pupils who needed it.

Reorganization of schooling in the borough and the city had increased the uncertainty of staff over their future employment, which was greatest for those in borough schools likely to be amalgamated. More progress had been made in the city, and all the heads we interviewed had been reappointed. However, several schools would merit fewer incentive allowances when they were reorganized than at present, implying that some of the staff would have to leave. Heads had no control over when and how reorganization would be implemented and were unable as yet to make detailed plans.

Changes in the teaching of religious education within the basic curriculum and collective worship appeared to have been implemented with few problems. Religious education was taught within LEA guidelines, covering a range of major world religions. Six of the schools with the highest proportion of pupils from minority ethnic groups, mostly with Asian backgrounds, had applied for determination in the county and the borough, thereby exempting them from the requirement that collective worship be mainly of a Christian character. The city LEA and SACRE encouraged a liberal interpretation of the 1988 Education Reform Act and liaised with minority ethnic groups, resulting in no applications for determination, even from the schools with a very high proportion of pupils from these groups. A national survey of SACREs (Taylor, 1991) showed that there was wide variation in the attitude of LEAs and their SACREs towards schools seeking determination, this factor being a strong influence on whether staff and governors in schools with a high proportion of pupils with a minority ethnic background would make an application. In our survey, only one head reported that parents from minority ethnic groups had pressed for collective worship to reflect their own faith.

## Limits to school-level control

A combination of factors originating at all levels of the education system had so curtailed the ability of staff in two city schools to control their situation that it was impossible to plan for change coherently. One school had experienced a 20 per cent drop in pupil numbers since the beginning of the academic year, leading to an anticipated 15 per cent cut in the formula-funded budget. As a result of the LEA reorganization strategy, many parents had decided to send their children to a nearby Roman Catholic school which had already been reorganized, to avoid a move to a middle school in its final years before closure. It was difficult to attract parents because the school was situated on the edge of the city's red light district. The head observed:

> Most of the girls down there are white, just as most of the people
> who live round here are black, and it is a source of grievance to the
> community. The respectable families here are tarred with the brush of
> that situation.

When the head was appointed in 1989 the school was well staffed thanks to the LEA primary-school project. The staff had undertaken several successful initiatives. Then three teachers were lost after the LEA project finished and the

LEA was unable to sustain the staffing level under the LMS formula. By the end of September 1990 the unexpected drop in pupil numbers threatened the jobs of four more teachers. Staff were now demoralized. LEA staff had questioned whether the building extension planned as part of the reorganization arrangements should go ahead now the school roll had declined. Pupil numbers were further reduced when a family took children away after investigation by staff brought a case of incest to light. The head pointed to the irony of endeavouring to protect children bringing financial loss under LMS.

Resourcing in the other school was also constrained by a unique combination of factors. According to the head:

> We are very close to a number of battered wives' refuges, so our pupil intake and withdrawal and admissions read like the 'Who's Who?'. In one school year I lose a whole school community and take a new one in.

Many mothers were single parents and could find only intermittent work. The head spent time helping them to claim the benefits to which they were entitled. The turnover of pupils was very high; many had special needs but had never stayed anywhere in the UK for long enough for the statementing procedure to be completed, so the school did not receive resources needed to give specialist support to these children. About 60 per cent of the pupils were from minority ethnic groups yet over one-third came from Arab countries and were not eligible for Section 11 support, although most could not speak English when they came. The school was a loser under LMS with a deficit of £26,000 despite reassessment by LEA staff. Internal rebuilding of the school (which was very dilapidated) was due to begin soon. The head had taken up post in 1988 and worked hard to make ambitious changes, but had been hampered by the lack of resources and now faced major staff changes: 'You cannot set a whole-school approach up in less than five years, I reckon. Given the kind of constraints we've got here. I won't achieve that when reorganization deals me another set of staff.'

Most factors in these extreme cases were beyond the ability of the heads and the (reportedly supportive) governors to control. These factors, alongside those affecting most of our survey schools, gave rise to very considerable environmental turbulence. The acute level of under-resourcing connected with some factors severely constrained heads and staff from making plans for change since little development comes resource-free. Both heads claimed that much of what they and their staff had intended to implement within their development plans was no longer possible. Without a minimum degree of school-level control over external innovations and resources for their implementation it seems impossible to sustain a coherent approach to development.

## TURBULENCE AND STABILITY

The interviews with LEA staff and heads revealed an array of factors affecting planning for change. For each school the combination was unique: national and local factors interrelated with those specific to the site; and some LEA-level factors, such as the level of local council spending, may have had less direct effect on planning in schools than others like the LEA development planning initiatives. Some site-level factors, including the requirements concerning religious education and collective worship, had less impact than others. It is possible to group the factors operating in some or all schools. Table 3.5 is a synthesis of factors which, within the national and local context we have outlined, appear to promote external or internal environmental turbulence. Table 3.6 summarizes those which make for stability at school level. The lists reflect the snapshot approach to data collection in the first phase of the research. Our subsequent case studies confirmed the influence of these and additional factors (see Chapter 7).

Planning for change must address the shifting balance between turbulence and stability to which these factors lead. The situation is complicated by the fact that factors connected with the management of planning directly affect the planning process. While development planning was designed to help keep the potential turbulence caused by multiple innovations within bounds, the fact that it was itself innovatory contributed to the turbulence experienced by school staff and, to a lesser extent, governors.

Some factors lie within their sphere of influence, and so it is possible that practical steps could be taken to reduce some sources of excess turbulence, by developing a routine procedure for adjusting plans, for example. Equally, it is possible deliberately to increase turbulence where deemed desirable to achieve

**Table 3.5** The impact of factors promoting turbulence on the planning process

| Factors promoting environmental turbulence | Impact on planning process |
| --- | --- |
| Abundance of external innovations, mostly compulsory | Coping with multiple, simultaneous goals and overload for staff |
| Low school-level control over external innovations | High proportion of reactive planning in response to external demands |
| Initiation by head of major innovations | Contribution to multiple goals and workload of staff |
| Crises and issues indirectly connected with innovations | Requirement for planned response, often including altering existing priorities |
| Ambiguity over and unpredictable changes in the characteristics and implementation requirements of external innovations | Adjustment of plans |
| Inadequate resources to achieve goals | Adjustment to reduce scale of activity, inhibition of implementation of innovations |
| External monitoring of progress with innovations | Planned response to deal with criticisms |
| Routine maintenance activity affected by external innovations | Adjustment of plans for managing routine activity |
| External innovations affecting management of planning (especially LMS, in-service training) | Creation of new tasks for managing planning and considerations that plans must take into account |
| External imposition of two overlapping planning cycles | Adjustment of plans according to stage reached in cycle |
| Conflict at school level over direction of development (especially governors or staff versus head) | Inhibition of planning, coping with lack of commitment to implementation |
| Innovatory procedures for managing planning for change (development planning), sometimes compulsory | Creation of new roles and tasks, implementation of formal procedures, sometimes to externally determined timetable |

**Table 3.6** The impact of stabilizing factors on the planning process

| Factors promoting environmental stability | Impact on planning process |
|---|---|
| Availability of clear and consistent information about external innovations | Facilitation of detailed planning |
| High level of control over innovations originating in school | Facilitation of detailed planning within available resources |
| Adequate resources to achieve goals | Facilitation of detailed planning |
| Lack of external monitoring of progress with innovations | Control over degree and timing of implementation |
| Consensus at school level over direction of development | Facilitation of detailed planning, commitment to implementation |
| Institutionalization of innovations | Termination of planning for implementation, reduction in staff workload |
| Development planning procedure | Establishment of priorities and implementation plans, provision of support, limitation of staff workload |
| Routinized and flexible procedures for adjusting plans | Ease of response to changing circumstances |
| Support among governors and parents for, or passivity towards, direction of development | Facilitation of implementation |

an educational purpose, as where headteachers adopted the role of innovators. Yet staff and governors are also at the mercy of factors over which they have little or no control, especially those connected with external innovations and the level of resourcing. The tables do not indicate the strength of influence of each factor, and indeed there was variation between schools. We hypothesize that the balance of influence from factors over which there was little school-level control was in the direction of turbulence. On the other hand, the influence of factors which were potentially more controllable varied between schools, leading us to suggest that there may be more and less effective ways of managing planning for change within a turbulent environment.

## Match between our findings and planning models

Our finding of pervasive environmental turbulence at school level is consistent with the importance attached to it in strategic planning. The LEA and school development planning initiatives followed the same logical sequence and occasional updating process as the DES guidance which, as we discussed in Chapter 2, the *strategic planning* model broadly shares. Evidence of adjustment of some plans within the development plan itself and the creation of plans for development outside it suggests that the process of planning for change in such a turbulent environment contains much that is *evolutionary*. We have suggested that the *flexible planning* model captures the relationship between planning according to two overlapping cycles and spasmodic response to changing circumstances dictating repeated adjustment of plans. But the findings give little indication of the dynamics of planning, to which we now turn.

# Chapter 4

# An Overview of the Six Case-Study Schools

Our purpose in this chapter is to offer an overview of each school as an advance organizer for the cross-site analysis to follow. A potential disadvantage of such a cross-site approach is that it can be difficult to gain a sense of each school, both as a context for planning activity and as an institution which is evolving over time. Therefore, bearing in mind the risk of a small degree of overlap with other chapters, we begin with an outline of each school and its site-level context. A brief summary is then given of how planning for change was carried out, highlighting some of the most important factors which affected the planning process.

## THE SITE-LEVEL CONTEXT OF EACH SCHOOL

In the previous chapter we discussed the national and LEA context which affected planning for change in our survey schools. The factors described there continued to influence planning activity at school level until the summer of 1991 when the second phase of fieldwork started. Here we home in on the site-level context of each case-study school. Common features were that the six head-teachers were women and all the schools were county-maintained. Variation between the site-level contexts is depicted in Table 4.1.

### Central Primary School

Central was a medium-sized primary school located in an old part of the main city within the county. The school was surrounded by streets of Victorian and Edwardian terraced houses and was close to a busy main road, lined with shops which led into the city centre. The catchment area was mixed and, although the majority of the pupils were working-class, there was a significant number of children from professional middle-class families.

    The school was built at the turn of the century: a solid, two-storey, red-brick building with wide corridors and wood-block floors. The classrooms were light and quite spacious, opening onto a central hall on each floor. The younger children were on the ground floor while classrooms for the 8-11-year-olds were upstairs. There was a lack of facilities such as sinks in the classrooms, and noise could also be a problem in the ground-floor rooms as the central hall was used for assemblies, physical education and meals. The rooms, halls and corridors were brightly painted and were decorated with plants, displays of children's work and photographs of school activities. One room, close to the entrance, had been furnished with comfortable chairs and tea-and coffee-making facilities and was used as a meeting place for parents. A group of mothers met there weekly for coffee.

**Table 4.1** Site-level context of case-study schools (summer 1991)

| Feature | Central Primary | Town Primary | Highway Middle | Heartlands Combined | Southside First | Northedge First |
|---|---|---|---|---|---|---|
| LEA | County | County | Borough | Borough | City | City |
| Pupil age range | 3–11 | 3–11 | 8–12 | 3–12 | 3–9 | 3–9 |
| Location | City centre, Victorian terraces | Urban, mixed private and council housing | Urban, mixed private and council housing | Urban, mixed housing | Inner-city, back-to-back Victorian terraces | Edge of inner city, Victorian terraces |
| Buildings | Edwardian, two-storey | 1930s, large playing field | 1940s, shared site with two other schools | Edwardian, two-storey, temporary classrooms | New building, temporary classrooms | Victorian building being refurbished, temporary site |
| Layout of classrooms | Separate rooms | Semi-open-plan | Separate rooms | Separate rooms | Semi-open-plan | Semi-open-plan |
| Number on roll | 260, 23-place nursery | 300, 20-place nursery | 240 (rising rapidly) | 420, 25-place nursery (rising rapidly) | 310, 39-place nursery | 450, 26-place nursery |
| Pupils from minority ethnic groups | 30% total including 15% Afro-Caribbean, 8% Asian | 70% total including 69% Asian | 20% total – 15% Asian, 5% Afro-Caribbean | 34% total including 15% Asian, 11% Afro-Caribbean, 3% Somali refugees | 90% total including 86% Asian, 2% Afro-Caribbean | 55% total including 22% Asian, 20% Afro-Caribbean, 10% mixed race |
| Socio-economic status of parents | Mixed working and middle class | Working class | Mixed working and middle class | Mixed working and middle class | Working class | Mixed working and middle class |
| Number of teaching staff including head | 13 | 15.3 | 12.4 | 16 | 18 | 23 |
| Teachers from minority ethnic groups | One appointed July 1991 | 2 | 1 | 0 (2 in past) | 0 (2 in past) | 2 |
| Percentage of staff interviewed appointed since head in post | 40% | 40% | 85% | 45% | 100% | 60% |
| Number of years head in post | 1 (2 years acting head) | 2 | 5 | 5 | 8 (+ 2 years as deputy) | 6 |
| Allocation of minority ethnic group support staff responsibilities | 2 f.t.e. Section 11 support 1 vacancy – filled July 1991 | 3 f.t.e. | 0.4 f.t.e. ESL support | 1.1 f.t.e. ESL support | 2 bilingual assistants 2 home–school liaison officers 1 peripatetic nursery nurse | 2 bilingual assistants 2 home–school liaison officers 1 peripatetic nursery nurse |
| Governors from minority ethnic groups | 0 | 1 | 0 | 1 | 2 | 4 |

There were two other buildings on the site; one housed the nursery and a music room, the other had originally been a secondary school and was now used as an adult education centre. The area around the buildings was covered in tarmac and was used as a playground. Though space was limited, the school was engaged in a project to improve this environment and a climbing frame had been provided, games had been marked out on the asphalt and flowers and bulbs had been planted in containers around the site.

The school had been given a fully delegated budget in April 1991 and, despite some teething troubles (including difficulty collecting all the information that was required about salary levels), the budget was being implemented with few problems. Several factors contributed to this situation: first, the school was not a 'loser' under LMS and had several young staff; second, LEA staff had made funds available for schools to appoint a finance officer, in this case the former school secretary who had experience in handling finance; third, the LEA had provided a computer for the school and training and support about LMS for headteachers and finance officers; and finally, one of the school governors who was a former accountant had played a key supporting role in the finance subcommittee.

All members of staff had a curriculum or organizational responsibility. The headteacher and her deputy worked closely together, meeting daily, and had a planning meeting every week. They formed a senior management team with the two B incentive allowance holders which met fortnightly to discuss school policy matters.

About 30 per cent of the pupils in the school were from a minority ethnic group: the majority were Afro-Caribbean, but an increasing number were from Asian families. There were also a few children from white minority ethnic groups, including Poles and Maltese. Many of the Afro-Caribbean families had been in the area for two or three generations and only a small number of Asian children came to the school unable to speak English. The Section 11 support was allocated to two projects: raising achievement of Afro-Caribbean children, and a language-acquisition project which was focused on the children in the lower school for whom English was a second language.

## Town Primary School

The second county school, Town Primary School, was located in a mixed area within a mile of the centre of a large town. The catchment area contained a council estate and semi-detached and detached private housing. The school was of medium size but was not full to capacity. There was some evidence that, as the number of Asian pupils increased, a few white parents were choosing to send their children to schools which had a predominantly white population. Approximately 75 per cent of the pupils were from a minority ethnic group and the percentage was rising in the lower school. The main ethnic group was Asian, from one region in Pakistan. Most of these pupils entered school not speaking English.

The school was built in the 1930s and was a single-storey, red-brick building, surrounded by extensive playing fields and set around a central quadrangle which was a tarmacked playground area. Organized as separate infant and junior schools from 1960, the school had been amalgamated into a single primary school in 1980. The site also housed a speech and language unit which was an LEA resource for children whose speech was impaired and a unit, which was staffed by social services, for pre-school children considered in need of support and care. The school was spacious: the classrooms were quite large and airy, all opening onto a wide corridor, and there were two school halls and a library. The rooms and corridors were decorated with displays of children's work and there were bilingual signs for the information of pupils and their parents. However, the classrooms were spread over a wide area, leading to high costs of heating and maintenance. The playing fields were large grassed areas but work had begun on a plan to improve the environment by, for example, planting trees and creating a wildlife garden.

The school had been given a fully delegated budget by the LEA in April 1991 and had received a computer and funding for a finance officer to support the implementation of LMS. However, the transition to LMS had not been particularly easy, partly owing to the fact that neither the headteacher nor the finance officer had time to attend computer training courses. In 1991/2 the staff was relying on manual systems of financial record-keeping and the headteacher was having to spend a considerable amount of time monitoring the budget. Though the school had experienced a budget cut, the total sum was considered adequate. There was some concern that, if pupil numbers declined in future years, the consequent reduction in the budget would be difficult to handle.

All members of staff had a curriculum or organizational responsibility. There were two B allowance holders who, in addition to their curriculum responsibility, acted as coordinators for the early and upper years (for Key Stage 1 and for Key Stage 2 within the National Curriculum). The headteacher and the deputy discussed school matters on a daily basis, and held a formal meeting once a week. With the two B allowance holders, they formed a senior management team which usually met fortnightly. Providing language support for bilingual children was a major priority for the school but there were only two bilingual teachers, one working on a Section 11 home-school liaison project, the other a mainstream class teacher. One other teacher was funded to work within a Section 11 project on language acquisition.

## Highway Middle School

Highway Middle, the first of the two borough schools, was a medium-sized 8-12 middle school whose roll had doubled in recent years. Situated close to a large run-down housing estate and railway line on one side and bounded on the other by a major road into the heart of the conurbation, the school shared a site with two others: a first school and another middle school. Highway had become more popular with parents in the five years since the present head had taken up her post and was increasingly 'poaching' children who lived in the catchment area of the other middle school on the same site, especially those from the few professional middle-class families. Fully 50 per cent of children from the catchment area of the other middle school now came to Highway.

Within the LEA proposals for reorganization of schools to take effect in September 1992 the three schools on the site were scheduled to be amalgamated to form a single 3-11 primary school of over 600 pupils. The chair of governors for Highway, a Labour councillor, had threatened to call for a ballot of parents to consider opting out of LEA control to protect the integrity of the present school. Perversely perhaps, a Labour councillor was attempting to make use of a national policy to which the Labour Party was officially opposed in order at the local level to thwart the reorganization policy brought in by the recently elected Conservative borough council! In the event it was decided that the school would be too small to be viable under LMS and plans for becoming a grant-maintained school had just been dropped. A temporary governing body was in the process of being set up to make decisions connected with the new school. There was great uncertainty over staffing, especially for the three heads - at least two standing to lose their present job.

All three schools were built of concrete blocks in the late 1940s, with asphalt-covered flat roofs. Sets of separate classrooms and specialist rooms opened off long corridors at right angles to each other, and each school was connected to another via one corridor so that the three formed a single maze. Although many plants and displays of pupils' work had made the interior bright and colourful, the effect was counteracted by buckets placed about the building to catch water leaking through the roof. Each school on the site had its own entrance and playground and the three shared a playing field. The site was prone to attacks by vandals and one classroom had been badly damaged by fire during the recent Easter holiday.

Highway was set to be a 'winner' by a substantial amount under LMS, but the transition arrangements meant that so far only 1 per cent of the promised extra funding had materialized. The LEA policy for introducing fully delegated budgets had been reversed when it was realized that 'ring fencing' - limiting eligibility for posts in the reorganized schools to existing staff within the borough - would be impossible in schools with full LMS. Governors would control the appointment and dismissal of staff and would be entitled to advertise nationally. Full delegation for Highway had been postponed from April 1992 to the following year, after amalgamation.

All teaching staff had a curriculum coordination role, even those in their first year of teaching, who served in an apprentice capacity under the supervision of the deputy head. The head and deputy had a strong working partnership, and an experienced teacher with a brief for coordinating work in the upper two year groups was included in the management team which met weekly to discuss policy issues.

The school had a small proportion of pupils from minority ethnic groups: about 15 per cent Asian Gujerati speakers and 5 per cent from Afro-Caribbean backgrounds. All these pupils spoke English and most were second or third generation in this country. Consequently the small allowance for specialist support under Section 11 was intended for vocabulary extension work.

# Heartlands Combined First and Middle School

Heartlands was located in a socio-economically very mixed area which included council housing, bed and breakfast accommodation, dwellings owned by housing associations, and owner-occupied housing. The school was very full, its roll having risen by 50 per cent in the last three years. The main building was an Edwardian block of two storeys with a row of classrooms leading off the corridor on each floor. There was a specialist room for science and home economics. A row of temporary classrooms lined one side of the main building, while the nursery was housed in a temporary classroom on the other side. The site was cramped, with a small playing field to the rear bounded by residential streets and on one side by a high school.

With a mainly mature staff, the salary bill was proving difficult to cope with despite the school being a substantial 'winner' under LMS. Full delegation was due in April 1992 and at the present level of funding, which included the damping effect of transition arrangements, it had been impossible to set a balanced budget. As the head remarked: 'The irony of it all is we were considered very successful because we retained very good experienced staff. And now in financial terms I'm unsuccessful.' A supernumerary Asian teacher had been employed until recently at the initiative of LEA staff and, according to the head, had brought a valuable cultural experience into the school. She regretted being unable to continue to employ this teacher once the school became formula funded; the budgetary constraints built into the partially delegated LMS budget would not allow it. Under the new arrangements the school, rather than the LEA, would now have to cover this teacher's salary.

All teaching staff had some curriculum or organizational responsibility, the core subjects within the National Curriculum being held by experienced staff. The head had been keen to dilute any sense among staff of separate first- and middle-school departments, so had divided the year groups into lower, middle and upper years, the latter two groups having a coordinator. Uncertainty over the LEA proposals for reorganization was less than at Highway, since the school would lose its oldest year group and become a 3-11 primary school.

About one-third of the pupils were from a minority ethnic background, of whom 3 per cent were Somali refugees from the civil war. They had been traumatized by the violence there and spoke no English when they came to the school. Ironically, part of Somalia was once a British colony, yet the country was now not a member of the New Commonwealth and so officially Section 11 funded specialist language support was not available for the Somali pupils. As there were no other resources in the school to help these children the head had bent the rules and they were given ESL teaching by the teachers funded through Section 11.

# Southside First School

Southside, with its brand new buildings surrounded by a spiked metal fence, contrasted dramatically with its grim surroundings. It was located in the poorest area of the city, a labyrinth of dilapidated back-to-back Victorian terraces. The local community consisted largely of Asian families from rural

Pakistan and Bangladesh, fairly recent arrivals in the UK who were the most disadvantaged minority ethnic group within the city. The head commented: 'Many of the fathers came over here to work in the mills and factories. And of course they are all closed down. If you are working in a mill or factory, actually spoken English is not a high priority. Many of the fathers didn't learn a lot of English so they couldn't be transferred to something else.' Unemployment was high and the head spent much time looking to the welfare of pupils and their parents. She had been deputy head before gaining the headship eight years before, and was now the longest-serving member of staff.

The original Victorian building had been burned down by vandals and the school was accommodated temporarily in the sixth form block of a nearby school. Then asbestos was discovered elsewhere in this school and teaching continued while the other buildings were demolished. The present building was completed in 1987 and immediately proved too small for the catchment area. It had remained full, with temporary classrooms occupying part of the playground. The nursery was included within the main building which consisted of semi-open-plan classrooms and shared activity areas with central corridors. One reason for the popularity of the school with parents was the great emphasis placed on their close involvement. There was a community room and provision of a wide range of activities including English classes for parents, a crèche, a mother and toddler group, and occasional events such as a trip for all pupils and their families to the seaside. As Muslims, many mothers were expected by their husbands to stay at home and thus had limited opportunities to learn English apart from their participation in school activities.

Children from the Asian community made up 86 per cent of the school population, many of whom spoke little or no English when they started school. Consequently there was a high level of provision of specialist support funded under Section 11. A bilingual nursery nurse and two bilingual and cultural support assistants worked with the younger children. As a legacy of the LEA's primary schools project, from which the school had benefited greatly in the past, two LEA-funded home-school liaison officers, both of whom were bilingual, promoted links between parents and teaching staff.

Uniquely among the case-study schools, the head had confined the allocation of curriculum and organizational responsibilities to staff holding an incentive allowance (including a brief for minority ethnic groups), leaving teachers on the main scale responsible solely for their own classwork. Three teachers were attached to each pair of classes in the same year group, one acting in a support role, reflecting the generous level of staffing provision in the city. Coordination of each year team was the responsibility of a senior staff member and year groups were also divided into lower and upper years.

The school was due to become a one-and-a-half-form-entry primary school from September 1992, the oldest year group staying on so that the school would cater for the full 3-11 age range by the following year. The head and deputy had been reappointed but all other posts were yet to be allocated. The LEA had ring-fenced appointments and had promised that there would be no redundancies. C grade incentive allowance posts were being dealt with now, then other allowance levels in turn, and finally main-scale teachers. Uncertainty about their future was fast becoming the main cause of stress among staff. The catchment area was also due to change, meaning that some pupils would not be able to continue to attend the school unless they won an appeal to the LEA.

## Northedge First School

Northedge was a large school whose Victorian buildings, situated on the edge of the inner city, were undergoing extensive refurbishment. Consequently the school had been moved to a temporary site a mile away, and was currently occupying a 1960s building in need of repair. For example, a water leak had opened up above the headteacher's desk. The nursery was housed in a separate building on the original site and the children had enjoyed the sight of heavy earthmoving and building equipment working on the refurbishment. The school was therefore split between the two sites and was due to move back at the end of the summer term. The impending move had become a major planning priority and staff looked forward to working in the refurbished building.

The area consisted of mixed housing, mostly Victorian terraces. Quite a high proportion of parents chose to live in the area even though they could have afforded to go elsewhere. The school was perceived by many parents to be desirable because of its evenly balanced mix of ethnic groups among pupils, which was unusual in the city. Most multiracial schools, including Southside, had a predominance of one minority ethnic group. Northedge was one of the few schools in the city with a broad range of ethnic groups. Of the 55 per cent of pupils from a minority ethnic background, 20 per cent were Afro-Caribbean or African, and those of Asian origin from the Indian subcontinent included 15 per cent Sikhs and 7 per cent Muslims. There were a few 'international children', Iranians whose parents were studying at the local university. Many parents, including a substantial number from the Afro-Caribbean community, were keen for their children to go to the school both because of the balance of different ethnic groups and because it was on the edge of the inner city, so perceived to have higher social status than neighbouring schools.

Northedge had also benefited from the LEA's primary-school project and had two home-school liaison officers, one from an Asian and the other from an Afro-Caribbean background. There were two Section 11 funded bilingual and cultural support assistants and a peripatetic nursery nurse. In contrast to the other case-study schools, there was quite broad representation of minority ethnic groups on the governing body, and a Sikh teacher and an Afro-Caribbean teacher were employed.

All members of the large teaching staff had some curriculum or organizational responsibility, with the major curriculum areas falling to more senior staff members. Each year team of two class teachers and a support teacher included a year coordinator, but the head was planning to create several cross-year teams when the staff moved back to the original site in order to adapt to the constraints of the building.

The refurbished site was to consist of suites of open-plan areas for pairs of classes, with the hall, a community room, a large multipurpose room and administrative rooms housed in the old part of the building. The site was on a hill and was to be split level, with a dining room and the nursery unit on the lower level.

Like Southside, the school was due to face radical change under the LEA reorganization scheme. The head and deputy had been appointed, but all other posts were yet to be allocated. The school would be overcrowded in the year between moving back to the main site and September 1992, when it would become a two-form-entry primary school. The LEA plan to change the catchment area for Northedge First had angered Afro-Caribbean parents because it would preclude many from keeping their children at the school after reorganization, especially as they could not afford to move into the more expensive houses within the new catchment area. They claimed that the proposal amounted to institutional racism because they would be denied a place for their children and the present much-valued ethnic mix in the school would be lost.

## PLANNING FOR CHANGE: SOME COMMON FACTORS

Planning in these schools, as already implied in Chapter 3, continued to be dominated by pressure from central government to introduce its reforms for schools. All but Highway Middle catered for children within Key Stage 1 of the National Curriculum, and the first annual national assessment of pupils at the end of this Key Stage was being implemented in 1991. According to government ministers (NCC, 1989), the results of this first run were not to be published (although later this policy was reversed). National Curriculum subjects were being phased in year by year for the whole age range covered by the case-study schools, children being required to follow the relevant programmes of study in technology from the beginning of the academic year 1990, geography and history in 1991 and art, music and PE in 1992. The staff were at various stages of implementing LMS and were all to be affected by the change in funding of specialist support for pupils from minority ethnic groups under Section 11.

The LEAs, as we saw in Chapter 3 and in the previous section, put pressure on staff in schools to implement the national reforms (LMS proving particularly problematic in the borough schools as a result in part of the inadequate budgets allocated under the LEA formula) and changes following from their own policies, most notably reorganization in the borough and the city. The development planning initiatives in the county and city included the mandate to complete and submit the LEA-designed document. LEA encouragement in the borough for schools to join the voluntary development planning initiative had resulted in Highway participating in 1991 and the head of Heartlands deciding not to take part but to continue using her own version, based on a flowchart.

Governing bodies in all the schools continued to give more or less active support to the professional staff, largely through the headteacher, making little attempt to initiate changes. Indeed their largely 'hands off' approach to change constituted a factor whose effect on planning was to help the heads to retain some control over the relevant process and the content of plans.

# THE DYNAMICS OF PLANNING FOR CHANGE IN EACH SCHOOL

There were many similarities and differences in the remaining factors affecting the planning process among the six schools, the combination and the relative influence of each being unique to the case in hand. Here we summarize the experience of planning for change, within and outside a development plan, during the four terms from the summer of 1991.

## Central Primary School

Development planning was a familiar process at Central as the staff had been involved in collaborative planning exercises for a number of years. In summer 1991 the headteacher was coming to the end of her first year of headship, but she had already been acting head for two years and had been deputy head for the previous four. Over this time she had helped to develop a school culture in which planning was regarded as a core activity.

At the start of the 1991 summer term the head and staff had completed their third development plan within the LEA scheme. The bulk of decision-making about school policy issues took place in staff meetings. A style of decision-making by consensus had been introduced, meaning that all teachers participated and agreed to support the decision favoured by the majority. The development plan was a well-read document, used to structure staff meetings and planning for in-service training across the whole year. It was formally reviewed halfway through the year and was referred to in staff meetings on other occasions. The staff were successful over a number of years in achieving the targets that they had set in the development plan. Where they failed to achieve particular objectives it was usually due to matters outside their control. One reason why the development plan could be used as a framework for organizing activity through the school year was that the priority areas that were identified closely paralleled the tasks that the school was compelled to undertake, including the implementation of the National Curriculum, national assessment and LMS.

However, though the broad picture at Central was one of relative stability, any impression that the school was incident-free would be misleading. In 1991/2 the school had several staffing issues to deal with: one of the Section 11 teachers followed a programme for a term to gain qualified-teacher status; the headteacher was on maternity leave and resigned at the end of the year; and the budget for Section 11 projects was cut, raising the possibility that one teacher would lose her job and disrupting work in the classroom. Yet despite all these unplanned events, the staff managed to continue to work on their development priorities.

## Town Primary School

The headteacher at Town was coming to the end of her second year in post in the summer of 1991. She had been able to appoint a deputy in April 1990, which she regarded as a key event as she and the new deputy had a similiar philosophy and ideas and were able quickly to establish a good working relationship. The school did not have a tradition of development planning but the introduction of the LEA initiative coincided with changes that were already under way in the school. Soon after her arrival the LEA inspectors had conducted a full inspection of the school and had produced some clear recommendations for change. Their suggestions mirrored ones that she and the staff had identified but the exercise had enabled staff to see that the changes she wanted to introduce were validated by an outside group.

The school had produced development plans since 1989/90 and in the summer of 1991 the headteacher was in the process of submitting the third plan. A copy of the development plan was issued to each member of staff. It was used as a framework for planning topics for staff meetings and training days, and was formally reviewed every year. The staff were successful over a number of years in achieving the targets they had set. In many instances these targets focused on tasks that were linked to the introduction of the National Curriculum and assessment, including revising the history and geography policies in line with attainment targets. Other development targets, such as encouraging parents to become more involved in the life of the school and improving the school environment, were seen as major issues that would be worked on for several years.

Though the staff were able to work steadily on their development targets in 1991/2, there were several incidents that interrupted the flow of events. Some of the problems were caused by the building, including a breakdown in the school boiler which forced an emergency school closure, and an unsafe perimeter wall. Other problems were caused by a cut in the Section 11 budget which seriously disrupted work on two projects and threatened a reduction in staffing, and by the deputy head's absence on maternity leave.

## Highway Middle School

The head had initiated many innovations in her first years in post, a factor contributing to high turnover among the staff she inherited, which had enabled her to appoint teachers who shared her educational views. She and the deputy worked closely together. There was a strong culture of collaboration among the mainly young staff and great support for the head.

The deputy took charge of the development plan, which was to span three academic years, taking plans well beyond the scheduled amalgamation with the other two schools on the same site. Part of the rationale agreed by the head and staff for taking part in the development planning project was to strengthen their position for negotiating with staff from the other schools after amalgamation. Staff conducted a major review, identified priorities, and began developing action plans.

The initiative was then abandoned, overtaken by an issue that turned into a crisis. Water leaking through the roof reached electricity cables, forcing the supply to be cut off. The school was split between two temporary sites for the autumn term while the roof was repaired. Planning for the implementation of external innovations was briefly resumed in the spring but was overtaken, in turn, by a new school-based innovation: to take vertical groups of pupils on a residential field trip. Towards the end of term, vandals set fire to three classrooms. Meanwhile the LEA announced that reorganization had been postponed for a year.

The head and colleagues in the management team had long established an approach to planning based on regularly updated flipcharts. This approach was sustained except during the move to the temporary sites. It covered both development plan priorities and all other areas. In this exceptionally turbulent case, rapid response to unexpected changes in circumstances beyond staff control was frequently required, although staff also contributed to turbulence through the field trip innovation. The planning approach which actually served the head and her colleagues was more flexible than the development planning cycle they began but, without external compulsion, soon abandoned.

## Heartlands Combined First and Middle School

The head had initiated a comprehensive overhaul of the school after taking up her post, originally encapsulated in a three-year plan drawn up by the deputy and herself. She had declined the invitation to take part in the LEA development planning initiative as she felt that her approach, based on a flowchart, worked well. The three-year plan had been extended each academic year.

There was an undercurrent of antagonism between some members of staff. The deputy had responsibility for a class and was perceived by the head as being unwilling to shoulder responsibility, while the deputy perceived that the head was equally unwilling to release her from her class and give her a full managerial role. Another teacher was regarded by the head as impulsive while he perceived her as blocking his ideas. Divided loyalties among the staff resulted in variable commitment to supporting the head and to planning as a whole staff.

This factor exacerbated difficulties during the summer term 1991 where lack of information on the LMS budget inhibited what would otherwise have been routine planning for the allocation of staff and classes for the 1991/2 academic year. The head did not receive the information needed for planning until shortly before the end of term. She felt depressed over the next few months, as her perception of her role became increasingly at odds with the role she was forced to play. The development plan was extended into the new academic year but not written up, both because the head was responding to other priorities and because she was aware that the deputy was applying for a post elsewhere, which she subsequently secured. The announcement in the spring term that the LEA reorganization plan had been postponed removed the urgency of preparing for reorganization.

The head eventually produced a supplement to the flowchart for her own reference, then successfully applied for a post elsewhere, beginning in the spring term 1993, and began planning for handing over the school to her successor. The development plan was an *aide-mémoire* for the head, rather than the whole staff, although the planning they undertook remained consistent with areas covered within the existing document.

## Southside First School

Southside had a slightly smoother experience than the other city school, although planning became severely inhibited in both cases as reorganization loomed closer. The head had been an initiator since coming to the school as the deputy, and since taking up the headship had appointed every one of the present staff. There was a very strong collaborative culture among the staff and widespread support for the head. She continued to press ahead with initiatives, especially in the area of support for pupils and their parents from the Asian community. She had held an annual school review with staff based on the GRIDS scheme for some years.

Her commitment to a consultative review and planning exercise was consistent with the process advocated by LEA staff within the compulsory development planning initiative. However, the head felt that much of the information required in the document was not useful to staff. She introduced the consultation process and the plan was duly submitted. Some in-service training followed the priorities identified but the head did not wait until the document was completed before starting work in certain areas. Priorities within the 1990/91 development plan were implemented broadly as expected, but only half of the priorities in the next development plan were addressed because the coordinator for two priorities had to take on additional duties as acting deputy, precluding her from tackling the work within the development plan. Planning for other changes took place independently, including arranging an induction programme for newly appointed minority ethnic group support staff, and bidding for funding within a new central government initiative to support inner-city schools.

The advent of reorganization dominated planning during the 1991 summer term. Uncertainty over staffing the new school remained as various posts were filled or vacancies created where staff gained posts in other schools. The deputy, who had taken maternity leave, resigned from her post shortly before she was due to return and the head took the opportunity of early retirement. The catchment area was also changed. No plans could be made for the period immediately after reorganization until the new staff could meet together during in-service training days near the end of the summer term. The 1991/2 development plan was not reviewed and LEA staff did not require another for the next two terms because of their top priority of enabling new staffs to settle into their reorganized schools. Staff morale remained high, despite the heavy workload and the prospect of the staff group being split up.

## Northedge First School

Since taking up her second headship at Northedge, the head had instigated many changes, making her educational beliefs and values known to staff and encouraging them to experiment within these parameters. She was now struggling to sustain initiatives such as team teaching in the face of central government reforms. She received strong support from the deputy and most staff, especially those whom she had appointed.

Planning for change was inhibited by the pressing short-term need during the summer term 1991 to plan the move back from the temporary site to the refurbished site. Subsequently responses had to be planned to problems that became apparent once the staff were settling into their new surroundings.

Most priorities in the 1990/91 development plan were implemented as intended. The review and planning exercise for 1991/2 had to be completed by the end of September 1991, when the staff were struggling to establish themselves on the refurbished site. It was duly completed, but the outcome was not disseminated to all staff, some of whom remained unclear about its content. The single copy of the document retained by the head was stolen with her bag early in the spring term 1992 and she did not request a photocopy from the LEA. The document gave no guidance for planning during the year, and no review was undertaken at the end of the cycle.

Of the four priorities identified in the 1991/2 development plan only the one relating to settling into the refurbished building was implemented as expected. The teacher responsible for one priority was too busy and another failed to retain her post in the school within the arrangements for reorganization and did not continue with work on the priority for which she was responsible. As with Southside, planning for changes including the inner-city initiative and reorganization was carried out more incrementally and without any link to the development plan. The LEA plan to change the catchment area under reorganization took up the head's time as she had to liaise with the Afro-Caribbean community and the LEA. Staff morale was lowered by the experience of moving back to the refurbished site, then by uncertainty surrounding reorganization and the anticipated dispersal of staff.

## MULTILEVEL CONTEXTS FOR CROSS-SITE ANALYSIS

The introduction to each school outlines the site-level context in which planning for change took place, nested within the LEA and national policy contexts described in earlier chapters. The summaries of the dynamics of planning provide a glimpse of the range of factors affecting planning for change in our case-study schools within these multilevel contexts.

In building up a more fine-grained analysis of the various factors and their interrelationship, the next four chapters each take a thematic look across the case-study school sites, beginning with an examination of the contribution - or lack of it - of different individuals and groups to the management of planning, and the arrangements made for carrying out the process of planning for change.

# Chapter 5

# The Management of Planning

We argued earlier that planning must be organized within a framework which has to be established, maintained, monitored, and modified where appropriate. The survey showed how many headteachers introduced new management structures and reallocated staff roles as high-priority school-based innovations during their early years of headship. Some of these structures and roles were central to planning and implementing other changes. Our first cross-site theme is the management of planning at school level: an examination of the elements contributing to planning as an orchestrated process. Potentially the boundaries of this theme are rather vague, so we will set out some of the parameters of our focus.

First, headteachers were key figures in the management of planning. Their actions in this area lay within their general management style, reflecting their managerial beliefs and values. All the case-study school heads expressed a commitment to consultative decision-making, but varied in how much consultation they enabled to take place within the planning procedures they had created. Equally, the actions of heads in managing planning were affected by differences in how far they had tried and succeeded in creating a climate of trust and mutual support and had established shared professional values among staff. Some put a greater emphasis on efficient administration than others. We confine our attention here to the planning process itself, other background factors being picked up in Chapter 7 according to their influence on the degree of turbulence or stability which surrounded planning for change.

Second, the management of planning for change (our main concern) and for maintenance were two aspects of a single enterprise in all the case-study schools, entailing many common features with differences arising at the level of detailed operation. As we shall discuss in the next chapter, development planning was an approach to managing a significant proportion of planning for change.

Third, managing planning for change embraces the school-wide level: developing and revising policies; ensuring that priorities are established among competing pressures for change; and arranging for detailed planning to be undertaken for the implementation of particular changes. This focus covers planning by individuals within their school management roles. For example, development of a new policy and planning to implement history and geography within the National Curriculum for all classes was led by teachers with responsibility for coordinating these curriculum areas. It does not extend to other individual tasks such as classroom management - as where class teachers planned their own work within history and geography.

Fourth, the school level covers individuals and groups who do not work within the institution but have a legitimate interest in the content of plans and therefore in how plans are made and how progress with their implementation is monitored. Legally, once LMS has been fully implemented, the governing body has major responsibility for the curriculum, staff appointments and finances (DES, 1988b) while, within the oversight of governors, the headteacher is 'responsible for the internal organisation, management and control of the school' (DES, 1989c). The head is required to 'consult, where this is appropriate, with the authority, the governing body, the staff of the school and the parents of its pupils'. The division of responsibilities between headteachers and governors envisaged by central government is spelled out in DES (1988c) guidance issued to each governing body:

> *Governors* have a general responsibility for the effective management of the school, acting within the framework set by national legislation and by the policies of the LEA. But they are not expected to take detailed decisions about the day to day running of the school - that is the role of the *head*.... A good head will discuss all the main aspects of school life with the governors and expect them to offer general guidance.
>
> (p. 7)

Other individuals and groups concerned with planning in state-maintained schools include headteachers, teaching and support staff, parents, other members of the local community, and external agents including LEA staff and central government officials. The survey of heads suggests that in practice the contribution of different individuals and groups to planning varied according to local circumstances in ways that did not necessarily reflect the legal position, as we explore further below.

## ELEMENTS IN THE MANAGEMENT OF PLANNING

Evidence from the six schools implies that there was a common network of five elements which constituted the management of planning:

- *orchestration* - creating and sustaining the framework within which the other elements contribute to planning;
- *constituencies* - individuals and groups at school level with a legitimate stake in the content of plans;
- *roles and tasks* - planning responsibilities of individuals and groups;
- *structures and procedures* - arrangements for carrying out planning;
- *sub-processes* - components of the overall planning process.

These mutually influencing elements were set within the wider local and national context discussed in Chapter 3, as Figure 5.1 depicts. It indicates that planning was *orchestrated* through the process of creating roles, such as responsibility for coordinating curriculum areas; defining related tasks (say, reviewing curriculum policies or implementing new programmes of study); and setting up structures for planning, including staff meetings or governors' working parties.

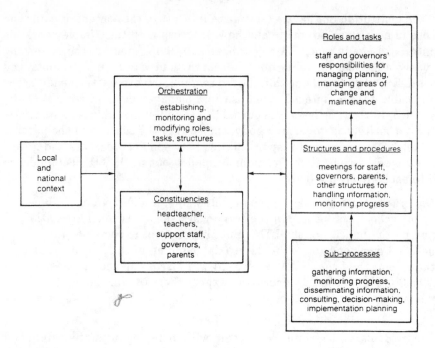

Figure 5.1 *The management of planning at school level*

The headteachers were not only central in orchestrating planning within the school, but also influential in creating some of the structures employed by their governing body. Orchestration of planning reciprocally influenced the four remaining elements.

We have already noted the range of *constituencies* with a legitimate stake in planning. The need to address these constituencies in some way, coupled with the heads' beliefs and values concerning how far to adopt a consultative style of management (especially in relation to teaching staff), affected the various planning *sub-processes*, including:

- gathering of information, especially connected with externally initiated changes;
- dissemination of information, including the content of decisions taken - whether internally to staff, or externally to governors or parents;
- consultation among different constituencies, where individuals represented their personal interests or represented the interests of particular groups;
- decision-making among priorities and for specific areas;
- detailed planning for implementation of decisions, especially those relating to school-wide changes;
- internal monitoring of progress with the implementation of plans.

These sub-processes underpinned the approaches to development planning which will be discussed in Chapter 6.

A complex *structure* of meetings between representatives of various constituencies was developed in each school, within which many of the sub-processes were carried out. For example, full staff meetings were often used for formal decision-making, and in-service training days might include extensive formal *procedures* for consultation. Other structures and procedures, not necessarily involving face-to-face interaction, were established for gathering and disseminating information - such as a system of folders for official publications about the National Curriculum. Arrangements other than formal or informal meetings for monitoring progress with implementation of decisions were less widespread. They included, in two schools, samples of children's work being sent regularly to the head.

Various structures and procedures were employed to deal with planning subprocesses by individuals whose *roles* included more detailed *tasks* connected with the management of planning (carried out primarily by heads) or the management of specific areas, such as LMS, for which planned activity was required. The roles and their associated tasks related, in turn, to the constituencies with an interest in the content of planning. For instance, the work of governors and headteachers in setting the annual budget within LMS included representatives of all the main constituencies.

All five elements affected each other. Management structures and procedures, for example, were employed by representatives of particular constituencies to consult others or in being consulted themselves. These structures and procedures were established and modified to meet the evolving needs of those constituencies. Similarly, they were influenced by the wider local and national context, as when HMI or LEA inspectors visited a school and gave feedback to heads, staff and governors, or when new information was received about externally initiated changes. Let us look now at some of the elements and their interrelationship in more detail.

## ORCHESTRATION

The headteachers used their authority to create roles, structures and procedures designed to include various constituencies. They allocated staff roles with varying levels of involvement of staff, according to each head's beliefs and values about consultation within this area of management. Most heads made a regular practice of consulting senior staff about role changes.

The allocation of curriculum responsibilities between staff at Central for 1992/3 was decided in discussion at a full staff meeting. The main considerations were to allow individual teachers to build on their interests and expertise and to ensure that no one had too heavy a workload. In Town School the senior management team (the headteacher, deputy and two B allowance holders) discussed how roles should be reallocated during the deputy's absence on maternity leave. The head at Highway had invited the teaching staff to discuss in her absence the roles for which incentive allowances should be offered. Staff made a presentation to the head and she and senior staff decided the allocation in the light of this open consultation exercise.

When she took up her present post at Heartlands, the head found that the first- and middle-school departments were run largely independently, with little continuity. Most management roles among staff were attached to a department. She held an informal appraisal interview with each person at which she discussed the possibility of changes in roles, giving her rationale of improving continuity across departments which was widely accepted among staff. She negotiated with individuals to ensure that curriculum responsibilities spanned the whole school. More recently, during an in-service training day, staff members had initiated a discussion about swapping curriculum responsibilities and asked the headteacher to approve their suggestions.

The heads also attended to the development of structures and procedures which were used for planning activities. Central had well-developed procedures for disseminating information. Teachers had a pigeon-hole in the staffroom and they received individual copies of key information sheets. The head reviewed any general documentation that came into the school and decided to whom it should be distributed. She produced a weekly newsletter about forthcoming events which was pinned up on the staffroom noticeboards and given to all members of staff. The noticeboards were also used to display details of dates and topics for staff meetings and training days for the year ahead; information about in-service training courses with relevant ones highlighted; and sheets of flipchart paper indicating how staff intended to organize their topic work in the following term. The staffroom was a regular meeting place for staff at morning break and the head would frequently use this opportunity to disseminate information, on occasion discussing issues that had come up at a headteachers' meeting.

At Southside voluntary working parties were convened to make recommendations on changes in particular curriculum areas, a legacy of participation in a school self-review project. The head commented: 'That really goes back to the old GRIDS system - if you want to get something done, get a group of enthusiasts together and they're the ones that are likely to do the groundwork.' She had also developed procedures (much appreciated by staff) for disseminating information internally about externally initiated changes, including using a highlighter to draw attention to key points on incoming documents. They were then placed on a table in the staffroom so that individuals had access to all the relevant information if they wished but could take the short cut of reading just the highlighted parts. For material that the head regarded as particularly important, staff were asked to tick their names on a list to indicate when they had read it.

Structures and procedures were monitored informally by the heads to ensure that they were effective and were modified if necessary. For example, the head at Northedge had instigated a procedure for writing school policies based on staff workshops:

> In the early days when I arrived I involved everybody. So every small group met, discussed the issue, wrote a small paper, gathered the papers together; we then had 'vertical groups' [of staff working with different age groups of pupils] and they discussed it, and it took a long time.

The advent of the national reforms, together with LEA initiatives such as the promotion of equal opportunities, had overloaded this system:

> At one time we had as many as five workshops who were having meetings every lunchtime and sometimes after school as well - which was quite horrendous. So I made a management decision in restricting the workshops to a limited number.

During the 1991 summer term, as the staff prepared to move from the temporary site to the refurbished main site of the school, the head asked them to put on hold the three workshops under way at that time, leaving unfinished business in two curriculum areas. She felt that staff had too much to do in getting ready for the move to continue with this curriculum development activity. The perusal of proposals by vertical groups of staff had to be abandoned. The principle of consultation which underpinned the head's approach to curriculum development was severely constrained by the weight of externally imposed demands.

Roles, structures and procedures employed by governing bodies in contributing to planning are largely laid out for them (see DES, 1988c), though there was some evidence of room for local interpretation. The formation of subcommittees and working parties varied among the six governing bodies. Both county schools had four subcommittees, the borough schools had working parties (with advisory powers only) for finance, and Southside did not have any subgroups. The head at Northedge had advised the governors to set up subgroups which were subsequently created for staffing, finance, curriculum and resources. However, monitoring by the deputy, who attended the curriculum and resources subgroups, led to the head suggesting that they be held in abeyance as they were found to be unnecessary. Here a structure intended primarily for governors was initiated, monitored and modified by members of staff.

Reorganization in the borough and the city dictated that Highway and the city schools must have temporary governing bodies whose sole responsibility was to plan for the newly constituted school, entailing the appointment of all staff. Setting them up was simple in the city, as the same people were members of both present and temporary bodies. The situation was more complex at Highway because the school was to be amalgamated with two others so a single temporary body was required, whose membership was drawn from the three present governing bodies. Staff were uncertain for some months how the two teacher representatives for the temporary governing body would be chosen from the three schools, and whether one school staff would not have a representative. The situation was resolved eventually through the cooptation of the teacher governor from one school.

## CONSTITUENCIES

Each school served the same range of constituencies, but there was variation between schools in the contribution of particular groups to planning and the structures and procedures designed to cater for them. The constitution of governing bodies is designed to ensure that the full range of groups is represented, and to exclude some overlap between roles. Heads and staff are not eligible to chair the governing body of a school in which they work, for example. The degree of overlap for individuals between the constituencies to which they might have allegiance varied markedly in practice. The legal position, as depicted in Figure 5.2, is for a fixed number of governors to be appointed to represent four constituencies. Headteachers may become governors or serve in an *ex officio* capacity. Co-opted governors are to include representation of the local business community, but co-optation may also be used to increase representation of other groups such as local community associations. LEA governors are appointed by the political parties that make up the local council. Governing bodies operate within a wider context that includes LEAs and central government.

The greatest overlap between constituencies either represented on the governing body or to which individuals might hold allegiance for other reasons occurred at Northedge (see Figure 5.3). Here a teacher governor also had children at the school and one of the minority ethnic group support staff, from the Afro-Caribbean community, was a co-opted governor. The headteacher was

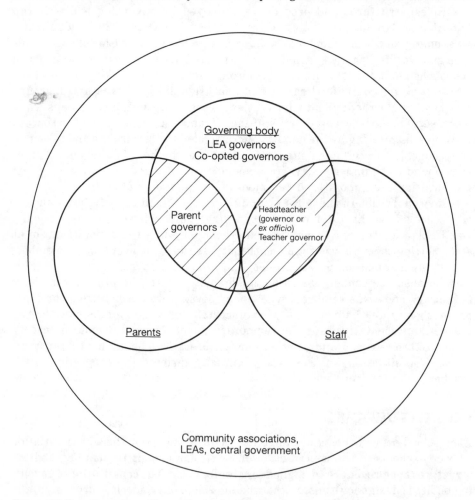

Figure 5.2 *Constituencies with a stake in planning at school level*

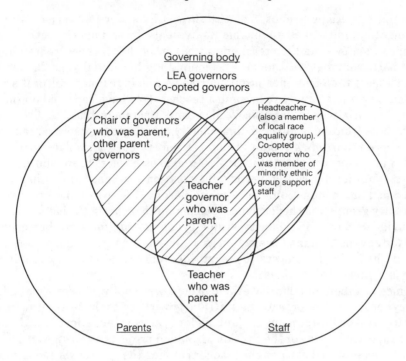

Figure 5.3 *Overlap between constituencies at Northedge First School*

a member of the city race equality group. Representation of different constituencies on the governing body creates the opportunity for the interests of each constituency to be taken into consideration in planning. Whether they are or not depends on other factors, including how far members of a constituency are consulted; the amount of consensus among members; the degree to which individual governors express a view; and whether particular vacancies on the governing body are filled.

## Representation of minority ethnic groups

Minority ethnic groups were under-represented among governors and teaching staff in comparison with their proportion among parents and the community at large. Of the case-study schools, only Northedge had a substantial number of governors from minority ethnic backgrounds. This school and Town had the highest number of teachers from minority ethnic groups, two in each school being Asian. Under-representation did not appear to be due to discrimination against black people at school or LEA levels, but resulting from wider economic and social conditions which meant that relatively few suitably qualified people from minority ethnic groups applied for teaching posts.

Appointing staff and governors from a minority ethnic background was a high priority for the heads, most of whom had made special efforts to recruit them. The head at Central had placed advertisements in the *Caribbean Times* without success. In general, applications had rarely been received from teachers from minority ethnic groups. Yet the three LEAs were at various stages of implementing initiatives to enable individuals from minority ethnic backgrounds to achieve qualified-teacher status. One of the teachers from a minority ethnic background at Northedge was completing her initial year, having been seconded part-time from her previous role as a bilingual and cultural support assistant in order to study to become a teacher. (We have reported on the relevant LEA initiatives in detail in Wallace and McMahon, 1993.)

Parents from some of the main minority ethnic groups represented among pupils were reported as tending to be reticent to put themselves forward for election as governors. The head at Town expressed her disappointment: 'We had a vacancy for a parent governor. Information was sent out in bilingual text and we had one nomination - for a white parent.' She was building links with community groups and the local mosque, hoping that this initiative would result in individuals from the minority ethnic group coming forward, but could not persuade anyone to stand for election as a governor. At Heartlands, the governing body had used its powers to co-opt governors from minority ethnic backgrounds represented in the school.

Since members of minority ethnic groups were not well represented in the two key constituencies of teaching staff and governors, their concerns were most likely to be taken into account in planning for change where efforts were made to gather their views. One of the Section 11 funded projects at Town was designed to foster home-school liaison. The teacher running the project visited families in their homes and met parents in school and so was able to gather information from at least some of the parents from minority ethnic backgrounds.

Evidence from all six case-study schools suggested that the heads and their mainly or wholly white teaching staff planned mostly according to their assumptions about what parents from minority ethnic groups would wish, in so far as it complied with their own educational and managerial beliefs and values. There was widespread consensus that different religions and cultures should be acknowledged, that racial stereotyping should be avoided, and that any racial abuse among pupils should be dealt with as a very serious matter. Examples from different schools included:

- assemblies taking themes from various religions;
- implementation of history and geography within the National Curriculum being planned to ensure that its ethnocentric bias was limited as far as possible;
- a uniform allowing girls to wear trousers;
- a white nursery teacher consulting black nursery nurses to ensure that books did not contain any racial stereotypes that they might find offensive;
- Muslim girls being allowed to wear tracksuits for physical education and games;
- procedures being established for following up any incidents where pupils made racist remarks.

On the other hand, in one school where some boys and fathers challenged the authority of staff because they were women, apparently reflecting assumptions about the status of women within their own culture, action was taken to assert this authority in line with staff members' managerial beliefs and values.

Few arrangements were made specifically for consulting parents from minority ethnic groups on religious or cultural issues. Both city schools included several black minority ethnic group support staff drawn largely from the local community, including staff with a brief for home-school liaison which included visiting the homes of all parents. They were consulted on occasion by the heads and they also reported back to staff the views of parents from both minority and majority ethnic groups, so providing a significant indirect route for the expression of minority ethnic group concerns. One of the home-school liaison officers from Northedge commented:

> Parents are more willing to come forward and express their views, but you'll never get 100 per cent of them and quite often you don't get the parents that really need your help. You have to go and seek them out. . . . You go on a home visit and a parent that you've probably seen on the street or in the playground that is quite shy and hasn't much to say, once you get onto their territory there's quite a lot of observation going on and it all comes out then.

## The professional staff

Within each constituency, individuals from minority ethnic backgrounds appeared to have a similar level of influence as their majority ethnic group counterparts over planning for change. Consistent with the findings of the earlier multiple innovations project reported in Chapter 1, the heads formed the most powerful constituency at school level, although their power was very far from exclusive. It was based on a combination of their legal authority and the adoption by governors of a support role. Not only did they initiate school-based changes and seek room to manoeuvre to adapt external changes, but they also tended to encourage their staff to take initiatives as long as they were consistent with their beliefs and values. The majority of teachers we interviewed in each school confirmed that the headteacher fostered initiative-taking, having made the acceptable parameters clear. Those staff who had been appointed by each head very largely shared her beliefs and values. A teacher at Southside said of the head:

> She's very supportive. If you see an area of weakness that you feel you want to change she says: 'By all means go ahead and do it . . . as long as you've thought it out and you can see how things can be improved - not just negative criticism.'

There was somewhat less consensus at Heartlands. Most teachers reported that the head had created a climate of change, but that resources had recently become a major constraint:

> There's been this feeling that one is free to institute change. But there hasn't been a specific directive. The ambience of the school encourages staff to take initiatives. . . . I have seen the emphasis change over the

last two years from what would be of great educational value to what we can afford.

However, as we mentioned in Chapter 4, a quite recently appointed teacher resented the way the head had challenged some of his ideas because he wished to have a free hand in initiating change. While he accepted that setting parameters for change was a legitimate part of the head's role he found it personally dissatisfying because of the limitations placed upon his freedom to innovate.

Teachers and support staff across the six schools reported that such changes as they did initiate generally lay within the bounds of their personal class-teaching, support or management responsibilities. In contrast to the heads, they were not a major source of large-scale, school-based initiatives. A fairly typical example was the initiative taken by a teacher at Northedge to set up a library of mathematics games which children could take home to use. She consulted the deputy and members of the parent-teachers' association first, then teachers of the younger pupils, including the reception year where she worked. The initiative quickly took off:

> It snowballed really, in that other year groups have approached me about trying to include them and developing it for other year groups. Parents have come to me and said how pleased they are and that it has been very beneficial to them. It gives them an insight into the kind of activities that go on in school and ways that they can help their children at home.

She commented on the head's support, indicating that the initiative lay squarely within the head's beliefs and values that had been communicated to staff:

> She has always made it known that she encourages parents' involvement in any way at all, whether it's parents coming into school for workshops, clubs or whatever. But this is very much direct contact with the home and therefore she really has been very enthusiastic about it.

A teacher at Central stated that the head encouraged staff to initiate changes although she liked ideas to be discussed with her in advance. She cited as an example her attendance at an in-service language course where the idea of organizing a writers' workshop had been discussed. She subsequently talked to the head about what seemed to be a good idea. The head suggested that they discuss it with the staff, resulting in several class teachers setting up writers' workshops.

Minority ethnic group support staff also took initiatives within their role. One of the staff responsible for home-school liaison at Southside noted how the introduction of his role had been innovatory for both parents and the teaching staff, and how home-school liaison officers had developed this role incrementally over the years. Once again, the support of the headteacher had been essential:

> It's not just the rhetoric, it's not just verbal, it's the actual practical commitment that's there, and I think that's important. The practical resources need to be made available by headteachers who wholeheartedly want it to happen, and that has been the case.

# Governing bodies

The varied - but in all cases minor - part played by the governing bodies in contributing to planning for changes (apart from the appointment of staff under reorganization in the borough and city schools) related to governors' interpretation of their role. All the governors we interviewed perceived the role of the governing body as supporting the professional staff, as long as staff did their job effectively, rather than the governors initiating changes for the staff to implement. The chair at Heartlands regarded the role of the governing body as

> one of supportive management. I consider the headteacher to be the managing director and I am the chair of the board who should be there to support the managing director. The board should be the final responsible body within the school and must accept the ultimate responsibility for what goes on in the school. But they should, in my opinion, leave day-to-day, week-to-week, year-to-year education matters to those who know best.

The chair at Southside hinted that the governors' non-interventive stance was contingent upon their trust in the work of the staff, and especially that of the head:

> Our main purpose is to support the professionals and keep an overall view.... I suppose the financial situation is the most important one. I have no views at all of taking over the professionals' jobs or responsibilities. Because in my opinion, and I may be fortunate, in this school there is an exceptionally good head and a very good staff.... I would not presume to tell them how to do a good job; the only thing is we would keep an overview of it all.

Well-established governors frequently had a close working relationship with the headteacher and other staff. The chair of governors at Central had been a governor there since 1969, and had been chair for eight years. She had served as a city councillor for eight years and was an experienced politician who was well able to organize campaigns on the school's behalf when required. She and the head had a formal meeting to discuss school business once a fortnight and as she lived only a few minutes' walk from the school she was able to visit frequently to collect her mail and speak to staff. The chair at Town also had a long relationship with the school, having been a governor since 1976. In order to help the members of the governing body become better informed about the school curriculum, they had recently instituted a system where an individual governor would go into the school for a day to see how a particular subject was taught and would then report back at the next governors' meeting.

The heads appeared able to retain much of their power to manage the schools, despite the policy framework created by central government which enabled governors to become more interventionist, as long as they established their credibility and gained governors' trust. The six governing bodies monitored the work of the schools, including progress with implementing innovations, primarily through the headteachers' reports to governors backed by informal communication, principally between the heads and chairs. It was the practice in both the county schools for teachers with curriculum management responsibility to attend the governors' meeting when the policy for their curriculum area was being discussed. Other staff, except those who served as governors, generally had little contact with the governing body. The relationship established between the heads and the governing bodies was therefore pivotal in enabling heads to retain a high degree of control over planning for change.

The six heads attempted to keep the governors informed about changes being planned within the school. At Heartlands the head arranged, over a year, for each teacher with management responsibility for an area of the curriculum to make a presentation at governors' meetings. Yet only the county school heads consulted governors, within the development planning process, over their preferences for change (see Chapter 6).

Individual governors did contribute to planning in areas where they had particular expertise or knowledge related to their position in the local community. One governor at Central, a former accountant, helped to organize the school finances after the introduction of LMS. The chair at Heartlands was a building surveyor; Southside's chair was a Labour councillor of many years' standing for the ward where the school was situated, which brought her into close contact with many parents. She actively supported the local Muslim community association and also served on the city council's education committee. A governor from the Afro-Caribbean community at Northedge helped to draft the school's antiracist policy.

## Parents

This constituency also played little direct or indirect part in contributing to planning for change. Although parents are regarded by central government as the 'customers' of schools and have been given greater powers through increased representation on governing bodies and the ability to exercise some choice over schooling, this policy thrust had scarcely penetrated the case-study schools. All six were popular with parents, and five were either full or were experiencing a rapidly rising roll. Indeed, as we noted in Chapter 4, the main concern expressed by Afro-Caribbean parents at Northedge was over the LEA's proposed change in the catchment area which would deny them the opportunity to continue to send their children to the school of their choice. Town was the exception, where some white parents were exercising choice by taking their children away to other schools with a lower proportion of pupils from minority ethnic groups.

Parents were welcomed into each of the schools and individuals were invited to talk to their class teacher about their concerns over the education of their own children. Heads also made a point of being accessible to parents. Staff attempted to inform them about changes, for example at open evenings held on particular areas of the National Curriculum. Yet parents as a constituency were consulted by the staff on their preferences for change on rare occasions. In the 1992 spring term, as part of their preparation for the 1992/3 development plan, staff at Central issued a questionnaire to parents asking them to identify what they felt were the strengths of the school, any problems or aspects of the school about which they were unhappy, and what needed developing. They received many responses and were able to implement several of the suggestions that were put forward. Elsewhere bounded consultation exercises were undertaken over specific issues. Staff at Highway wrote to parents to ask them whether they would support an innovatory residential field study trip; parents at Northedge were consulted on their wishes for a school uniform.

Where parents expressed preferences that were not congruent with the educational beliefs and values of the professional staff, staff attempted to 'educate' them by persuading them to accept the staff's professional views. The main desire, expressed by a minority of parents, was for a more formal education than any of the schools provided. Some parents from minority ethnic groups were reported by the minority ethnic group support staff as basing their view upon the more formal approach they had experienced in their country of origin. Their concern was also shared by individuals from minority and majority ethnic backgrounds educated in the UK.

The issue was more widely expressed in the case-study schools catering for the youngest pupils. It took the form of questioning the educational value of learning through play, including the rationale for the use of construction toys. The nursery teacher at Southside, who was leading a school-based initiative to give pupils in the nursery greater responsibility for their own learning, perceived a need to 'share with the parents our philosophy about how children learn'. She commented: 'I think there is always the suspicion that parents would like to see children sitting down and doing something like writing, something that is producing an end product.'

Other preferences were also expressed. Some parents at Central complained that the school sports day was not competitive enough. This issue was discussed by the staff, who decided that as they valued their present approach they would not change it. The teacher responsible for home-school liaison at Town reported that many parents would like more mother-tongue teaching, particularly in the early years. However, the school did not have the resources to employ community language speakers who could work alongside the class teachers.

While parents' wishes had little influence on planning for change, their needs as perceived by the professional staff were a major factor in stimulating the planning of school-based initiatives. The head at Southside had spearheaded a series of such initiatives, gaining considerable financial and staffing support from the LEA, to build close links with the largely Muslim community. Many parents were illiterate both in English and in their first language, having experienced very little formal education. Innovations included a shared reading project: on one evening each week a teacher and a member of the support staff with responsibility for home-school links visited the homes of pupils who needed extra support with reading. They taught parents or older brothers and sisters who were literate in the English language how to help the children learn to read. In addition, a regular reading workshop during the school day was organized where parents and children could learn to read together. An educational toy library was provided to help compensate for the lack of toys in the homes of many pupils. Their parents reportedly either did not perceive the learning potential of educational toys or were unemployed and could not afford to buy them. In sum, the staff made great efforts to help pupils' families to educate themselves and to participate in the children's learning according to the teachers' views of good practice.

The head extended her support for all parents, many of whom faced severe social and economic difficulties, well beyond the bounds of education. One of the home-school liaison officers reported that:

> She is very helpful. I never saw a headteacher welcome parents so much. Any problem they come with, she tries to solve it. Not only with school, their own problems or whatever. Even if she goes to somebody's house and sees they don't have any furniture she will phone round everywhere and she will hire a van herself and take some to them. That's why I think the parents like her so much. Even if they can't talk in English, all the time they come to her.

Local community associations connected with minority ethnic group religions existed within the area of two of the case-study schools. The heads liaised with these associations but they did not exert a major influence on school-based changes. The overall picture was that at school level the professional staff, led by the heads, had by far the greatest impact on planning for change; the staff were also strongly influenced by their beliefs and values in respect of the other constituencies.

## ROLES AND TASKS

Apart from the chairs, the roles of most governors were undifferentiated. Individuals elected to serve within particular subgroups and, in the city, one governor took special responsibility for liaising with the staff concerned with pupils who had special educational needs. Much more differentiation was evident in the allocation of management responsibilities among teaching staff, and hence the greater contribution to planning made by staff with incentive allowances. In all cases allocation of management responsibilities was based on the hierarchy of salary levels, all incentive allowance holders having more responsibility than main-scale teachers.

Heads were able to delegate responsibility for maintenance tasks and for planning the implementation of particular changes, coordinating implementation activity, procuring necessary resources, and monitoring implementation. Various parameters governed the potential for delegation, including:

- the possibility within the conditions of service for teachers (DES, 1989c) that all except probationers (teachers in their first year of service) could be given some management responsibility;
- the incentive allowances allocated to staff before each head took up her present post;
- the number and grade of incentive allowances made available by the

LEA within national limits, dependent upon the number and age of pupils;

- the adequacy of the LMS budget allocated to the school within the LEA formula, determining whether all available incentive allowances (with their additional salary costs) could be awarded;
- the number of qualified full-time teaching staff;
- the number of probationary teachers on staff, who could not be expected to undertake full responsibility for areas beyond their classwork.

The distribution of management responsibilities relevant to planning for change is summarized in Table 5.1. The national reforms appear to have influenced the content of responsibilities. In different ways, each school covered subjects within the National Curriculum, together with religious education, and had some arrangement for coordinating the work of groups of classes (such as Key Stage 1 and Key Stage 2 at Town). The larger schools also covered other curriculum areas like health education; administrative responsibilities such as looking after audio-visual equipment; and other school-wide coordination responsibilities including assessment, provision for pupils with special needs, staff development and in-service training, the use of computers, equal opportunities, and (in the city schools) multicultural education.

The borough schools appeared to be most tightly constrained in the range of responsibilities that the heads could delegate, partly in consequence of the tight LMS budget. The head at Highway Middle (the smallest of the case-study schools) had employed an exceptionally high proportion of probationers in 1990/91, which kept the staff salary bill down but meant that they could not be allocated full responsibility for a curriculum area. They did accept a gradually increasing level of responsibility as their probationary year progressed, within a developmental 'apprentice' arrangement where they were supervised and supported by the deputy. At Heartlands, the head had withheld an A allowance because the budget was so tight that it would not stand the marginal claim upon it from the extra salary payment.

In sharp contrast, the city schools experienced a much more favourable level of staffing within a more generous LMS budget. The two extreme cases provide an instructive comparison. Southside First had fewer pupils than Heartlands Combined, which catered for older pupils who represented a larger per capita contribution to the budget than the younger children. On the other hand, Southside benefited from the weighting within the city LEA's LMS formula based on the proportion of pupils (nearly half) entitled to free school meals. Not only did Southside have more teaching staff overall, but the school also had more A allowances.

Certain roles, such as coordination of provision for pupils with special needs and responsibility for the National Curriculum core subjects of science, mathematics and English, were allocated to experienced allowance holders in more than half the schools. All deputy heads were responsible for administrative areas but otherwise their roles varied markedly, reflecting, in part, the

**Table 5.1** Distribution of management responsibilities (summer 1991)

| Teaching staff | | Central Primary | Town Primary | Highway Middle | Heartlands Combined | Southside First | Northedge First |
|---|---|---|---|---|---|---|---|
| | | | | | School | | |
| Probationary teachers | Number | 3 | 0 | 4 | 2 | 0 | 2 |
| | Responsibilities | – | – | Apprentice curriculum area | – | – | – |
| Main-scale teacher (full-time) | Number | 7 | 7 | 3 | 5 | 9 | |
| | Responsibilities | Curriculum area | Curriculum area | Curriculum area | Curriculum/ administrative area | – | Curriculum/ administrative area |
| A incentive allowance holders | Number | 2 | 2 | 1 | 1 | 4 | 4 |
| | Responsibilities | Curriculum area | Curriculum area | Curriculum area, community links | Curriculum area, administrative area | Curriculum area/ coordination (e.g. nursery) | Curriculum area/coordination (e.g. equal opportunities) |
| B incentive allowance holders | Number | 2 | 2 | 1 | 4 | 4 | 5 |
| | Responsibilities | Two curriculum areas/coordination (e.g. special needs) | Curriculum area, coordination (e.g. in-service training) | Special needs, upper-school coordination | Curriculum area, coordination (e.g. special needs) | Two curriculum areas/coordination (e.g. home–school links and multicultural education) | Curriculum area |
| C incentive allowance holders | Number | 0 | 0 | 0 | 0 | 0 | 1 |
| | Responsibilities | – | – | – | – | – | Special needs |
| Deputy heads | Number | 1 | 1 | 1 | 1 | 1 | 1 |
| | Responsibilities | Curriculum area, coordination (class teacher) | Curriculum area, coordination (class teacher) | Unspecified range (no class) | Curriculum area, administrative areas (class teacher) | Two curriculum areas (no class) | Curriculum area, administrative area (no class) |

overall staffing level of the school and their working relationship with the head. For example, the head and deputy at Highway had developed into a highly collaborative small team. As the head said: [The deputy] and I are becoming more interchangeable - it's wonderful!' The head had ensured that the deputy was neither given full responsibility for a class nor tied to particular management responsibilities. The deputy was very versatile, stepping in wherever necessary. She regularly covered classes, supervised two of the probationers, and took charge of the development planning process. At Heartlands, the head was subject to greater financial constraints and, as we saw earlier, also perceived the deputy to be unwilling to take sole responsibility for major management areas. The deputy's management responsibilities were confined to a curriculum area and administrative duties such as the staff duty rota.

## Staff involvement in planning

Within their management roles, staff led planning for the implementation of particular changes through structures and procedures developed in each school. In general, they would draft policies for discussion by colleagues, lead meetings of staff, attend in-service training courses provided in the main by LEA staff, run development activities for colleagues, procure resources and give informal encouragement to individuals.

In addition, heads worked more or less closely with some experienced members of staff with substantial management responsibility in considering choices between priorities, planning the implementation of changes and maintenance work for which the heads were primarily responsible (including the allocation of classes and staff roles), and monitoring across the school. The heads at Southside and Heartlands involved their deputies less in school-wide planning than did the others. There was variation in arrangements, some of which changed during the period of fieldwork, reflecting the efforts of heads to find the most effective mixture of meetings in a frequently changing context. When the head at Central and the deputies at Town and Southside took maternity leave, senior staff in the schools 'acted up', taking the place of these people temporarily.

All heads brought together a group of the most senior staff for some form of consultation on plans but their frequency of involvement varied widely. At one extreme, a weekly meeting of the management team (consisting of the head, deputy and a B allowance holder) was held at Highway. At the other, all incentive allowance holders, the head and deputy met once a year at Southside to discuss the development plan priorities. The regular senior management team meetings at Heartlands were occasionally postponed by the head because she found them unproductive. There was evidence of conflicting expectations among the members of this group, some of whom perceived that the head should be providing the agenda. The head saw the purpose of the meetings as consulting senior staff about their own concerns, so the agenda should come from them. At Northedge the head decided to move from a regular meeting of such a group to one where teachers from each team based on paired classes were represented by one of their number who attended an equivalent meeting in rotation. This arrangement led to occasional difficulty over communication within teams, as the system relied on whoever attended relaying information to their colleagues.

## Monitoring

There was considerable variation in how far the work of staff was monitored by the head and by staff with management responsibility for particular areas. Most monitoring was carried out in the county schools and least at Northedge but in no case did it extend to regular observation, except for probationary teachers. The level of monitoring by heads in the case-study schools was consistent with the national picture. HMI inspections in 1992 revealed that

> there was little monitoring and evaluation of the curriculum by
> headteachers, although a majority of them visited classes on a daily
> basis. In less than a sixth of the schools were heads engaged in explicit
> monitoring of the work with an eye to evaluating the curricular
> strengths and weaknesses of the school as a whole and dealing with
> inconsistencies in the quality of teaching.
>
> (Office for Standards in Education, 1993, p. 11)

None of the schools had yet implemented teacher appraisal within the framework set by central government ministers. Nevertheless, planning was informed by a range of formal and informal structures and procedures. Heads and their staff were beset by what they perceived as the higher priorities of planning to implement a multiplicity of changes and, as with all primary-sector schools, there was limited 'non-contact time' when staff could be released from their classroom for monitoring activities.

The head at Town made her criteria about what constituted good practice explicit by talking about her philosophy of teaching and learning at staff meetings, and tried to model good practice in her own work. She also praised good practice when she observed it in different parts of the school and drew it to the attention of other staff. She used a range of informal and formal methods of monitoring teachers' work. The informal methods consisted of regular walks around the school and visits to classrooms, acting as a substitute teacher when someone was away, and noting the inputs that teachers made in meetings.

On a formal basis teachers handed their termly plans of work to the headteacher for comment; periodically she would go through the folders of work from a whole class. The head engaged in very detailed monitoring for certain tasks: when teachers were writing reports on individual pupils for parents she gave the staff guidance and then read each teacher's comments. Where she was unhappy with a statement she asked the teacher to rewrite it. She had also prepared a detailed analysis of the school's Standard Assessment Task (SAT) results as a means of informing a special needs initiative. Though appraisal had yet to be introduced, the head conducted an annual professional discussion with each member of staff which provided an opportunity to discuss and clarify the teacher's job description, to identify professional development needs and to raise any other issues of mutual concern.

The other heads expected staff to inform them of progress and monitored informally as they walked about the school, went into classes, talked to individual members of staff and participated in conversations in the staffroom. More formal approaches included examination of teachers' written forecasts at Heartlands and Southside, and review meetings with individuals in the borough schools.

Few arrangements were made by heads for staff to carry out formal monitoring, beyond what was required for probationary teachers. Most staff with management responsibility stated that they monitored informally: by making themselves available to teachers on request; making a point of asking them about progress; or observing casually as they went round the school. More formal activities were rare, limited mainly to working alongside colleagues in the county schools to support implementation of particular changes. In Town school, exceptionally, time was provided for a teacher to take on a support role for colleagues in science and physical education, two priorities within the 1992/3 development plan. Feedback on the progress of staff apparently made a small contribution to planning compared with the effort to establish priorities and implement changes, and some of that feedback was limited where it was based upon teachers' perceptions of their progress.

The work of headteachers was subject to little monitoring at school level. As we have seen, governors relied largely upon the heads' own account of progress. The head at Town had been appraised during 1991/2 and found it a very positive learning experience. Her appraisers were two people who knew her well: the LEA school liaison officer and a fellow headteacher for whom she had great respect. The head at Heartlands was the only other headteacher who had also begun her own appraisal process by the end of our fieldwork.

External monitoring by LEA staff or HMI was sporadic and happened very rarely. Where inspection in some form did take place, heads generally took recommendations for improvement seriously and subsequently worked on them with staff (Table 5.2). LEA staff in all three LEAs had revised the way in which they monitored schools, as we described in Chapter 4. Town Primary received a full LEA inspection and a short follow-up visit after two years; Central and Highway received a short visit, resulting in a written report, shortly before or during the period of fieldwork, and Heartlands experienced such a visit in two successive years. The city schools received no LEA monitoring visit, although Southside had been subject to a full HMI inspection in 1989. External monitoring appeared to offer a useful stimulus for planning, but did not happen sufficiently often to make a major contribution.

## STRUCTURES AND PROCEDURES

The principal structure in which planning took place was the pattern of formal meetings among staff and, to a lesser extent, between staff and members of other constituencies. The structure of meetings among staff is portrayed in Table 5.3 (pp. 106-7). Despite considerable variation at the level of detail, the groups brought together for meetings and the opportunities for consultation with other constituencies were broadly similar across all six schools. A few meetings for staff were held during the school day, including those between

**Table 5.2** External monitoring since 1989

| | School | | | | | |
|---|---|---|---|---|---|---|
| Features | Central Primary | Town Primary | Highway Middle | Heartlands Combined | Southside First | Northedge First |
| Time | Autumn '91 | Autumn '89; follow-up autumn '91 | Spring '91; autumn '91 | Autumn '90 | Spring '89 | – |
| Agent | LEA inspectors | LEA inspectors | LEA inspectors | LEA inspectors | HMI | – |
| Type | Monitoring visit | Full inspection | Monitoring visit | Monitoring visit | Full inspection | – |
| Duration | One day | One week (one day follow-up) | One day | One day | One week | – |
| Impact on planning | Staff worked on recommendations, e.g. information technology | Capitalized upon by head to initiate changes | Staff worked on recommendations, e.g. speaking and listening | (Autumn '91): head reviewed communication with parents | Staff worked on recommendations, e.g. investigations in mathematics, science, technology | – |

the head and deputy at Northedge; the management team at Highway; and the lower and upper school meetings at Southside, which occurred while the head took an assembly. The large majority of meetings for staff took place in 'directed time' after school or during in-service training days. In all cases, the head ensured that under normal circumstances a regular opportunity was available for formal consultation and decision-making among staff. (The lack of full staff meetings at Highway during the term spent split between two temporary sites was consequently of major concern to all staff.) A variety of informal meetings took place when individuals or groups perceived the need, as in Southside, for example, where year groups would meet at breaks, lunchtimes, or after school at least once a week to coordinate their day-to-day work.

Working parties were employed in the borough and city schools although, as we saw earlier, they had to be curtailed at Northedge. A typical procedure at Southside was followed for the task of developing a list of famous people within the programme of study for Key Stage 1 History. The coordinator for geography and history asked colleagues for a volunteer from each year group across the school, on the grounds that teachers currently working with pupils at Key Stage 2 might teach younger pupils in future. The group met ten times towards the end of the school day when pupils were read stories, enabling some staff to be released. Generous staffing provision allowed each pair of classes to have a third teacher acting in a support role. The coordinator chaired the meetings and presented the completed list for the headteacher's approval. The working party was subsequently reconvened to consider resource requirements.

The advent of so many externally initiated changes, coupled with the way in which some of them evolved, made it imperative that all members of staff were kept informed about those changes which directly affected their work (and that governors were also kept up to date). We noted earlier how the heads actively gathered information and disseminated it internally. Each LEA had some form of occasional meeting for headteachers, where they were addressed by LEA staff and could exchange information with colleague heads. Memberships of LEA consultative task groups of some kind was a source of specialized information for a few individuals. The head at Heartlands served on a borough committee for assessment and one of the teachers was a member of the humanities working party, for instance. Staff in all six schools received or had sight of central government and LEA documents on particular changes and attended staff meetings and school-based training. Those going to in-service training courses gathered information from the course content and from informal exchange with colleagues from other schools. At Southside, a minority of staff mentioned how useful they found the information disseminated by colleagues who had been on courses.

Several other sources which lay outside formal structures and procedures were drawn upon by individuals to varying degrees. The mass media, especially the education press and specialist primary teaching magazines, were quite widely consulted. Professional association documents were used but tended to be perceived as offering a union perspective. Television was less used, and a minority of teachers commented that programmes were biased. A substantial minority of staff referred to an informal network of friends among teaching staff and, in a few cases, LEA staff.

## Training for planning

Only the head at Highway had experienced any training in models of planning. She had been pressurized to adopt rationalistic procedures offered during an advanced degree course but she found them ill-matched to her preferred - more intuitive - approach:

> I was getting really hung up about those systems and my mind doesn't work like that. I'm not saying I'm not systematic ... but I felt it was slowing me down going laboriously through this (procedure) when my mind worked in a different way.

All the heads, however, had experienced some training for LMS and those in the county and the city had been introduced to the development planning process advocated by the LEA.

A variable proportion of coordinators had attended LEA courses in their area of management responsibility. These courses had covered the content of particular changes and had helped coordinators with planning how they would introduce changes to their colleagues in school. Such input was widely perceived to have been of some practical value for the task in hand but it had not made any significant impact on the planning process across the school. It seems that staff had learned how to manage planning and to carry out the sub-processes entailed within it very largely through their experience in the job. This experience included development planning, located within the elements for managing planning discussed in this chapter. We now move on to examine how development planning fared at school and LEA levels.

**Table 5.3** Meetings among staff where planning took place (summer 1991)

| Type of meeting | | Central Primary | Town Primary | Highway Middle | Heartlands Combined | Southside First | Northedge First |
|---|---|---|---|---|---|---|---|
| | | | | | *School* | | |
| Head and deputy | Timing | Weekly, school day | Daily, school day | Daily, school day | Daily before school | Occasional, variable times | Weekly, school day |
| | Contribution | Review and short-term planning | Short-term planning | Short-term issues, day book | Short-term issues | Short-term issues | Medium-term planning, 'think tank' |
| Management team | Timing | Fortnightly, after school | Weekly, after school | Weekly, school day | Fortnightly, lunchtime | Annually | Fortnightly, after school |
| | Contribution | Development planning, decision-making | Development planning, decision-making, organizational issues | Coordinating planning, decision-making | Consultation | Development planning | Consultation |
| Department | Timing | – | – | Occasional, lunchtime | Variable – weekly to once a year depending on staff perception of need | Weekly, school day | – |
| | Contribution | – | – | Upper school, short-term issues | First, middle departments, lower, middle, upper years, short-term issues | Lower and upper-school consultation, decision-making | – |
| Year group | Timing | Weekly | Weekly | Termly, school day | Weekly | Termly, school day | Weekly, lunchtime |
| | Contribution | Planning topics and other work | Planning topics and other work | Planning topics | Short-term issues | Planning topics | Discuss proposals from full staff meeting and feed back |

|  |  | 1 | 2 | 3 | 4 | 5 | 6 |
|---|---|---|---|---|---|---|---|
| Staff | Timing | (i) Weekly, after school (ii) Fortnightly, lunchtime | (i) Weekly, after school (ii) Briefing, weekly, before school | Once or twice weekly | Fortnightly, after school | Half-termly, after school | Fortnightly, after school |
|  | Contribution | (i) Consultation, decision-making (ii) Routine business | (i) Consultation, decision-making (ii) Student progress | Consultation, decision-making | Consultation, in-service training, decision-making | Consultation, decision-making | Consultation, decision-making |
| Training day | Timing | Five per year | Five per year | Five per year | Five per year | Five per year | Five per year |
|  | Contribution | In-service training and development priorities | In-service training and development priorities | Consultation, supporting implementation | Consultation, supporting implementation | Consultation, supporting implementation, preparing for reorganization | Consultation, supporting implementation, preparing for reorganization |
| Working party | Timing | – | – | Occasional, for duration of task | Occasional, for duration of task, lunchtime | Occasional, for duration of task, school day | Occasional, for duration of task, lunchtime |
|  | Contribution | – | – | Development planning, planning within priorities | Drafting policies | Planning within priorities | Drafting policies |

# Chapter 6

# School Development Planning

Our second theme is to take forward the story of development planning. Here we take a close look at the development plan documents, the operation of the development planning process in the six schools, and factors which influenced the fate of development planning as an innovation at both school and LEA levels.

The national policy context (including the recommendations of the national project on development planning) and evidence of LEA and school-level responses across the country were outlined in Chapter 1. The assumptions underlying the development planning model put forward in central government guidance were explored in Chapter 2, and the change process entailed in the implementation of development planning was highlighted. The main features of the development planning initiatives launched within the three LEAs we studied were summarized in Chapter 3 and issues were raised relating to their implementation as innovations for both schools and LEAs. The survey of headteachers provided insights into some of the factors affecting the implementation of development planning and the content of plans. Chapter 4 previewed the present discussion by summarizing how development planning fared in each case-study school, and Chapter 5 discussed elements of the management of planning: the context into which development planning in the schools was fitted and of which it was part.

Development planning offered a procedure for managing some or all innovations and other changes at school level. As such, it had to be implemented as part of the approach adopted in each school for the management of planning for all areas of change and maintenance of existing practice. We will see how the heads orchestrated development planning, involved certain other constituencies and used structures, procedures, roles and tasks connected with planning.

## THE DESIGN OF DEVELOPMENT PLAN DOCUMENTS

The documents making up the plan recorded decisions relating to future development work made during some form of review and planning procedure, and an agenda for action and deployment of resources during the implementation period. Completed documents were a tangible outcome of whatever planning sub-processes were encapsulated in the procedure adopted for compiling them.

Their format depended on who was designing the document for whom. The head at Heartlands used her flowchart solely as a source of reference for guiding planning in the school where she worked. The documents developed by LEA staff in the county and city, in common with many other LEAs, were intended to serve all three purposes identified in Chapter 1: guiding planning in schools across the LEA; collecting information for LEA staff to provide support for development, principally through provision of in-service training courses; and collecting information which could be used in LEA monitoring of schools. The interests of the designer profoundly affected the design. How far the LEA documents would prove useful at school level depended upon the degree to which these interests coincided. Some of the information needed by LEA staff turned out to be superfluous as far as staff in school were concerned because it was not needed to guide their planning efforts.

## Documentation for the county schools

The LEA *Guidelines for School Development Plans* had been revised in the light of the first year's experience, and the 1990/91 document was quite lengthy, being organized into two main sections:

- an introduction and rationale for development planning with advice on the content of plans and the planning process. This section also contained copies of the forms that the schools had to return to the LEA;
- practical advice and instruments that might be useful when producing, implementing and evaluating the development plan.

Information required from the school consisted of:

- a short statement of the school's aims;
- a summary of the previous year's development plan and in-service training programme;
- details of the development planning process;
- an outline three-year plan for up to six priorities;
- an action plan for each priority;
- information about the intended use of the five annual training days, their focus and estimated costs;
- the staffing structure;
- an annual curriculum return;
- details of delegated budget expenditure (where appropriate);
- a summary of the estimated in-service training costs.

The bulk of this information related directly to the school development plan and only outline details were required. The plans submitted by Central and Town ran to about twelve pages. Figure 6.1 illustrates how the priorities in county school development plans could span from a few months to over three years.

## Documentation for the borough schools

As we saw in Chapter 3, heads in borough schools designed such documents as there were to suit their own purposes while LEA staff collected information on

| Outline three-year plan for SDP priorities | Central School | |
| --- | --- | --- |
| | Start date | End date |
| **Target 1**<br>To implement the National Curriculum Attainment Targets and programmes of study in the core subjects, English, maths and science, so that each child receives the NC through our thematic approach | 9/88 | 7/91 |
| **Target 2**<br>To implement the assessment policy to take account of National Curriculum legal requirements so that each child's achievements will be carefully monitored within an NC framework | 6/89 | 12/92 |
| **Target 3**<br>To implement the National Curriculum Attainment Targets and programmes of study in the foundation subjects so that each child receives a balanced curriculum within the NC framework | 4/90 | 7//92 |
| **Target 4**<br>To initiate and monitor a financial system to take account of formula funding and local financial management so that we may effectively use our budget to meet our aims | 4/90 | 7/92 |
| **Target 5**<br>To develop our outside areas so that we can ensure purposeful and safe play by children and increase the area's potential as a rich learning resource | 4/90 | 12/91 |
| **Target 6**<br>To develop a behaviour policy for our school which takes account of links with parents, our community and pupil management so that we may enhance the quality of the relationships in school as outlined in our school documents. | 4/91 | 12/91 |

Figure 6.1 *Priorities in Central's 1991/2 development plan*

in-service training needs by other means. At Highway the development planning initiative never got as far the completion of a document. The consultative review and planning process was curtailed after leaks in the roof led to the school being split between two temporary sites. The only documents were ingredients of the review and planning process, including questionnaire sheets, a collated list of priorities, and individuals' ideas relating to each priority recorded on flipchart paper. On the other hand, the system for planning recorded on sheets of flipchart paper was sustained and some priorities from the review and planning exercise were subsequently incorporated within it.

The head at Heartlands had developed her own flowchart as a very succinct recording device for development work. The document, which covered one sheet of A4-sized paper for each academic year, did not need to be self-explanatory to individuals outside the school. It was an informal working document on which she wrote amendments as the year progressed. Tasks to be undertaken each term were set out for:

- the curriculum - updating curriculum and other policy statements such as equal opportunities, reviewing the distribution of time for different curriculum areas, writing curriculum plans for each year group to be sent to parents, and writing individual staff forecast sheets and reviewing their effectiveness;

- record-keeping and assessment - developing and using records for various aspects of pupils' work, reviewing record system, preparatory training for teachers of Key Stage 1 classes, selecting and storing samples of pupils' work;

- in-service training - consulting about needs, meeting needs arising from National Curriculum subjects, establishing a programme for staff meetings and training days;

- furniture, equipment and resources - replacement of furniture for classrooms and for staff, budgeting for resources and developing a new ordering procedure within LMS, ordering material to implement the equal opportunities policy, appointing a coordinator to supervise resource areas, and updating an inventory of furniture and equipment.

Part of the flowchart addressing furniture, equipment and resources is reproduced in Figure 6.2. The plan for the forthcoming academic year was written in the summer term marking the end of the previous year. It could be extended year by year by attaching a new sheet of paper to the right hand side of the existing document.

## Documentation for the city schools

The LEA development plan for primary-sector schools focused on the curriculum and consisted of forms broken down into five sections, only the last of which was the plan itself for the present academic year. Some of the information required had been collected previously through other forms, and heads were encouraged to append photocopies of this information to the development plan document. Southside's plan for 1991/2 consisted of some thirty-one pages, including a two-page questionnaire for staff constructed by the special-needs coordinator in connection with one of the development priorities.

The amount of background information required meant that the completed document provided a detailed account of the context for the summary of current intentions for curriculum development. Like the document used in the county schools, it was designed to be self-explanatory to someone who did not know the school: the content would inform LEA staff not only about development priorities and some in-service training needs but also about contextual factors that might be relevant when reading through the completed plan in preparation

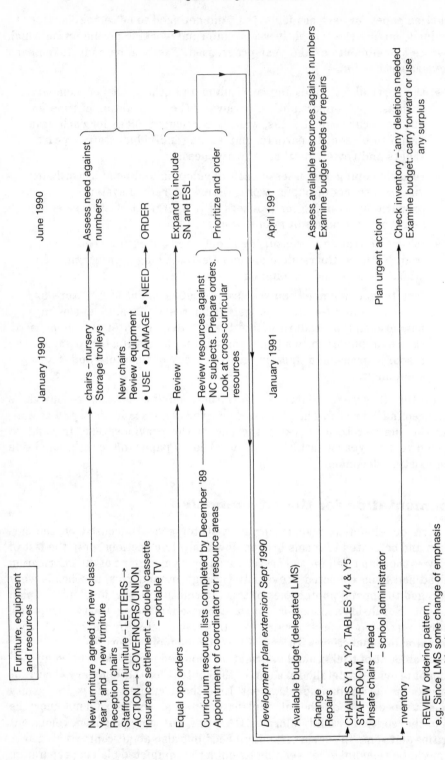

**Figure 6.2** *Excerpt from the Heartlands developments plan*

for an inspection. A significant proportion of the content related to the document's role in demonstrating that the LEA was holding schools externally accountable for the use of LEA and central government resources. One instance was the requirement for a statement of the use of in-service training days and a list of courses attended in the year prior to the period covered by the plan, together with an account of their effectiveness. The content for the 1991/2 Southside plan was as follows:

Part One: Context of Present Curriculum Provision

- School profile
  - school type
  - age range of pupils and number on roll
  - summary of current staffing
  - nursery admissions and summary of nursery staffing
- School context
  - area served by the school
  - number of free school meals
  - number of children with a statement of special educational needs
  - number of pupils for whom English is a second language
- School buildings
  - number of teaching areas and class units
  - use of additional rooms
- Staffing
  - copy of part of the current LEA staffing and organization return giving details of teaching and other staff
  - description of other support agencies regularly used in school (e.g. educational psychologist)
- Pupil organization
  - copy of part of the current LEA staffing and organization return giving details of the number of pupils in each year group
- Parents
  - statement of evidence of parental expectations concerning the school
  - list detailing current parental involvement in school
  - list of other initiatives for building home-school links
  - strategies employed to communicate with parents about the school philosophy and curriculum
- Governors
  - ways of updating governors about the school
- Community links
  - links with local schools to which pupils will transfer when they leave the primary-sector school
  - collaborative activities with other schools
  - links with industry
  - other community links (e.g. visits to the local Gurdwara)
  - community use of school facilities

Part Two: Philosophy and Aims of the School

- copy of statement

Part Three: Current Curriculum Statement

- list of all current documents on curriculum and organization (e.g. policy for racial harmony)
- summary of identified strengths and weaknesses of the school
- summary of use of training days in the previous year
- list of courses attended in previous year by each member of staff
- account of evidence of the effectiveness of these training days and of the courses listed
- issues raised by the school-wide review in relation to the curriculum, staff development and individual children

Part Four: Gaps between Current Curriculum and National Curriculum Requirements

- table showing for which subjects a new or revised scheme of work was needed

Part Five: The Plan

- up to four targets for the next academic year
- an action plan for each target
- a special-needs questionnaire for staff (appended by the head)
- statement of implications of the plan for physical, financial and human resources (without financial details)
- account of the use of devolved in-service training money for the previous financial year

Compared with the amount of other information required, very little detail of the plan for the coming year had to be supplied. The plan for three priorities and statement of the implications for resources ran to just four of the thirty-one pages. A considerable proportion of the remainder consisted of information that had already been supplied on other forms or information which had not changed since the previous year. The statements relating to parents in the first part of the plan were virtually identical in Southside's 1990/91 and 1991/2 plans, for example.

Action plans completed in both the city school plans were brief. Figures 6.3 and 6.4 show what was stated for two development priorities within Southside's 1991/2 plan (slightly modified to preserve anonymity). Most of the action to deal with the priority relating to special educational needs had been implemented before the development plan document was written up. It is evident that the review procedure had enabled an issue to surface of which senior staff had been unaware: a testimony to the impact of this procedure which the head had used annually since the early 1980s. Yet the completion of the relevant section of the development plan document could not have contributed to the formulation of

**School development plan 1991/2**

NAME OF SCHOOL _____

PART FIVE : THE PLAN

E1 PRECISE TARGETS 1991/92

(a) Priority 1       (b) Target Date for:       (c) Named
                                           Staff Leader

*Speaking*       Commencement *6.9.91*       *(English coordinator)*
*and Listening*

                 Completion:

---

(d) Action Plan

*(a) Form working party to develop existing guidelines on speaking*
    *and listening – to extend to Key Stage 2*
*(b) Minutes to be kept*
*(c) Evaluate children's progress*

DRAMA     6.9.91     *(art and craft coordinator)*

*It was agreed that more work in drama could lead to better spoken English and extension of language.*

*a) Coordinator to contact LEA adviser for drama*

Figure 6.3 *Southside's development plan - priority 1*

action taken in response to the emergence of this issue. Questions arise over how far the documentation fulfilled one of its purposes of guiding action in school and the degree to which it was an encumbrance for planning while fulfilling the purpose of informing LEA staff.

## THE FATE OF DEVELOPMENT PLANNING

In each of the six schools, the introduction of development planning initiatives entailed the use of existing elements within the management of planning. The review and planning procedure covered some of the sub-processes highlighted earlier in Figure 5.1. Information-gathering, consulting and decision-making were central sub-processes in all cases and, apart from Highway whose initiative foundered, the procedure included, to a varying degree, implementation planning and monitoring of progress. Yet dissemination of information to staff and

| (a) Priority 2 | (b) Target Date for: | (c) Named Staff Leader |
|---|---|---|
| *Special educational needs* | Commencement: *6.9.91*<br><br>Completion: | *(Special needs coordinator)* |

(d) Action Plan

*When the survey of staff opinion GRIDS was completed special educational needs was highlighted as an area of concern.*
*To further pinpoint the areas of concern the coordinator produced a questionnaire for staff to write in their opinions.*
*When the questionnaire was analysed we found that new staff did not understand needs identification procedures and exactly what was involved in statementing.*
*The coordinator then held a staff meeting to clarify these areas.*
*This led us to the fact that it was not special needs that was the concern but that our staff induction policy needed to be reviewed.*

*Staff induction*

*Staff handbook has been updated and a section on special needs and equal opportunities added.*
*Staff tutor to be given a set time to consult with new staff.*

Figure 6.4 *Southside's development plan - priority 2*

governors (as opposed to informing the head or LEA staff) was a strong feature only in the county schools.

Heads orchestrated the use of roles and structures and the degree of involvement of different constituencies in carrying out such sub-processes as each development planning procedure encompassed. Existing arrangements for managing planning were employed in all cases: staff meetings, for example, were the forum for review and planning exercises covering the sub-processes of monitoring progress, consulting and decision-making within the development planning review procedure. Even at Highway planning for some priorities identified was taken forward within the customary procedure based on flip-charts. In a very few instances new elements were created, such as responsibility for managing the development planning process, which the head at Highway delegated to her deputy.

## Development planning in action – county schools

In the summer of 1991 the county schools were putting the finishing touches to their development plans for 1991/2. Procedures for completing plans were well-established in both schools and were carried out with little apparent difficulty. Central began with a detailed evaluation of the previous year's plan. Progress in meeting the specific targets was reviewed regularly throughout the year in staff meetings and at governors' meetings. The procedure followed in 1991 was that ideas about what should be the school's priorities for 1991/2 were discussed with the staff. They were also invited to make their views about school targets and their personal professional development interests and needs clear to the head by completing a short questionnaire.

The head and deputy worked together to produce the first draft of the plan. This effort entailed identifying priority targets, thinking through details of the in-service training support that would be required, and considering the budgetary implications. The draft was circulated for comment, first to staff and then to governors. Where necessary, the head subsequently amended the plan. Only when consensus was reached was the plan forwarded to the LEA. This consultative process was the normal mode of decision-making at Central; but in adopting this style LEA advice was followed which asked school staff to describe 'the methods by which consensus was reached' when giving details of the planning process.

A further example of this consultative style occurred in the spring of 1992 when, in preparation for the 1992/3 plan, the staff issued the short questionnaire to parents and governors that we mentioned in the previous chapter, inviting them to identify features that they liked about the school and to highlight any problems. The response rate was higher than the staff had anticipated and they found it a very helpful exercise. Several issues that parents raised as concerns were dealt with very quickly. Each year, once the development plan had been finalized, the head and deputy planned the topics for training days and staff meetings for the year ahead.

The vast majority of the staff thought that the development plan was useful. The deputy commented: 'It encouraged you to analyse what you had done and what you had achieved over the past year as well as looking forward.' One of the B allowance holders reported that the plan 'gave a focus to work in the school, it encouraged people to sit down and think what they were good at, what they were not good at and where they needed to target'.

Central staff had established the practice of conducting a formal review of their school development plan once it had been under way for six months. The 1991/2 plan was reviewed at the end of September 1992 in a full staff meeting. A full copy of the school development plan was held by the four members of the senior management team, there was a staffroom copy, and all staff had been given a copy of the priorities and specific objectives. The review at the staff meeting was conducted relatively informally, each target being discussed in turn; progress was assessed and, where necessary, implementation plans were adjusted to try to ensure that the targets were achieved. However, because the development plan figured very prominently as a means of managing planning, staff rarely found themselves seriously off target or behind schedule.

A further reason why the staff managed to follow the plan reasonably faithfully was that the priorities related to initiatives such as the National Curriculum and assessment which they had to introduce anyway (see Table 6.1). Indeed, the head's main complaint was that, because of the pressure of external innovations, there was no real opportunity to focus on internal school priorities. In 1991/2 only two of the six priorities were not concerned with externally imposed innovations.

The implementation strategy was agreed when the development plan was drawn up. Typically one teacher would be given main responsibility for each

**Table 6.1** Development plan priorities in the county schools

| | | School | | |
|---|---|---|---|---|
| | Central | | Town | |
| Time | Priority | Implemented as planned? | Priority | Implemented as planned? |
| 1990/1 | National Curriculum English, maths and science 9/88–7/91 | Yes | Maths, English, science and technology to July 1993 | Yes |
| | Assessment 6/89–12/91 | Yes | Assessment of resources 10 December 1990 | Yes |
| | Foundation subjects 4/90–7/92 | Implementation delayed till final orders received from NCC | Parental involvement to July 1992 | Yes |
| | LMS 4/90–7/92 | Yes | Review planning and recording methods used and develop policy on this July 1991 | Yes – timeline for working policy document extended to October 1991 |
| | Outside environment 4/90–7/91 | Yes | | |
| | Links with parents 4/90–12/92 | Not as much progress as anticipated because of time required for targets for National Curriculum and assessment – did not get place on county behaviour policy training scheme | Create and implement a behaviour policy to April 1991 | Yes |
| 1991/2 | National Curriculum English, maths, science 9/88–7/91 | Yes | English, science and technology to September 1992 | Yes |
| | Assessment 6/89–12/92 | Yes | Special needs to September 1992 | Yes |
| | National Curriculum foundation subjects 4/90–7/92 | Yes, history and geography. No final orders in other subjects – delayed | Parental involvement to July 1992 | Yes – timeline extended |
| | LMS 4/90–7/92 | Yes | Review planning and recording methods and develop policy to July 1991 | Yes |
| | Outside areas 4/90–7/92 | Yes | To implement LMS to July 1992 | Yes |
| | Behaviour policy 4/91–12/92 | Yes – but rather less progress than anticipated | | |

priority. Time slots at staff meetings and on training days would be allocated for work with staff on the target area. The plan provided a framework for development work in the school over the year and progress was kept under review by the headteacher and the senior management team, providing considerable stability. Several priorities had an implementation period longer than a year (the time span allocated to the implementation of the assessment policy extended from June 1989 to December 1992, for example), enabling the staff to work on the priorities incrementally. Most staff felt they had been adequately consulted and were content with their level of involvement in the planning process.

The value of the development plan in providing a framework for action was demonstrated in the 1991/2 school year when work on the targets continued despite some changes in staffing and the head's absence on maternity leave. If the teacher leading work on a particular target area changed, the new person was expected to continue with the same implementation strategy. The staff experienced a particularly turbulent time in the 1992 spring term when it appeared that some existing Section 11 support would be lost. Although staff fought a vigorous and time-consuming campaign to oppose the projected cut they were not deflected from their development plan priorities.

The experience of development planning at Town was similiar in many respects. Staff undertook a process of consultation to evaluate the current year's plan and to identify priorities for the next. Unlike Central, they did not set aside time for a formal mid-year review. However, all members of staff had a copy of the development plan and it was referred to from time to time in meetings. It appeared particularly helpful to those teachers who had been designated to lead work on a particular priority area. The teacher with responsibility for special needs (a priority for 1991/2) reported that she regularly referred to her copy of the plan, finding it very useful because:

> there was so much going on that without something like that you did become very disorganized ... it helped to clarify priorities. Previously all we were doing was identifying loads and loads of things that had to be done and of course there wasn't time to do all of them.

The way the plan was compiled was similiar to Central and was in line with the LEA recommendations. Broad priority areas were identified at a staff meeting and the head then produced a draft plan in consultation with the deputy and the B allowance holder who was responsible for in-service training. The draft was discussed at a meeting of the senior management team and subsequently at a full staff meeting and a governors' meeting. Only when all these groups were satisfied did it go to the LEA. The heads at Central and Town stated that they had not received help from the LEA in compiling their development plans but that, had they considered it necessary, they could have called upon the assistance of their liaison officer.

Priorities at Town reflected the pressure of external innovations, although two of their five targets in 1991/2 were initiated at school level. As at Central, the major area excluded from the plan was work conducted through the Section 11 projects. Since Town had a higher proportion of students from a minority ethnic group the proposed cuts in the Section 11 budget in Spring 1992 caused a major problem; yet staff were still able to continue working on their development targets.

They identified additional priority areas through the year to a greater extent than staff at Central. For instance, during 1991/2 the head and a few other staff were working on a project to improve the school environment. They produced a ten-year plan to improve the grounds and were successful in gaining some external sponsorship and in winning awards for this work; yet it did not feature in the school development plan until 1992/3. A more typical example was where, during the course of the year, they introduced within one of their priorities aspects of work which had not been specified in the original plan. In 1991/2 the headteacher launched an intervention project which was designed to give students with special needs a short period of one-to-one help from a member of staff. This work was congruent with the priority relating to pupils with special needs but staff had not planned the project when the development plan was drawn up. In this case the development plan provided a broad framework for the school's work and enabled the staff to focus their energies in particular directions but they did not feel constrained by it. A majority of staff were satisfied with the level of involvement in the development planning process; one teacher who would have welcomed greater involvement had been appointed after the plan was compiled.

## Progress with the development planning initiative – county LEA

The development planning initiative was monitored by LEA staff and continued to be a high priority. Whereas in the first year the emphasis had been placed on briefing all the relevant groups about the implications of the plan and on giving advice about the planning process, in the following year the focus shifted to evaluation. The in-service training inspector organized meetings for headteachers to address the evaluation of school development. Questions tackled in these meetings included:

- How successful had the school development plans been?
- How would staff know?
- What factors had taken them off course if they hadn't succeeded in meeting all the targets?

The inspector discussed the idea of success criteria. She felt this investment had paid dividends because at the end of that year she was impressed by the quality of the evaluations that schools submitted with their plans for the following year.

The guidance produced by the LEA was kept under review and was modified as seemed necessary. School staff were not required to submit a statement of the school aims or a copy of their annual curriculum return within the documentation for 1991/2. In 1992 a group of inspectors and advisers conducted a review of the LEA guidance for schools about development planning and simplified it further. One adviser involved in this exercise noted that when the guidance was originally drawn up there was an emphasis on in-service training to follow up and support work on school priorities. This focus had become much less significant as now funds devolved to schools had to be spent on nationally identified priority areas. The working group set up in 1992 reviewed the documents that schools sent in as part of their development plan and reduced them considerably. In the 1992/3 plan staff were required to submit just a single sheet which contained the outline plan for their priorities. The summary of the evaluation of the previous year, the overall implementation programme and the action plans for each target, which staff were asked also to complete, were to be kept in the school for discussion with the governing body and the school liaison officer.

The principal inspector reported in 1992 that, after more than three years' work supporting schools in development planning, she felt that the LEA did not need to support the initiative so heavily. At first, school staff had been pressurized to complete a plan but the LEA had nevertheless always tried to emphasize that it was the school's plan. The message had been that, although LEA staff could use and learn from the plan, it must be of practical use to the school. In 1992 soundings were taken with several headteachers about whether it was sensible to continue to use standard forms for the development plan or whether schools should be left to design their own. The general response was that the standard form was useful and people were familiar with it so it should remain. The authority would continue to support development planning, albeit in a more low-key manner, by continuing to issue guidance and by including it as a topic in induction courses for new headteachers. The inspection system was an additional means of motivating headteachers to complete a development plan as inspectors would always ask to see it and would comment on it in their report.

## Development planning in action – borough schools

Staff in the two schools had very different experiences. A National Curriculum development plan had been completed at Highway prior to engaging in the development planning initiative, which the head had found helpful in sorting out the timing for implementation of different subjects. The head's rationale for working on the development plan, in addition to raising staff awareness and agreeing priorities for the medium term, was unique among our case-study schools. Her aims were to help sustain the existing collaborative and improvement-oriented professional culture among the staff in the face of the threat posed by prospective amalgamation with the other two schools on the same site under LEA plans for reorganization; and to put the present Highway staff in a strong bargaining position relative to staff from the other schools after amalgamation was effected in September 1992. Soon after starting the head commented on the value of the exercise:

> Very useful, especially in the current climate where we could so easily fall apart with everybody just looking after their own back yard ... and now we're coming into the academic year which will be the final year; it's really hit people that this is the end. ... We are doing something and we are working on a process, and we actually discussed why we were doing it in the light of the impending changes. So I think it has been a support to us as well as all the other things we would hope to get from the process ... From the outset we were looking at it as a long-term plan and acknowledged that we were not going to exist after one of these years. ... If we were prepared to go into the new school and we actually had our priorities sorted, even if the other two schools didn't, at least we would then have some influence on the direction in which the new school would go ... we are boldly going, as they say, towards the new school with as much of the team intact as can be. ... Otherwise I think you would have seen mass movement of the staff out of the school.

The development planning initiative may be interpreted as an attempt to stabilize what promised otherwise to become an even more turbulent period leading up to the amalgamation if staff began to seek posts elsewhere and the present level of enthusiasm and mutual support among staff was lost. The willingness with which the staff participated implies that the existing collaborative culture nurtured by the head was a precondition for their full commitment to the development planning process.

The LEA project team had suggested that school staff should have a free hand in working out a procedure, and accordingly offered a range of ideas and materials. The head asked the deputy to take charge and refrained from joining the steering group, which consisted of five teaching staff - all those who volunteered. The group designed, administered and collated questionnaires for teaching and other staff. Teachers were given an opportunity at a staff meeting to write down more detail or raise issues connected with each of the ensuing twenty priorities and associated targets.

The top priority reflected the openness of the consultation procedure and the constituencies involved: to improve the level of heating throughout the school. Others related to national innovations including assessment, history, geography and religious education. A substantial minority of priorities represented small changes which could be addressed rapidly. The head treated the development planning process flexibly, asking staff to start work immediately on priorities such as history and geography because of the urgency of complying with the central government timetable for implementation of these subjects within the National Curriculum, although the formal action planning exercise had yet to be undertaken.

Staff with relevant management responsibility estimated the resources that might be required to address each priority but decisions were delayed because LEA staff had not informed the head of the final budget for the current financial year until two months into the year in question. Voluntary working groups were formed to work on an action plan for each priority and time was made available during in-service training days scheduled immediately before the start of the autumn term. The deputy anticipated working with the head to produce a master sheet with the suggested timing for implementing activities within each priority, which would be presented to the staff for approval. Staff were very satisfied with their close involvement up to this point.

The process gave way to the higher short-term priority of organizing a move to temporary sites while repairs were carried out to the roof of the school. It was never completed but senior staff continued to refer to the top ten priorities in monitoring progress with the relevant changes. A new process was launched the following summer term (at the end of our fieldwork), this time for a one-year rather than three-year plan, after staff learned that the LEA reorganization plan had been postponed and was now rescheduled for September 1993.

As we highlighted in Chapter 4, this was but half of the story: the head and her two colleagues in the management team continued to use their system of short- to medium-term planning, into which priorities from the development planning process were incorporated. At the beginning of each term the management team brainstormed management tasks that ideally should be dealt with in the next few months. The list was divided into items which were more or less urgent, deadlines were set for completing them and, for some items, individuals were allocated to tasks. A related list of topics to be discussed at staff meetings was drawn up. All details were recorded on flipchart sheets and the lists were reviewed at weekly management team meetings or more frequently by the head. Items were ticked when completed, and the list updated either with new deadlines or additional items (see the excerpts in Figure 6.5). Reference was also made to these lists during the following term in generating a list of topics and identifying staff who would take responsibility for leading related activities at a series of staff meetings and meetings between other groups, including the management team.

The management team was able to preserve a degree of stability throughout an exceptionally turbulent year by means of this simple tool for planning changes and routine maintenance activities. It was consistent with the flexible planning model outlined in Chapter 2 although it catered mainly for the short term, providing a flexible approach for regular and *ad hoc* creation, monitoring and adjustment of priorities and action to be taken to achieve the associated tasks. No more was written down than management team members considered necessary as the tool was designed solely for the purpose of guiding their planning. The National Curriculum development plan, together with the priorities identified within the development planning process, provided a framework of longer-term priorities upon which members of the management team were able to draw.

For different reasons most planning work in borough schools took place outside the formal development planning process. The approach adopted by the head at Heartlands also foundered for a time owing turbulence, but (as described in Chapter 4) the reasons were connected with problems over the introduction of LMS and antagonism between the head and some members of the senior staff. The latter issue constituted a growing internal source of turbulence which militated against full commitment to consultative planning.

The process was developed by the head to meet her planning needs, and she retained the only copy of the flowchart during the fieldwork period, although one had been put up in the staffroom previously. There was a long gap for other staff between the review at a staff meeting early in the summer term 1991 and the meeting at the beginning of the following spring term with the senior management team to discuss the head's draft extension into the next academic year (which was by this time nearly halfway through). On each occasion staff were invited to respond to the head's proposals and to put forward their own view of priorities and in-service training needs. The head perceived that much of what the plan covered, like the annual cycle of resource audits and the review of curriculum policies, was now a regular part of maintenance planning and staff did not need the document.

Indeed, procedures which had hitherto been written down on the earlier plans continued to be carried out, including a review of curriculum and other policies led by a teacher with responsibility for policies. In so far as the development planning process was a management tool for the head alone, she was able

**Management issues**

| Objective | Date(s) allotted | Deadline | Completed | Notes |
|---|---|---|---|---|
| Development plan 1) Plan stage 2) Financial costs in relation to priorities | 17 June (see below, coordinators' bids) | | Staff working groups on each issue Completion on training day day in September | |
| Coordinator bids | 23 May (discussion) | Bids by 3 June | Discussion 19 June | Dependent on budget outcome from LEA |
| B Allowance | 10 June – revised (advert 24 July, 3 June) | | Appointed | |

**Staff discussion (staff meetings)**

| Issue | Date proposed | Date actual | Notes |
|---|---|---|---|
| Assessment | 12 June, 7 September, 24 June | Delay till complete appointment ✔ | |
| Budget/finance | 3 June | 12 June | Small groups feedback September training day |
| Development plan | 3 June | 12 June | } together ✔ |
| Inspection report | 20 May ✔ | | |
| History and geography | Introductory session Practical session organized (coordinator and deputy) | July? | |

Figure 6.5 *Excerpts from planning flipcharts at Highway (summer 1991)*

to orchestrate planning in the knowledge of staff responses to the consultation exercise without necessarily having to write down the outcome. Equally, staff were involved in planning and implementing changes without reference to a development plan document. Most staff interviewed stated that they were satisfied with their existing level of involvement, although there was some confusion about whether individuals had been consulted about the development plan, as they had not seen a copy of the flowchart since the last review. Governors were not involved during the fieldwork period, although the previous version had been presented to them.

## Progress with the development planning initiative – borough LEA

The turbulence caused by the postponement of the LEA reorganization of schools affected LEA staff as much as those in schools. The development planning project team had sent the draft of their guidance document to staff in all schools in the first two phases of the project and had amended it in the light of feedback. The planned dissemination of the document to all schools in the LEA was delayed and training support for the final phase of the project had to be rethought. LEA staff wanted heads to be appointed to amalgamating schools before the document was released so that it could form part of a set of materials on 'shaping the new school' which would be backed by in-service training provided by the LEA.

Inspectors had switched their support work for 1992 to introducing appraisal for headteachers, and the inspectorate was being restructured again as a result of the 1992 Schools Act, with the likelihood of redundancies. One inspector noted how the LEA record as a pendulum authority (see Chapter 3) meant that LEA staff were well versed in dealing with a high degree of turbulence and the responsive planning it entailed:

> We are continually having to adjust and readjust. We are always drawing up time scales for when things have to be done. As an LEA we've got much better at that ... we are continually juggling the priorities and trying to make them fit. Since we're an LEA that has had to adapt quite a lot from the different political changes, people just see it as a part of life here and seem to be better able to face it, somehow. There are a lot of people who are able to see where the opportunities are going to be and to gear things up for that.

## Development planning in action – city schools

The implementation of development planning in both city schools included an element of compliance with the LEA directive rather than full commitment to the process and the documentation forming the core of the initiative. We saw in Chapter 4 how the development planning process was very similar in both schools, confined almost entirely to an annual formal review and planning procedure entailing consultation with staff which culminated in the head compiling and submitting the document to the LEA adviser with pastoral responsibility for the school. At Southside, the process was assimilated within the annual GRIDS review to which the head had been committed for some years. The chairs of both governing bodies did not recall seeing the completed document but had discussed some of the priorities.

Once the document had been submitted, the heads retained the only copy.

While the head at Southside very occasionally referred to the document to check progress, her colleague at Northedge did not consider it necessary to contact LEA staff for a copy to replace hers after it was stolen. Staff were unaware of any LEA monitoring of the development plan and knew little about the LEA advocacy of a consultative review and planning process. Unlike the county document, there was no section for an evaluation of progress with the previous development plan. Therefore, unless some form of monitoring visit was paid and the relevant evidence sought, any LEA members of staff who might have read the document would not have been able to assess progress in relation to the priorities. As we showed earlier in Table 5.2, neither school was inspected during the time of our fieldwork.

Heads and staff generally gave more credence to the annual consultation and decision-making sub-processes than to the document. For the head at Northedge, 'the authority's development plan is like a reminder and it's a structure and it's a sort of kick in the ribs'. However, she believed that staff were aware anyway of the main priorities that affected staff across the school. The head at Southside acknowledged that the process 'certainly makes you clarify your ideas and it makes you accountable as well', but was also critical:

> You fill in these pages and pages of details, like the numbers in the school, the area of the school, how much your building is used, and all the rest of it. The school philosophy - and you wonder, at the end of the day, who is going to look at it? I don't know if anyone does. And the bit at the back: 'what are your priorities?' These are the things we would have been doing anyway.

Compiling the document was an onerous task which fell largely to the heads, yet they were unclear why so much background information was required. Constraints on the choice of priorities for development imposed by the timetable for implementing each subject in the National Curriculum led to the deputy at Northedge questioning the necessity for such a plan:

> We are not initiating changes, we're responding. ... The problem is that we sit down and we look at it and there are four priorities in this development plan. And most of these are dictated by something else. In next year's one history and geography will obviously be one of them, but we haven't got to grips with technology yet and we haven't really got to grips with maths. And we're still struggling with science. And those are just the curriculum changes we've had to go through. If we could sit down without the pressures it would be a really good exercise ... but you have to put all your energy to what's coming on stream in the National Curriculum.

Even finding time to work through the review and planning procedure could prove difficult in a context of so much change. At Northedge the head delayed consulting staff during the 1991 summer term because of the greater urgency of coping with the impending move back from the temporary site to the refurbished building: 'Used properly it can be a very helpful and effective jolt, but it's when there are so many other things and you are all the time having to juggle them.'

Other staff had little or nothing to do with the development plan document. Several were confused between the consultation procedure for identifying staff development needs in outline and the separate procedure for identifying priorities for the development plan (see Chapter 3). A few teachers could not remember being consulted about the development plan. Main-scale staff at Southside, who did not have a management responsibility, tended to be less clear about the role of the development plan than the senior staff, who were more centrally involved in consideration of priorities.

Staff other than the head were, in the main, reasonably satisfied with their level of involvement in the development planning process but a minority pointed to the limits of what could be delivered. While staff were encouraged to identify school-wide priorities for development and to articulate their individual development needs, only the priorities on which there was the highest level of agreement tended to be addressed. Staff development was directed towards these priorities at the expense of other individual needs. One inexperienced teacher at Northedge was reluctant to consult colleagues with curriculum responsibility because they were so busy:

> It might be slightly different for people who are in the profession for so many years but I started teaching only two or three years ago. I feel that I have a lot of problems but, as for taking others' time, you never seem to because of the pressure on them that stops finding time to do those things.

Two teachers at this school noted how the plan did not address new external demands to which they had to respond during the year. One pointed to the requirement for flexibility, referring to the recent central government announcement that the number of attainment targets for mathematics and science would be drastically reduced:

> It's a nice idea but probably unworkable. Because our experience - certainly looking at the current situation over the last couple of years - has been that there have been so many needs to respond to things at rather short notice that are actually major changes that I would have thought anybody making a development plan will be looking at it almost tongue in cheek: this is what we would like to do; we'll see if they let us. Because if you plan that these are the areas of the curriculum that you think are the most important, then somebody may well come in and say, 'Actually we are throwing out all the attainment targets in maths and science, and you have got to rejig it.' If there continue to be things of that nature which become an immediate problem that we will have to look at, and have to see how that fits into things, it will constantly be throwing out the things that you had decided to make a priority. Certainly my perception of how things have gone on in the last couple of years hasn't been that people are not wanting to plan or not bothering to, but that there has been a constant need to respond, almost on an *ad hoc* basis, to the various pressures coming at us from elsewhere.

She perceived that because of the pattern of external pressures staff were forced to prioritize, as development planning encouraged them to do, but also to resist being pushed into trying to do more than they could realistically address:

> Probably one would have to make some kind of stand where we say we will do this but we will do it at a pace that is reasonable to expect of the staff in the present circumstances. And not to meet deadlines. Especially when we have had the experience of going ahead with things like science and maths and they in their wisdom eventually turn round and say, 'Well, we've given you something that is unworkable' - which we could have told them before - 'and now we are going to change it again.' Those sorts of things are very undermining when people have put long hours and extra time in . . .

However, the head indicated how the legal status of much external pressure posed a threat which limited how far heads were willing to prioritize and therefore to decide what *not* to take on:

> Heads particularly are paranoid about the legality. I say to somebody, 'Is it legal? Do I have to?' If I don't then I can say, 'Right, it can go to the bottom of the list of priorities.' But if it's legal then I've got to fulfil it, otherwise I can find myself in a mess.

The changes which were identified as priorities in the development plan documents for the two schools are listed in Table 6.2. Most priorities related to national reforms, while 'settling in' at Northedge was related to the move back to the refurbished site in September 1991, and so linked to an LEA initiative. Special needs was the sole priority not directly linked to externally initiated changes. In both schools, fewer priorities were addressed as set out in the development plan during 1991/2 than in 1990/91, largely because of additional priorities which inhibited staff from undertaking the anticipated activity. These priorities made heavy demands on time and resources, the most significant being preparation for reorganization.

What the table does not show is the high proportion of changes addressed in both schools that the development plan did not cover. Much planning was unrelated to the development plan. Its main impact seems to have been two-fold: annually to formalize certain considerations connected primarily with the curriculum which, with the exception of special needs at Southside, were already evident to the heads and some staff; and to constitute a time-consuming task in itself which had to be fitted in alongside other planning work. It appears that the LEA development planning initiative represented a framework for managing a limited amount of planning for all changes. This framework made no allowances for unanticipated shifts in priorities between consultative review and planning exercises.

**Table 6.2** Development plan priorities in the city schools

| | | School | | | |
|---|---|---|---|---|---|
| | | Southside First | | Northedge First | |
| Time | Priority | Implemented as planned? | Priority | Implemented as planned? |
| 1990/1 | History | Yes | Science | Yes |
| | Geography | Yes | Special needs | Yes |
| | Assessment and record-keeping | Yes | Technology | Yes (in 1992) |
| | Religious education | Yes | PE | No – other priorities for staff training and resources |
| 1991/2 | Speaking and listening | No – other priorities, English coordinator acting deputy for a term | PE | No – other priorities for staff training and resources |
| | Special needs and induction | Yes | Settling into refurbished building | Yes (but unanticipated problems) |
| | Science | Yes | Mathematics | No – other priorities |
| | – | – | Art | No – coordinator felt existing practice within legal requirements |

# Progress with the development planning initiative – city LEA

Experience with implementing the innovation at LEA level of designing and implementing a development planning initiative for schools (see Table 2.2) had led LEA staff to undertake a major review. An adviser commented:

> We felt that after three years it didn't just need tinkering with: it needed a complete rethink as to where we are, what the purpose is, and let's have something that is going to be more suitable. We admit that in the last plan the format was given careful consideration but within a very short time window and with very little consultation because we had to have something up and running.

The 1991/2 version of the development plan document had been shortened by a few pages through the removal of information that had proved to be of little use to the LEA or the schools. Advisers had responded to requests from school staff for whom they had pastoral responsibility to help with compiling their development plan.

The thinking of LEA staff was informed by the report of a study commissioned by a group of LEAs on improving the links between LEA strategic planning and development planning in schools (Counselling and Career Development Unit, 1992). This report highlighted how LEAs tended at this time to seek a partnership with schools in which LEA councillors and staff could retain the ability to take initiatives, while staff in schools emphasized their need for a 'listening and enabling LEA' which was largely responsive to concerns expressed at school level. Central government policies discussed in Chapter 1, designed in part to curb the power of local government, were beginning to take effect and LEAs were found to be moving towards a 'service delivery' mode of operation where schools would increasingly be making the running. In other words, the LEA context was going through a rapid transition which affected the parameters within which the development planning initiative was set. The city LEA was much more powerful relative to schools when the development plan was launched in 1989 than it was likely to be in 1993, when all schools would have fully delegated budgets under LMS.

Feedback had been gained in referring to completed development plan documents during LEA inspections. Advisers had been able to examine progress with the implementation of particular priorities, and to check the list of courses attended by staff in the previous year to see whether heads were releasing colleagues readily enough. The documents had proved quite useful to LEA staff in planning the provision of in-service training but a procedure had yet to be developed to match stated priorities with the availability of courses. Detailed course requirements of schools were still gathered by independent means: one adviser sent out a form for history and geography courses, asking school staff to indicate whether they wished to send someone and whether history and geography were priorities in their development plan.

Advisers were aware that, in many schools, the development plan was viewed in a similar way to any other form for collecting information needed by LEA staff. The aim of enabling school staff to take ownership of a simpler, more workable process and document (that would remain compulsory so that LEA staff were provided with information they required to fulfil their monitoring and support obligations) underpinned a major consultative exercise beginning in 1991. When the 1991/2 development plan document was first sent out to schools, staff were invited to put themselves forward to serve on an LEA working party. Its membership included headteachers, advisers, an officer concerned with finance, and a trainer from a higher education institution. Members split into subgroups to consider the curriculum, staff development, finance and management. A newly designed development plan document was drafted, requiring less background information but sharpening the section on priorities to cover targets, timescales for action and success criteria. This draft went out to consultation with LEA advisers, school staff and governors. It was designed to cover the 1993/4 financial year (bringing it into line with the county initiative).

Advisers anticipated that conditions in schools would not be favourable for compiling a development plan after reorganization in September 1992 until the new staffs had been integrated. An interregnum was planned for the autumn term 1992 and spring term 1993 where no development plan would be required. During this period, it was expected that school staff would work on the construction of a new development plan for the reorganized school.

## IMPLEMENTING THE INNOVATION OF DEVELOPMENT PLANNING

We showed earlier how development planning represented an innovation spanning different levels of the education service; this chapter demonstrates how the fate of this innovation at school and LEA levels was inextricably linked. The recent LEA survey conducted by Mortimore *et al.* (forthcoming) indicated that the teaching staff, deputy and governors were involved in the planning process in over 80 per cent of LEAs. This finding reports perceptions at LEA level of a consultative approach; our findings suggest that the level of involvement of different constituencies may actually be quite diverse among schools within and between LEAs.

The implementation gap between LEA-level aspiration and the reality of practice was quite varied in the six schools we studied. (In exploring the factors that led to such gaps we do not seek to generalize across the LEAs nor to extrapolate beyond the limited period of our fieldwork.) The implementation gap was smallest in the county, where the school staff experienced less turbulence overall than in the other LEAs, both LEA and school staff had most experience of development planning, and the plan was the most comprehensive in design. The innovation was more or less institutionalized in county schools by 1992. The gap was larger in the city, where the document reflected a tension between the purposes of collecting information needed by LEA staff and guiding action in school, and the advent of reorganization inhibited medium- to long-term planning. It was greatest in the borough where the two heads were free to decline the LEA invitation to adopt the innovation, to postpone it, or to employ their own approach.

## Characteristics of the innovation

It is evident that a number of the factors and themes identified in research on the management of planned change (see Chapter 2) operated in combination. Let us focus on the characteristics of the innovation. First, LEA staff perceived a *need* for a development planning initiative, this need being largely imposed upon the LEA by central government demands. Similarly, heads of the borough schools acted on their perception of need - within the LEA project at Highway and through the head's own version at Heartlands. The head at Central had been involved in developing the LEA initiative and was committed to this approach to planning. It was less evident that a need, rather than compliance with an LEA requirement, was perceived in the other schools.

Second, as the initial survey suggested (see Chapter 3), *clarity* about the goals of development planning and how to implement it was difficult to retain at LEA level where (as recounted above) the policy context changed, dictating that the development planning initiative itself evolved. There was greatest clarity at school level in the county. Within the borough, staff at Highway were only beginning to come to terms with the innovation when it was postponed, and at Heartlands the head did not share what was her personal approach fully with other staff. Staff in city schools were not sure why LEA staff required much of the information specified in the plan.

Third, the innovation as designed was most comprehensive in its coverage of planning issues, and therefore most *complex*, in the county: development planning encompassed LMS and addressed the widest range of other changes whose implementation had to be planned at school level. Allied with complexity was external pressure, staff in county schools being strongly encouraged to implement the innovation in the depth required for them to reap such benefits as it could offer. For Highway, the complexity of the innovation related to the unfamiliarity of staff with this way of planning, which contrasted with the simpler and more flexible approach the management team habitually used. Lack of compulsion, coupled with the unexpected crisis of the move to temporary sites, led to its postponement before any benefits - beyond a list of priorities - could be gained.

Fourth, the *quality* of the innovation varied: the pressure for city LEA staff to launch the development planning initiative led to modifications later to 'debug' the innovation. However, as we noted above, the changing policy context also contributed to the need for the innovation to evolve in all three LEAs. Quality also related to the ability of the innovation to fulfil its designed purposes, whether for LEA staff, school staff or governors. Development planning was limited in its purpose of guiding planning in all six schools in so far as modifications to priorities had to be made or additional priorities had to be addressed between major review and planning exercises. Equally, the innovation in the county and the city did not completely fulfil its purpose of keeping LEA staff informed of shifting school-level needs for external support, or its monitoring purpose for which up-to-date information on current plans should ideally be available.

Fifth, related to quality was *practicality*. The consultative review and planning procedure was feasible in all the schools where it could be accommodated largely within existing arrangements for the management of planning, although at Highway and Northedge other priorities forced its postponement. Yet the formal development planning procedures and documents gave little help with retaining flexibility to respond as circumstances changed.

## Implementation themes

Each theme associated with successful implementation of improvement efforts related to the innovation of development planning at both LEA and school levels. First, the LEA vision for development planning appeared to be both communicated and shared in the county schools. Acceptance of the vision related to the amount of consultation that took place when the LEA guidance on development planning was being written, and to the high level of support and feedback that school staff received from the LEA when they first started development planning.

The vision in the borough was only communicated to those who took up the invitation to participate in the development plan project. As the city LEA adviser noted, the LEA vision appeared not to have been communicated to staff at Southside and Northedge, who consequently had little ownership of the innovation. It may be significant that, when the head at Northedge described the purpose of the development plan, she referred to it as the LEA's (see above). How far heads articulated a vision to staff depended on their sense of ownership: the head at Central believed in the form of development planning taken by the LEA initiative, whereas the heads of the city schools were less enamoured with their LEA version.

Second, there was little evidence of *evolutionary planning* at either level, except in so far as LEA staff reviewed and modified their initiatives as the policy context changed. At Highway, senior staff did develop their approach incrementally as far as the process went; in the county and city schools the central focus of implementation was the completion of the document, which had to be carried out in accordance with the LEA timetable. The head at Heartlands modified her approach, however, both incorporating financial considerations in her flowchart and delaying the consultation process as her circumstances changed.

Third, the development planning initiatives fostered different levels of *initiative-taking and empowerment*. One aim in each LEA was to enable school staff and governors to gain greater control over the destiny of their school by establishing priorities and directing resources towards them. Yet the enormity of the externally imposed central and local government agendas for change severely restricted the ability to make choices at school level. There was con- siderable room for initiative-taking by LEA staff, as the range in scope and degree of compulsion upon schools among the LEA initiatives illustrates. Yet the boundaries of this scope were also tightly drawn by central government directives including the National Curriculum development plan, requirements for LMS and for provision of in-service training. Initiative-taking in the county and city schools focused upon limited choice of priorities and determining the process for completing the LEA document. In the borough, heads were able to take the initiative of not participating or postponing work on development planning.

Fourth, *staff development and resource assistance* was limited, consisting primarily of in-service training for county and city heads when the initiatives were launched and participation in the LEA project for the deputy at Highway before and during the early implementation stage. Training for coordinators, as we described earlier, focused on the content of plans for individual areas and the process of introducing the relevant change to colleagues. The consultative review and planning procedure was largely incorporated within existing elements of the management of planning and was not, therefore, a focus of much training support. By and large, school staff coped with development planning within existing resources.

Fifth, *monitoring and problem coping* were also limited in scope. LEA monitoring in the county and city focused on the content of the document and the implementation of plans under priorities identified within it. Monitoring of the process was confined to the county, where reliance was placed upon the account given by headteachers. The borough LEA development plan project team invited feedback from schools on the draft guidelines but did not monitor activity in participating schools systematically. At school level, monitoring of development planning appeared to be confined to progress with particular priorities, and was largely informal.

Finally, the LEA development planning initiatives offered the promise of *restructuring*: a procedure for managing planning to implement a range of innovations and other changes. Most impact on shaping management roles, structures and procedures had occurred in the county schools. The head at

Heartlands had also shaped her own approach to planning through her initiative and that of staff prior to the period of fieldwork. At Highway the staff began to assimilate the process within elements of the management of planning, as the LEA initiative encouraged; and in the city schools the procedure was also assimilated, the main novelty being the completion of the document.

Development planning in the six schools appears to have been subject to many of the implementation problems which may beset any other innovation and to have met with varying success. It was institutionalized only in the county schools, whose staff experienced less environmental turbulence than those in the other LEAs. The analysis of factors and themes helps to account for some of the variations in implementation that we found. However, this analysis is limited by its exclusive focus upon development planning. Planning for change consisted of more, and in some cases much more, than development planning. As we move on to discuss in Chapter 7, development planning was set within a wider context of multiple changes and other ongoing work. The way changes including development planning were introduced, together with other factors, affected the shifting balance of environmental turbulence and stability, and so the tension between seeking coherence and flexibility that the approach to planning for change in each school had to tackle.

# Chapter 7

# Factors Affecting the Planning Process

The six schools were all busy places. Just how busy is indicated by the range of changes for which staff made plans of some kind. Our third theme is to explore how the characteristics of each change, the combination of changes, and the way in which they were introduced into the schools affected the ever-shifting balance of turbulence and stability which, in turn, impacted upon the planning process. Our starting point is the set of interrelated factors promoting turbulence or stability which we identified in our initial survey (Tables 3.5 and 3.6). The findings from the six case studies enable us to extend this list and to depict how the planning process was rendered a more complex and fluid affair than the development planning procedure and documents would suggest. Since the factors were so closely linked, it should be borne in mind that most examples which will be used to illustrate one factor also reflected the operation of others.

Most of the changes were innovations intended to improve the schools in some way. Some innovations were part of a larger whole: if we regard the 'basic curriculum' as an innovation, each of the ten subjects within it may constitute a significant sub-innovation, depending in part on how closely existing practice in any school matched the central government requirements. In addition, staff in each school addressed one or more unplanned changes, either in planning a response to a crisis or longer-term issue, or in planning a change in a routine procedure.

## THE BURDEN OF CHANGE

The *abundance of external innovations* was striking. While plans for particular externally initiated innovations or sub-innovations ranged from the adoption to the institutionalization or postponement phase - and not all plans led to implementation efforts - each represented a claim upon the finite capacity of staff to cope with change. Planning in all six schools addressed four innovations (development planning, LMS, assessment of the National Curriculum, and bids for Section 11 funded projects) and five sub-innovations within the National Curriculum (history, geography, art, music and physical education). Other innovations were associated with schools in particular LEAs. Reorganization of schooling affected the borough and city schools in a big way; heads from the schools in the city LEA put in bids to participate in an initiative for inner-city schools; both county school staffs undertook campaigns to preserve their Section 11 staffing, worked on improving the school environment and participated in projects on managing pupil behaviour. Plans were made in one or more (but not all) of the schools for a variety of innovations related to the curriculum (a whole school 'technology week'), pedagogy (team teaching) or management (procedures for assessing and supporting pupils with special educational needs).

Table 7.1 shows the full range of innovations and other changes addressed in one or more of the schools. The first two rows reveal how most external innovations originated as policies, ultimately, of the Conservative central government. The contribution of local government councillors as initiators of change was minimal in comparison, except perhaps at Northedge, where moving back from the temporary site and settling into the refurbished building dominated planning for several months.

The impact of the plethora of external innovations on planning was for staff to be juggling at any moment with plans directed towards a multiplicity of goals. Innovations would be at different phases of their introduction into the schools and the group of goals on which planning activity was focused shifted over time. During the early part of the autumn term 1991 the profile of external innovations and sub-innovations at Northedge for which plans of some kind were in hand consisted of:

- development planning (implementation phase) - how to fit in the consultative review and planning procedure, which had been postponed from the summer term, and writing it up;

- LMS (implementation phase) - how to find time to learn to use a computerized information management system which had just been delivered to the school;

- reorganization (early implementation phase) - the head, in consultation with the deputy, had drawn up job descriptions for B incentive allowances and submitted them to the LEA. She had been informed that the present C allowance holder would retain this post and was waiting to hear the LEA decision about which teachers with B allowances from Northedge or elsewhere were to be allocated to

**Table 7.1** Origin of changes addressed among the schools

| Origin (ultimate → immediate) | Change |
|---|---|
| Central government | Assessment, English, mathematics, science, technology, history, geography, art, music, physical education, religious education and collective worship, pupil registration procedure |
| Central government → LEA | Development planning, LMS, reorganization, appraisal, Section 11 bids, inner-city initiative, pupil-behaviour initiative |
| LEA | Refurbishment (Northedge) |
| LEA → school | Nursery expansion, team teaching, antiracist policy |
| School | Development planning (Heartlands), special needs initiatives, nursery teaching project, innovatory field-study trip, increase in pupil numbers, fire damage, stock and furniture audit, arts festival, staff turnover, school environment initiatives, maths club, 60th anniversary celebrations |

the school in September 1992. She was also liaising with governors, city councillors and representatives of the Afro-Caribbean parents who were objecting to the LEA proposals for the new catchment area, as their children might not continue to be eligible to go to Northedge. The proportion of pupils from different ethnic backgrounds, and hence their needs for specialist support, depended on whether city councillors held to their present decision;

- inner-city initiative (adoption phase) - the head had been notified a week before the deadline for submission of an LEA initiative to secure funds announced by central government officials during the summer holiday. She had consulted senior staff and compiled a bid, commenting: 'A week is too short to do accurate costings or to do anything in depth. Everybody was thinking frantically of a quick easy answer.' Staff were waiting to hear if the bid had been accepted;

- settling into the refurbished building (implementation phase) - several major problems had come to light after the beginning of term, including poor acoustics which led to very high noise level since sounds were not absorbed, insufficient space in the children's cloakrooms leading to a request to parents to refrain from entering the building and a subsequent backlash as they felt they were being unfairly excluded, and a drop in the morale of staff, whose high expectations of the refurbished building were not fully met. A response to each problem had to be planned;

- assessment of the National Curriculum (adoption phase) - staff were waiting to receive official documents from the central government agency for year-two pupils;

- Section 11 (implementation phase) - the head had been informed by LEA staff that the school was to be allocated two new support assistants and had appointed one and was advertising for another;

- technology, history, geography art, music and physical education (adoption or early implementation phase) - staff with the relevant management roles were responsible for making detailed implementation plans.

These areas of planning were supplemented by smaller-scale innovations originating in school, including the development of an antiracist policy, the promotion of team teaching and expansion of nursery provision.

## External pressure and internal consequences

A second aspect of this factor was that the external innovations were *mostly compulsory*, or technically optional but tied to resources that staff could not afford to ignore. We have noted above how the head at Northedge made a very rapid response (as did the head at Southside) to the LEA invitation to bid for funding within the inner-city initiative. She felt a moral obligation to make it a top planning priority:

I'm in the business of getting the best for my children. The deputy said at the time, 'Throw it in the bin, we haven't got time for that.' I said, 'No, I've got to make a stab at it even if I don't get anywhere for the very reason that I would be denying the children that bit of extra resource and support.' If I don't get it, OK - at least I could rest my conscience because I'd tried.

All the innovations and other changes listed in Table 7.1 whose ultimate origin lay with central government were compulsory or technically optional. There was little possibility of avoiding planning activity at school level, whether for provisional adoption of innovations which were the subject of a bidding process, or for implementation of compulsory innovations and sub-innovations. The sequence of the various externally imposed deadlines dictated the pace of planning at school level, on occasion forcing adjustment of existing planning priorities when information was received about the implementation requirements of these innovations.

The inner-city initiative is a clear example where space had to be made at two points within the existing workload of planning and other managerial activities. Not only was the original invitation to bid squeezed in during the very busy period at the start of a new academic year, but planning for the subsequent initiative was also carried out in a short period between learning at the end of the spring term 1992 that the two city schools would be able to take part and full implementation in school during the early part of the summer term. Moreover, the innovation, a 'sustained reading intervention', bore little relationship to the bids submitted by the heads the previous September, requiring a rethink of the original ideas.

A third aspect of the abundance of external innovations was the sheer quantity of change confronting every member of staff, resulting in varying degrees of overload for individuals (especially headteachers) at particular times. The weight of the burden of change may be illustrated by examining the innovations along the four dimensions introduced in Chapter 2: size, complexity, relationship with other innovations, and degree of compulsion. We have grouped the external innovations being addressed in each school according to our classification of their initial dimensions. Table 7.2 provides a summary of our classification of the external innovations and sub-innovations. Whether or not they were implemented as their originators intended is of course another matter, as we saw in the case of development planning in the previous chapter.

The greatest impact on staff capacity to cope with change tended to come from those innovations which were by design a combination of major (involving most or all staff), complex (entailing sub-innovations), interrelated (linked to other innovations) and compulsory. Although the planning and implementation effort varied to some extent according to factors such as the degree of disparity between existing practice and that dictated by any innovation, and the response at school level, these innovations generally took up much staff time, energy and emotion. LMS, for example, was designed as:

- major - to underpin decision-making by governors and staff about most areas of school activity which require financial resources, many

**Table 7.2** The external innovation load

| Initial dimensions | School | | | | | |
|---|---|---|---|---|---|---|
| | Central Primary | Town Primary | Highway Middle | Heartlands Combined | Southside First | Northedge First |
| Major, complex, interrelated and compulsory | LMS, National Curriculum, assessment, development planning | LMS, National Curriculum, assessment, development planning | LMS, National Curriculum, assessment, reorganization | LMS, National Curriculum, assessment, reorganization appraisal | LMS, National Curriculum, assessment, reorganization | LMS, National Curriculum, assessment, reorganization |
| All other major or intermediate in size | Section 11 | Section 11 | Development planning | | Development planning, Section 11, inner-city initiative | Development planning, move to refurbished site, Section 11, inner-city initiative |

of which either had not been carried out at this level before, or had not included financial considerations;

- complex - including sub-innovations such as operating an annual budgeting cycle, employing a computerized financial information system, and new consultative structures and procedures involving governors;

- interrelated - directly linked to the exercise of new powers by governors and in county schools to development planning, and indirectly linked to material resources and staffing related to implementation of the National Curriculum and religious education;

- compulsory - the form and timing of implementation of the innovation was set by LEA staff within parameters dictated by central government legislation.

If we add to these external innovations the others which along our first dimension were major or intermediate in scope, it is evident that the total external innovation load was very considerable. While some school staff had somewhat fewer external innovations to deal with than others, in all cases staff pointed to the less than ideal amount of attention that could be given to planning and implementing any innovation or sub-innovation, given the multiplicity of demands from the others, together with the burden of additional changes and the rest of their ongoing work. This difficulty was exacerbated in the many instances where little preparatory training or ongoing support was available for implementing innovations.

Teaching staff were most directly affected by changes in the curriculum. A teacher at Heartlands gave an example of how staff could reach saturation point: 'At the beginning of the term we tried to have some discussions on the history and geography and planning for this year. But I think that people were just overwhelmed with taking on something else and almost unable to take in new information.' The coordinator responsible for these areas of the curriculum commented:

> We can plan, we can accommodate most ideas from the legal require-
> ments, educational ideas that come up in the National Curriculum
> documents. But there are only a limited number of hours in the school
> day; primary schools have so many other calls upon time. . . . At a
> parents' meeting the other night I compared it to a runaway train.
> We've got this National Curriculum runaway Intercity and the teacher
> is running between the tracks trying to keep away from the train, and
> the train is coming closer. There might be a period of two weeks when
> you can run ahead of it, just keeping in control, but eventually it will
> steamroll you down - and it will come at a time like Christmas when in
> a primary school it's a different world!

Given the multiplicity of demands for change, some staffs attempted to hold to higher priorities: at Town the head stated that her main priority was to help the pupils become fluent and literate in English. The decision was taken not to give a great deal of attention to history and geography in Key Stage 1.

*Low school-level control over external innovations* resulted from the high degree of compulsion over the implementation of all those which were major. The characteristics of each innovation and the timing of its implementation were very largely dictated outside the schools, constraining the room for manoeuvre of heads and staff. Much planning for implementation was reactive: a direct response to external demands, rather than an outcome of school-level decisions over the direction and pace of development. The imposed timing of so many innovations and sub-innovations was the main cause of loss of control. Their content offered opportunities for heads, on the one hand, to capitalize upon some external innovations to further their own agenda for change while, on the other, leaving little room for taking initiatives in other areas.

*Initiation of major innovations by heads* was more or less curtailed, although they worked to keep up momentum with the implementation of innovations they had initiated in previous years and (as we described in Chapter 5) encouraged staff to implement a few innovations which were classified as minor or intermediate in scope. The head at Town was developing a strategy to raise teachers' expectations and increase the standard of pupils' achievement, which would take several years to implement. She introduced several minor innovations, such as a paired reading project and a short-term intervention project giving pupils one-to-one tuition (including support for able and gifted children), and also interpreted externally imposed innovations in a way which supported her central goal. For example, she made use of the requirement that teachers must write a report on each pupil by demonstrating to staff the form of reporting on pupil achievement that she considered acceptable.

The only major innovation initiated by a head was the residential field study trip at Highway and, in this case, she was responding in part to the enthusiasm of staff to offer the same trip to all pupils and to take them in vertical groups. The exercise was planned to contribute to an existing school-wide theme of cooperation between pupils, and to cover some aspects of the National Curriculum. The response from parents was double what the staff had expected but they felt committed to giving the opportunity to all pupils who wished to go. The decision to proceed led to a major planning exercise, so that different groups of pupils and staff could go on the trip over most of the 1992 spring term while the remainder continued with normal work in school.

Another goal was therefore added to the those imposed by external innovations, and planning for their implementation was largely postponed until the trips had finished and all staff could meet together. However, staff retained a *high level of control over the innovation, which originated in school.* Planning for implementation went relatively smoothly, at the pace set by staff, helped by the knowledge that the resources needed were available internally. The turbulence caused by the innovation was offset by the stabilizing influence of being able to control the change process from within the school.

# Interrelationship and interaction

Three factors which did not emerge in our initial survey were highlighted by our
analysis of the dimensions of innovations affecting the case-study schools and
the way these innovations interacted over time. As the summary in Table 7.3
indicates, they each promoted a degree of turbulence. The first concerned external innovations which were intended by their originators to interrelate with
each other. These innovations promised to promote greater stability once they
were institutionalized, as the grand design was to provide the framework for a
coherent approach to managing schools. We discussed in Chapter 1 the national
policy context from which so many external innovations came. The Conservative central government reforms constitute a strategy for developing a new
combination of centralized and decentralized control over the content and the
management of schooling within an educational marketplace. The National Curriculum, its assessment, LMS and increased powers for governors, for example,
were designed as a package of policies spawning innovations which would
change the nature of state schools across the country. The originators of other
innovations, notably development planning and reorganization of schooling,
were directly influenced by central government concerns. Yet the way in which
these interrelated innovations were developed and introduced led, on occasion,
to increased turbulence at school level prior to their institutionalization in so far
as one innovation depended upon another. In other words, there could sometimes be *conflict between the implementation requirements of interrelated
innovations*.

The prescribed content of the National Curriculum subjects and the areas
to be covered in the assessment of pupils at the end of Key Stage 1 were
designed to be integrally linked. The coverage of the statutory annual assessment procedure was reduced repeatedly, leading to staff (especially those in
the five schools catering for Key Stage 1) giving top priority to the core subjects of mathematics, English and science once central government ministers
announced that technology, history, geography and the other foundation subjects would definitely not be subject to compulsory testing.

Material resources and staffing levels needed to implement the National
Curriculum and the very time-consuming Key Stage 1 assessment procedures
were governed by the level of funding within the LMS formula. At Heartlands,

**Table 7.3** Additional factors promoting turbulence and stability in the planning process

| Factors promoting environmental turbulence | Impact on planning process |
| --- | --- |
| Conflict between interrelated innovations | Adjustment of plans to accommodate implementation requirements of each innovation |
| Negative interaction between innovations | Inhibition of planning |
| High staff turnover (especially under reorganization) | Responsive planning for replacement, induction of new staff |
| Factor promoting environmental stability | Impact on planning process |
| Mutually supportive staff culture including commitment to improvement led by headteachers | Facilitation of planning and implementation |

where the LMS budget was both inadequate and subject to repeated changes during the summer term 1991, the head was unable to employ extra staff or to support teachers in obtaining additional material resources. Far from enabling the necessary decisions to be made at the local level for the implementation of other external innovations, for a time the LEA strategy for implementing LMS inhibited these decisions from being taken.

Each National Curriculum subject was divided into a set of attainment targets and, within them, several levels of achievement. The core subjects (the first to be implemented) had more attainment targets than the other foundation subjects. Assessment of the core subjects by teachers, record-keeping, and the statutory areas to be formally assessed each year were designed within the framework provided by the attainment targets. As additional subjects were phased in, evidence accrued that assessing pupils within the increasing range of attainment targets was becoming unmanageable. Late in 1990 a central government proposal was announced to reduce the number of attainment targets for science from seventeen to around six, and for mathematics from fourteen to about five (*Times Educational Supplement*, 1990). Official documents from the National Curriculum Council were received in the case-study schools early in the 1991 summer term. In consequence, recording documents, whether produced by LEA staff or developed within schools, had to be redesigned and curriculum plans rethought.

A second new factor was the unintended consequence of *negative interaction between innovations*, some of which had not been designed to interrelate. The main impact of this factor was to hinder planning and implementation of these innovations. Such interactions occurred in all the schools to an extent, but most frequently in Highway and the two city schools which were strongly affected by impending reorganization. Negative interaction between innovations was especially marked at Northedge:

- the consultative review and planning exercise, which was the first stage of the development planning process, was held up for a time by the priority of preparing for and settling in after the move back to the refurbished site;
- settling in also took precedence over implementing National Curriculum requirements;
- building work to refurbish the site had been delayed because of expenditure being diverted by LEA staff to other sites in preparation for reorganization;
- during the run-up to reorganization planning for change was increasingly hindered because some existing staff would be redeployed elsewhere and those due to come from other schools were not yet in post;
- work on science had been stopped before the National Curriculum requirements had been fully implemented because of the subsequent demands to deal with technology, history and geography;
- Key Stage 1 assessment activity had swamped the development of a

code of conduct in consultation with the pupils in each year group (an earlier initiative influenced by the central government response to the Elton Report);

- the LEA offer to enable minority ethnic group support staff to study to become teachers was threatened because of demands from heads and governors of secondary schools that more centrally withheld funds must be devolved or they would seek grant-maintained status in order to benefit from central government financial inducements.

A third new factor we identified as promoting turbulence was the *high turnover of staff*. As the Northedge example above illustrates, staff turnover entailed within reorganization interacted negatively with other innovations, its main impact being to inhibit planning beforehand and to dictate that heads gave top priority to planning for the integration of new staff after reorganization had taken place. However, staff turnover connected with individual careers and career breaks also variably affected the other schools. We mentioned earlier how the head at Central and the deputies at Town and Southside took maternity leave, for instance.

## Crises and issues

Each school was affected from time to time by *crises and issues indirectly connected with innovations*. Although they were few compared with the number of external innovations, they could have a significant impact on planning, mainly by diverting time and energy away from other tasks and precipitating a planned response from heads. In Chapter 1 we noted how in an earlier exploratory study into the management of multiple innovations some crises and issues related to central government policies with no direct bearing on education. In the case-study schools any crises and issues were more closely (if indirectly) linked with innovations. So pervasive was the influence of external innovations that crises and issues were either the unintended consequences of innovations or had implications for them.

For example, the head at Southside was troubled throughout the fieldwork period by bills for the use of water in the school that were much higher than the estimates made prior to partial delegation within LMS. The issue only came to light because of LMS, but was thought to be due to a leak somewhere on the premises. Not only did the head have to take into account the heavier than expected demand of the water bill on the LMS budget, but she also spent time working with staff to save water and liaising with LEA staff who, in turn, spent time trying to trace the suspected leak (which was not found).

An issue for the head at Heartlands, also indirectly linked with LMS, was that she had great difficulty in persuading staff that financial, rather than educational, considerations were now a major determinant of and constraint upon the resources which could be afforded to support planned changes:

> Things like finance, that side of the school, it did not seem to matter how much you accessed them to information because of the real block a lot of them have about it. It is the principle they don't like: they just

won't receive it ... they did not want to receive the message if there ain't no money.

At Highway, the long-term issue of water leaking through the roof became a crisis when electricity cables were affected and the electricity had to be turned off. The head had been trying to persuade LEA staff to carry out more maintenance work for some time. She had put much effort into arguing her case but had been unable to convince the authorities concerned that the extent of the leaks constituted a major repair, and therefore an LEA responsibility, rather than a series of minor repairs which would be paid for through the school's LMS budget. An unintended consequence of the distribution of financial liabilities under LMS appeared to be a stand-off between the LEA and school where each party was protecting its own interests and trying to make the other foot the bill. According to the head:

> We've had this whole year of: 'When is a patch not a patch?' Because the LEA guidelines clearly said that a patch is the school's and major roofing repairs isn't. In our case we had lots and lots of patches and nobody would come up with the criteria for what was a patch. So nothing got done.

Crises could occasionally have a positive spin-off for the school. The staff at Town had to close the school unexpectedly for two days in 1991 when the heating system broke down, but were able to use the time for extra staff meetings to address various policy concerns.

## CHANGES IN THE CHANGES

In the minority of cases where sufficient *clear and consistent information was available about external innovations*, planning for implementation was reasonably straightforward. LMS was assimilated quite smoothly in the city schools, for example. Most external innovations turned out to be less clear cut from the perspective of staff. All the schools were affected in some way by *ambiguity over and unpredictable changes in the characteristics and implementation requirements of external innovations*. Let us unpack this rather convoluted factor. Dependence at school level on information about external innovations led to three kinds of problem. First, planning was hindered while awaiting information necessary for implementation of particular innovations. Ambiguity lay primarily in the lack of information related to innovations that staff were expecting to implement. Medium- to long-term planning in both borough and city schools was inhibited by the anticipation of staffing changes, as described earlier.

In the borough schools, delay by LEA staff in producing the out-turn figures at the end of the 1990/91 financial year until a couple of months before the start of the 1992/3 financial year hampered planning for all changes and maintenance activity requiring LMS funds. During the interim, decisions had to be made on the basis of estimates. The borough's LMS scheme, a complex innovation at LEA level in its early stages of implementation, appeared not to have taken into account a range of contingencies. Both borough schools had received enough applications from parents during the 1991 summer term to admit an extra class of pupils for the next academic year. Yet LEA staff were unable to confirm that money to cover the salary of an extra teacher and other resources needed by the pupils would be added to the LMS budget until shortly before the end of term.

Anomalies turned up frequently within the LEA record of expenditure under LMS in both schools. Heartlands was charged for the caretaker's private telephone bill and his overtime while he worked at another school, the salary of a clerical assistant while she worked part-time at another school, and the salary of a teacher who had transferred elsewhere in the borough. Highway was charged for bussing of pupils to the temporary sites while the roof was repaired and for cleaners, caretakers, heating and electricity on these sites, in addition to the charge for heating the original building to dry it out. The school was repeatedly charged for items which applied to the whole site, consisting of three schools. The effects of these anomalies were to increase the level of ambiguity for heads and governors over the financial situation and to take the time of heads in negotiating with LEA staff to get the anomalies removed.

Second, new information sometimes contradicted that which had been received earlier. Occasionally the information came from the LEA: the head at Heartlands had saved money from her 1990/91 LMS budget but was informed by LEA staff that it would not be carried over to the next financial year. She enlisted the support of the governors and three months later the money was returned. More commonly, contradictory messages were received from central government. We have seen how attainment targets in mathematics and science were reduced in number. Central government arrangements for formal assessment at the end of Key Stage 1 fared no better. The well-publicized time-consuming and disruptive impact of the Standard Assessment Tasks for Key Stage 1 implemented in 1991 led (before the testing was finished) to a central government promise to simplify the arrangements and reduce the areas to be tested for 1992, culminating in revised Standard Assessment Tasks (*Times Educational Supplement*, 1991b). Some staff who were directly affected became increasingly cynical, as this teacher of a year-two class from Northedge indicated:

> We have had the experience of going ahead with things like science and maths and they in their wisdom eventually turn round and say, 'Well, we've given you something that is unworkable' - which we could have told them before - and now we are going to change it again.' Those sorts of things are very undermining when people have put long hours and extra time in and then they turn round and say, 'We have got it wrong.' Because we could have told them that about the SATs. The fact that they actually announced while we were still doing them that they had got it wrong was one of the worst bits of PR that I have come across in educational circles ... then to keep getting little snippets of information about how they might change it which doesn't seem to reflect what teachers have been saying to them all along.

The decision of local councillors in the borough to postpone reorganization of schooling for a year was the direct consequence of a central government decision to approve the application from several secondary schools to become grant maintained. This decision served to prolong the uncertainty for heads and staff, especially those at Highway who were faced with the prospect of amalgamation.

The county schools, and especially Town, were deeply affected by the threatened outcome of the bids for Section 11 support. Here an LEA commitment was affected by a shift in central government policy. Ministers at the Home Office discovered that not all eligible bids for education services could be funded at the rate to which LEAs aspired and announced that 15 per cent less grant would be offered than the sum for which successful LEAs had applied. There were three minority ethnic group support teachers at Town in September 1991: two on temporary contracts, the other on a permanent contract. They worked on language acquisition and home-school liaison, and were beginning to make an impact on policy across the school. In addition to their classwork they were developing monitoring forms so that they could log the pupils' level of language acquisition. A concern among staff was that some pupils who came to the school not speaking English had not reached level 1 in the Key Stage 1 English tests, yet had made considerable progress in learning English, which they wished to record.

The head was informed by LEA staff in the middle of the 1992 spring term that Section 11 support would be reduced to two staff and that temporary contracts would not be renewed after Easter. The project on home-school liaison would in future be administered centrally. Great stress was caused in the school, the head immediately launching a campaign with colleague headteachers to oppose this directive, writing to the LEA, the Home Office, the local member of parliament, local councillors and the press.

The campaign achieved some success, the head being offered funding for 2.6 full-time equivalent staffing. County councillors had voted to increase spending to compensate for the shortfall in Section 11 funding from central government. In the meantime the school suffered. The two teachers on temporary contracts found alternative employment; the existing Section 11 team was broken up; the initiatives they had started were left unfinished; and work on the projects was severely disrupted in the middle of the school year. At the point where our fieldwork finished, the vacancy caused by the departure of one teacher on a temporary contract had not been filled. Pupils could not be given the level of support they needed and to which they were entitled.

The third problem over information was the short notice given in a few instances, forcing staff to make a rapid planned response. We described earlier how the city schools were given little time to prepare a bid within the inner-city initiative and to implement the very different project that eventually resulted. As reorganization of these schools approached, there was a flurry of staff interviews across the LEA as the remaining unfilled posts, mostly for main-scale teachers, were dealt with by heads and LEA staff. Heads did not know who their full complement of staff would be until the end of the summer term. Certain documents for Key Stage 1 assessment in 1991 did not arrive until just before the half term, as a teacher at Northedge noted:

It was a very, very short period of time where we actually had the information in our hands - the final documents - before we actually began. It meant that the only way we could do it was to work to do the planning in the holiday period before we came into school to start it.

One or more dimensions of a few external innovations or sub-innovations shifted towards the heavyweight end - more major, complex or interrelated, tallying with an increase in turbulence. History and geography within the National Curriculum were conceived as discrete subjects but became interrelated as staff in all six schools engaged in the complex planning task of integrating these subjects within broad topics or themes, thereby adapting these sub-innovations to fit in as far as possible with their existing practice. In this case, greater interrelationship was associated with some turbulence because of the considerable range of planning activity entailed in making the subjects fit a thematic approach to the curriculum while ensuring that the separate programmes of study and attainment targets were covered. The borough schools were granted more support from the LEA than had been requested in their Section 11 bids; the innovation became more major in scope and led to adjustment of plans for the proposed projects.

Every innovation or other change required resources of some kind for implementation. Detailed planning was simplified in so far as there were *adequate resources to achieve the goals* being pursued by staff. The city schools were generously staffed and financed, and comprehensive in-service training support was offered in the form of LEA courses. To varying degrees, though, all the schools were affected because *resources were inadequate to achieve all goals*. Lack of time needed for thorough and consultative planning and for full commitment to implementation of innovations was a major constraint even for the city schools; lack of finance hindered the heads in the borough schools from employing staff and procuring material resources. Where the goals were greater than the sum of the resources available, plans were adjusted accordingly to limit the scale of the change effort.

We noted in Chapter 5 how *external monitoring of progress with innovations* was sporadic (see Table 5.2). When it did happen, external monitoring stimulated the creation of a few new priorities and adjustment of a minority of existing plans for the implementation of changes. This adjustment was undertaken soon after the inspection, whatever stage had been reached in any formal development planning process, and independently of it.

*Institutionalization of innovations* did occur in a few instances, mainly in the county schools, reducing the planning load for staff as the new practices became an integral part of their work. At Central, for example, the LMS process was institutionalized by 1992 and was no longer a development priority.

## BLURRING THE EDGES

Much *routine maintenance activity was affected by external innovations*, a combination of LMS and reorganization of schooling making a particularly strong impact on planning in the borough schools. Working out the staffing and the allocation of pupils to classes was an annual task which heads would normally expect to carry out early in the summer term for the following academic year. The necessary decisions depended upon information on projected pupil numbers and, with the advent of LMS, information about the budget, the large bulk of which covered staffing.

At Heartlands, interaction between LMS and allocation of classes and staffing was exacerbated by lack of information. Considerable fluctuations in pupil numbers had been experienced among the schools within the locality. By the middle of the 1991 summer term the head was facing the likelihood that the number of children coming from the nursery into the reception year and the number of older pupils could not all be fitted into classes of a single year group. She could not make firm plans until she received the admission number from LEA staff with details of the school roll for the next term. Even then, it was possible that appeals by parents could result in changes to the number attending the school in September.

The final budget figure for the present financial year had been due before April but, two months on, LEA staff had yet to inform the head, and she and governors had been unable to set the budget. However, a provisional figure indicated that the school would be in deficit. The LEA formula, based on average staffing costs as dictated by central government, could not take into account the high proportion of mature teaching staff, whose salaries were around the top of the incremental scale. The transition arrangements made by the LEA meant that, although the school was due eventually to receive more than its historic allocation, little of this money was scheduled to be included in this year's budget. Nor had the out-turn figures for the financial year 1990/91 been received. Under these circumstances, the head was unwilling to appoint additional staff and risk pushing the budget further into the red.

Within the LEA plans for reorganization, all the pupils from years six and seven would transfer at the end of the next academic year to secondary schools whose intake would therefore change to take pupils at age 11 instead of 12. It was not yet clear whether the teaching of French would continue in what would then be primary schools, and the head was unsure whether to make plans now to discontinue teaching this subject in September 1992.

At this stage, the head was considering having a vertically grouped reception and year one class and a year four and year five class and had consulted teachers individually about the classes they would prefer to teach next year. A teacher had stated, after the deadline for giving notice for the summer term had passed, that she wished to resign from her post. The head had been unable so far to secure a replacement who was young enough and therefore affordable within the constraints of LMS.

After much time spent contacting LEA staff she was given the provisional admission number for the older pupils a few weeks before the end of term. Armed with this information, the head and staff made contingency plans to have several vertically grouped classes:

> My year six and seven staff have decided - we've yet to agree with parents - that we will go for three vertically grouped classes of year six and seven because we feel that this would facilitate the transfer of all

of them to high school more effectively. Because otherwise there is always going to be one, perhaps the year six group, who don't achieve quite the same importance because they are not the top of the school. And we feel they should be given that opportunity to be at the top of their school.

The final LMS budget for 1991/2 was received from the LEA, containing extra money, the head and governors were able to set a balanced budget three months into the financial year, and the head appointed an additional part-time teacher.

In September, more younger pupils came into the school than had been expected, as a result of LEA decisions on parents' appeals. They were accommodated within the allocation planned at the end of the summer term. However, the rationale for vertically grouping years six and seven in preparation for reorganization became redundant early in 1992 with the announcement of the LEA decision to postpone reorganization for another year, contradicting the earlier proposals which had informed plans for the allocation of classes and staffing.

Maintenance activity could also be affected by externally imposed changes in day-to-day procedures. At the beginning of the 1991 autumn term heads received details of a new central government requirement about the completion of pupil registers (DES, 1991b). The rationale of ministers was to collect information about truancy rates. Unauthorized-absence figures were to be published in the prospectus and annual governors' report for each school from the beginning of the following academic year, so as to inform parental choice of schooling. LEA stipulations in accordance with this demand included recording of latecomers and unauthorized absences. School staff in the borough were expected to telephone parents each day about any unauthorized absence and to insist upon written absence notes.

This procedure was largely carried out already in the six schools and little change was made in existing procedures. All the heads pointed out that truancy was not a problem in their school. The policy appears to have been more relevant to secondary schools, where a recent study revealed that about half the year seven and year nine pupils interviewed had 'skipped a day here and there' in the previous year (Keys and Fernandes, 1993).

The deputy at Highway undertook to check that staff used the new codes in marking their registers and to collate the figures from each class. She and the head were concerned to ensure that the procedure conformed to the legal requirement. Although staff had previously followed up on absences, the procedure now became more time-consuming because of the necessity of obtaining written confirmation from parents before an absence could be marked as 'authorized'. The figures for the school showed more unauthorized absences than was actually the case because some parents could not be persuaded to write a note. Just two pupils had played truant without their parents' knowledge in the last year and the staff had identified them; it was more common for parents to keep a healthy child away from school for various reasons. While not a major extra task in itself, following up absences represented a daily additional claim on the time of the deputy and the head, who were already hard pressed.

LMS was the main *external innovation which affected the management of planning* in all six schools. A moderate degree of turbulence was caused in so far as staff and governors had to come to terms with the new budgeting procedure and the much wider range of items of expenditure to be considered. Previously the only sums controlled at school level had been a capitation allowance for classroom resources (representing no more than 5 per cent of the LMS budget) and income generated from parents and other sources (HMI, 1992a). Major turbulence only resulted when the novelty of LMS was combined with insufficient finance and with a lack of clear and timely information, as we described above in the case of the borough schools.

Staff and governors in the county schools welcomed the additional flexibility they had gained through having a delegated budget. Extra secretarial and ancillary support was purchased at Central, and some classrooms at Town were redecorated and sliding partitions provided in two rooms. However, the head at Town anticipated that the school would soon suffer a funding crisis as numbers among younger children were dropping.

Similarly, *external imposition of two overlapping planning cycles* led to some readjustment of plans according to the stage reached in the financial and academic yearly cycles. Readjustment was less evident in some schools than others, related to the stage reached in the transition to greater school-level planning and budgeting. Development planning, LMS and devolved in-service training were designed to interrelate closely only in the county schools, and only here were the procedures associated with each innovation at an advanced stage of implementation. The county schools usually received details of their delegated budget for the next financial year towards the end of March, coinciding with the completion of development plans. Since the LMS formula was no longer radically altered from year to year the staff were able to make a broad estimate of what the school would receive, which aided planning.

These were also the schools least affected by factors promoting turbulence which influenced each cycle. We noted earlier, for example, how a significant and rapid increase in the number of pupils in both borough schools, coupled with tight LMS budgets and uncertainty at school level over securing a proportionate increase in the budget, led first to hindrance and then to adjustment of plans as the situation was clarified. Reorganization in the borough and the city effectively imposed an end date for all detailed planning and consideration of resources until arrangements for the reorganized schools were more or less complete.

In the borough and city schools, where development planning, LMS and devolved in-service training were both less major in scope and less interrelated by design, planning for each was addressed to some extent independently of the others, so the stage reached in one cycle would not necessarily affect planning within another. Development planning in the city schools was largely confined to the curriculum and did not encompass LMS: budgets were not to be fully delegated until after reorganization. Devolved in-service training money covered a small proportion of the training received by staff compared with that provided and paid for centrally (which covered most curriculum priorities in the development plans), so the stage reached in the cycle of allocation of this money had relatively little impact on plans for in-service training. Overlapping planning cycles led to adjustment of plans only where planning within one cycle was designed to dovetail with that of another. It seems likely that the lack of coordination between planning cycles and related procedures we encountered was widespread at the time. An evaluation of LMS carried out by HMI (1992a), which included longitudinal studies of LMS pilot schools, found that in the large majority LMS was not fully integrated with school development plans.

Compared with the conflict between governors and heads of a few schools in our initial survey, there was little evidence of *conflict over the direction of school development* at school level. It was confined to occasional tension between the teacher who wished to take individual initiatives and the head at Heartlands. Antagonism among senior staff may have affected the degree to which the head was willing to consult senior staff in setting the direction for change, but did not appear to hinder planning for implementation of external innovations, all of which were compulsory anyway. The analysis of the different school-level constituencies in Chapter 5 showed that *support among governors and parents for or passivity towards the direction of development* was marked in all the schools, effectively promoting some stability for staff because their plans were very largely unchallenged.

Not only was there a high degree of *consensus at school level over the direction of development* in all the schools, but there was also variable evidence of a factor promoting stability which we did not identify in the initial survey: *a mutually supportive staff culture which included a commitment to improvement led by the headteacher* (Table 7.3). The strength of this culture was most marked in Central, Highway and Southside. The head at Central had worked with most of the staff for some years and the other two heads had appointed virtually all the present staff (see Table 4.1). The high level of consensus over educational values, coupled with acceptance of the head's leadership, was a background factor which facilitated planning and implementation of changes through the commitment and enthusiasm of staff to engaging wholeheartedly in the process.

The head and other staff at Central had a close collaborative working relationship, brought about and sustained by several factors. First, the head made her philosophy of education explicit and modelled the behaviour that she wished staff to adopt. This philosophy was reportedly widely shared among staff. Second, the head's preferred approach to decision-making was to try to enable each member of staff to make a genuine contribution, describing herself as a 'facilitator' rather than a 'boss'. She aimed to build a strong relationship with each member of the teaching and non-teaching staff, stating: 'If I look after the staff, the staff will look after the children.' Third, the staff appeared both to like and to trust each other; discussions were lively but good-humoured and staff took care as a group to ensure that individuals who needed help were supported and that workloads were distributed as equitably as possible.

A teacher at Southside referred to the school's recent 'institutional history', when staff had worked in very difficult circumstances in temporary accommodation designed for sixth-form pupils after the original site had been burnt down by vandals. They had then experienced overcrowding and very large classes when they transferred to the new building, but had been able to sustain their work through mutual support:

> The planning and the teaching has to go on. And we seem to manage somehow - I think we're so used to changes. . . . A lot depends on the staff, and if the staff in the school weren't as flexible - we get on very well despite a high turnover of staff. This staff teach well together and they mix well together and they support one another. And if it weren't for that we'd go under.

Collaborative staff relationships went further than support with day-to-day coping; the institutional history of Southside included intensive and sustained development work, especially in relation to the local community. This finding is consistent with the North American research reviewed by Fullan (1991) which shows that effective principals play a key role in orchestrating change as a 'collaborative leader of continuous improvements in the school as an organization'. Elements of this culture were evident, but less marked, in the other schools. One of several possible factors may have been the lower proportion of staff whom the heads had been able to appoint since coming into post.

## WHERE DEVELOPMENT PLANNING FITS IN

The account of development planning in Chapter 6 confirmed the findings of the initial survey that, as an *innovatory procedure for managing planning for change*, development planning promoted turbulence in so far as new roles, tasks, structures and procedures were entailed in the planning process. Equally, in the county and city schools and to some extent at Highway, the LEA initiative helped to stabilize a potentially even more turbulent situation by highlighting a restricted range of priorities. However, staff were very limited in their ability to fend off external innovations because of the high degree of compulsion over their content and timing of their implementation. Development planning made the greatest contribution to stability in the county schools, partly because it was most comprehensive in scope and the closest to being an institutionalized innovation, and partly because these schools also faced the least turbulence. The annual cycle was not designed to cope with changes in the range of priorities during the year, although the process had been adapted at Central to ensure that the plan was updated halfway through the cycle.

*Routinized and flexible procedures for adjusting plans* existed to a greater or lesser extent in all the schools independently of development planning, helping to stabilize in some small measure a context where multiple changes had become one of the constants of school life. A less formal equivalent of the wall-chart approach at Highway was carried out in all the schools where the heads and, in most cases, some senior staff, monitored internally and externally and made plans in response to changing circumstances.

In order to determine how far planning for change was continual, as the model of flexible planning introduced in Chapter 2 implies, it is necessary to track the evolution of information about changes and the related plans. The next chapter therefore examines the planning flow during the period of our fieldwork.

# Chapter 8

# The Flow of Plans

How far was planning for change a continual process and how far did it follow the annual development planning cycle? In this chapter we examine how plans evolved through a broadly chronological account of the shifting focus of plans for the range of changes addressed in the schools (elaborating on the summary given in Chapter 4). The degree to which the flexible planning model (see Figure 2.1) matched the practice of staff, under the leadership of the headteachers, will be assessed in each case.

The flow of plans for each school is summarized in a table (see below) which lists the range of changes, including the innovation of development planning, other innovations and any significant crises or issues. An impression of activity connected with planning for each change is given by indicating when, during the four terms of fieldwork, it formed a major focus of planning efforts. In Tables 8.1 to 8.6 we have classified planning effort at any time according to three categories:

- a continual line represents a period when the change was a major focus of planning activity, especially for heads;
- a broken line implies that the change was in the background and planning activity was confined to awaiting further information, monitoring progress, or detailed implementation activity;
- a blank area indicates a period when the change did not feature significantly in planning activity.

It must be kept in mind that these categories relate to a continuous dimension, from no planning effort at all to a central focus of planning activity, and there can be no clear-cut distinction between, say, background and focus. Our judgements about when a change was the focus of planning activity or in the background are based upon periodic interviews with staff. A sense of planning flow has been obtained by extrapolation to cover the time between visits to the schools, according to informants' accounts of planning activity since a previous visit. The tables are no more than a crude heuristic device designed to illustrate how planning addressed a multiplicity of changes at any time and how the focus for planning activity varied between these changes as time passed in response to factors outlined in Chapter 7.

## PLANNING FLOW AND FLEXIBLE PLANNING

Each change that was included as a priority in the schools' development plan is marked with an asterisk (*). A cursory glance at the tables indicates how, despite variation between the schools, there were important similarities in the planning flow:

- the period when development planning was a focal point of planning activity (mainly the consultative review and planning exercise) largely coincided with the focus for most changes prioritized within the development plan - although some additional planning work was required for particular priorities;
- more changes were addressed than were included in development plan priorities, some of these arising after the point where development planning was focal;
- changes outside the development plan became the focus of planning activity at different times;
- several changes were the focus of planning activity at any point and the mix shifted over time.

A comparison with the account of development planning in each school (see Chapter 6) confirms how some identified priorities did not lead to focused planning activity in most schools. These priorities do not appear in the tables. The findings reinforce our argument that planning for change based on an annual cycle (as advocated in so much advice on development planning discussed in Chapter 1 and certain models reviewed in Chapter 2) was only part of the story in the case-study schools. In order to illustrate how the planning process actually operated, a brief account is given of the flow of plans for each school, and the variable balance is highlighted between the cyclic, spasmodic and continual components of the flexible planning model.

## Central Primary School

The development plan in the county schools was drawn up for the financial year (Table 8.1). In the 1991 summer term Central staff had identified priority areas for work and had just submitted the development plan to the LEA. Implementation of LMS provided a focus for planning, but proceeded smoothly. The staff had been able to fund an additional twelve hours per week of general assistance, thirty-two hours of clerical time and a half-time teacher post from the school budget. The school's SATs results had been analysed and, although the staff were not enthusiasts for this form of assessment, they were reassured that their results were broadly in line with those of similar schools in the county.

Two issues were causing concern. The first was the fact that one of their Section 11 projects had ceased as the teacher responsible had left and a replacement could not be found. The second was a more general staffing issue: the three probationers who had been appointed in September 1991 were coming to the end of their probationary year and the head and staff were anxious to monitor their progress and provide necessary support so that they would pass their probation. One had resigned, meaning that a suitable replacement had to be found. There was a flurry of planning activity towards the end of term when in July an Asian teacher was appointed to the vacant Section 11 post. This teacher was

**Table 8.1** Flow of plans at Central Primary School

| Change | Summer 1991 | Autumn 1991 | Spring 1992 | Summer 1992 |
|---|---|---|---|---|
| Development planning | – – – – – –→ —————→– – – – – – – – ——→ | | | |
| *LMS | – – – – – – – – – – – – – – – – – – – –→– – – – – –→ | | | |
| *Assessment | ——————→ – – – – – – – – – – – – –→ ——————→ | | | |
| *National Curriculum maths, English, science | – – – – – – – – – – – – – – – – – – – – – – – – –→ | | | |
| History and geography | – – – – – – – – – – – – – – – – – – – – – –→ | | | |
| *Art, music, PE | Music | | | |
|  | – – – – – – – – – – – – – – – – – – – – – –→ | | | |
|  | | | | Art ——→ |
|  | | | PE ——————————→ | |
| Section 11 | – – – – –——————→– – –→ ——————→ | | | |
| *Behaviour policy | ——————————→ – – – – – – – – – – –→ | | | |
| *Environment | – – – – – – – – – – – – – – – – – – – – – – –→ | | | |
| Licensed teacher | ———————————→ | | | |
| Maternity leave | ——————→ – – – – – – – – – – – –→ | | | |
| Staffing issues | ——————→ ——————→ ——————→ | | | |

experienced, but did not have qualified-teacher status as she had trained in India. In consultation with LEA staff, the head arranged that the teacher should follow a school-based teacher training programme. This strategy had implications for work in the following term in that one of the other staff undertook to act as a mentor; the teacher herself could not work full-time on the Section 11 project as, in order to gain QTS, she had to demonstrate that she could work as a regular class teacher and she also had to spend some time attending external initial training sessions.

A key planning task in the autumn term was to make arrangements for running the school during the head's absence on maternity leave. The deputy was going to become acting head and the intention had been that she should spend the first part of the term free from class-teaching responsibilities so that she could be inducted into the role. However, one of the A allowance holders was absent through illness for several weeks and the deputy had to substitute for her. The staff continued to work on their priority areas. The six-monthly review of their 1991/2 development plan revealed that they had remained on target.

Additional priorities had been thrown up by a visit from two LEA inspectors in the early part of the term. Their report had been broadly positive but they had identified two areas in need of development: the use of computers in classrooms, and the differentiation of work within one year group. The headteacher had been aware of both these issues but now had to give them a higher priority. A further unanticipated innovation, albeit relatively minor, was introduced that term when in response to a central government initiative the staff had to introduce a new method of taking the registers and recording pupil absence.

The 1992 spring term was dominated by the campaign against the proposed cut in Section 11 funding and the reduction in the school's Section 11 staffing allocation from two to one. The teacher most at risk was the only Asian teacher in the school; she had successfully completed her licensed teacher course in December 1991 and had gained QTS. The acting head and staff noted that she had proved invaluable in building links with the community as she was able to intrepret for parents who did not speak English. They were anxious to keep her on the staff. The campaign against these cuts occupied considerable senior staff time. During the term one teacher resigned as she was leaving the area, causing further difficulty as she had been taking one of the two year-two classes who were doing SATs. In the event the acting deputy, who was also a designated Section 11 teacher, worked alongside her in class for the last few weeks of term and took over responsibility for the class and the remaining SATs in the summer term. The threat of redundancy for the Asian teacher was removed but, as a result, the resources for the Section 11 projects were reduced.

Further issues which arose that term and occupied planning time, especially for senior staff, were the resignation and replacement of the school caretaker and a concern that the school might not be able to continue to subsidize swimming lessons (though the governors wished to do so). In mid-term the staff began a review of priorities in preparation for the 1992/3 development plan and for the first time a short questionnaire was distributed to parents and governors.

The main priority areas were unchanged in the 1992/3 development plan and work proceeded on them throughout the summer term. LEA staff had been persuaded to reduce the proposed cut in the Section 11 staffing allocation from a full-time post to just half a post. In the 1992 summer term the acting head had requested a supply teacher for this half-time post as the deputy was going back into the classroom and she had been allocated a member of the central Section 11 staff. This experience had not been especially successful as the substitute provided was not a trained teacher but had previously been employed making videos for the multicultural support service.

A considerable amount of planning for the new school year took place in the second part of the term. Two members of staff had to be appointed; several teachers were planning to change their class-teaching responsibilities; the acting head was exploring the feasibility of finding money within the LMS budget to paint some classrooms and install sinks in one or two rooms; and detailed planning was under way to manage the large intake of pupils anticipated in the lower school. Towards the end of term, the headteacher announced her resignation. The staff were immediately plunged into another busy planning period as people in acting posts realized they would probably hold them for a further term rather than giving them up in July as they had anticipated.

## Link with flexible planning

This school followed the cyclic model of planning which the LEA had recommended and the staff were able to work on the priorities that had been identified in the development plan. There appeared to be several reasons why cyclic planning proved possible. First, the staff and governors had had several years' experience of planning and had established the relevant procedures. Second, the priority areas were few in number and, of necessity, largely replicated the innovations that primary schools were compelled to introduce following central government legislation. Third, because the development plan operated on the financial year, the staff knew what financial resources would be available to support the implementation of the plan. Fourth, the staff did not experience any major crises in the year in question.

Nevertheless, the period 1991/2 included spasmodic changes in information about external innovations outside the development plan, which led to responsive planning activity. Most notable was the cut in the Section 11 budget. The headteacher's absence on maternity leave and her subsequent resignation constituted a significant issue throughout the year, leading to changes in staffing arrangements. In addition, a large amount of short-term planning was undertaken to cope with unexpected events like the aftermath of the inspectors' visit; the new procedure on registration; and modifications to the schedule of topics for staff meetings and in-service training days caused by delay in documentation produced by the National Curriculum Council. Overall, the environment remained relatively stable. Staff continued to work as a close, cohesive group and were able to follow the broad framework of their development plan with only minor modifications.

There was also a continual element to planning for change. The head and, later, acting head sought information about external innovations, monitored progress with changes, and adjusted plans in small ways as circumstances changed.

## Town Primary School

The 1991 summer term was relatively uneventful at Town in that there were no major crises which interrupted the normal flow of events (Table 8.2). The development plan for 1991/2 had been submitted to the LEA and staff were committed to working on the identified priorities. Additional money from the capitation budget had been allocated for work on two priority areas: special needs and science. The headteacher was concerned about how to raise the levels of teacher expectation and pupil achievement. Senior staff had analysed the school's SATs results, which had shown a correlation between the children's test scores, the length of time that they had been in school and their command of the English language. The finding had confirmed the headteacher's view that work on special needs should be a major priority for 1991/2, and planning for work in this broad area was undertaken.

This emphasis began in the summer term when the teachers were, for the first time, required to write a report for parents on each child. Staff meetings were held to discuss what kind of information should be included on the reports, and the headteacher underlined the importance of writing positive and constructive comments about the pupils. For a few weeks report writing became a high-priority issue in the school.

The start of the autumn term was unusual for the staff as, with one exception, they all changed their class-teaching responsibilities. Each class had a

**Table 8.2** Flow of plans at Town Primary School

| Change | Summer 1991 | Autumn 1991 | Spring 1992 | Summer 1992 |
|---|---|---|---|---|
| Development planning | ──→ | – – – – – –→ | ─────→ | – – – – |
| *LMS | ──────── | ──────→ | ──────── | ──────→ |
| *Assessment | ─────→ | – – – – | – – – –→ | – – – – |
| *National Curriculum maths, English, science | – – – – – – | ───────→ | – – – – – – | – – – – |
| History and geography | – – – – – – | – – – – – – | – – – – – – | – – – –→ |
| Art, music, PE | – – – – – – | – – – – – – | – – – – – – | – – – –→ |
| Section 11 | – – – – – – | – – – – – – | – – – – – – | ──────→ |
| *Parental involvement | – – – – – – | – – – – – – | – – – – – – | – – – –→ |
| *Special needs | – – – – – – | ───────→ | ─────→ | – – – – |
| Environment | – – – – – – | ───────→ | – – – – – →| – – – – |
| Building refurbishment | – – – – – – | – – – – – – | ──────→ | – – ───→ |
| Staffing | – – – –→ | – – – – – – →| ──────── | ──────→ |
| Classroom reorganization | ──→ | – – – →| | |

budget for the purchase of teaching materials and there was some initial concern because a number of the teachers had spent practically all the budget the previous summer leaving the 'new' teacher little flexibility. New teaching partnerships had to be developed between pairs of teachers. The staff continued to work on the priority areas identified in the development plan and the work on special needs was given special emphasis. The teacher responsible for this area was allocated one and a half days per week from September 1991 to develop a policy statement for the school and to work on raising staff expectations of able children. In addition all the staff started work on the 'short-term intervention' project which gave individual children a period of one-to-one help from a teacher each day for number of weeks. The staff continued their long-term project to increase parental involvement in the school.

An unexpected crisis which disrupted school life was a breakdown in the heating system necessitating the school's closure for two days. The staff were able to use this time positively by meeting to review the science policy document. Work on assessment procedures proceeded and the three teachers working on Section 11 funded projects devised a monitoring form for the staff which could be used to record a child's progress in spoken and written English. Shortly before the end of term the school was inspected by two LEA inspectors, a follow-up to the full inspection which had take place in the 1989 autumn term. This had proved to be a very encouraging experience as the inspectors had given the staff and the governors very positive feedback about the quality of work that they had seen.

Life in school became more problematic in the 1992 spring term. First, the school lost the half a day a week additional support it was receiving for special needs from a teacher from the LEA general support team, as the person doing the job resigned and could not be replaced. Staff initiatives in this area were weakened in consequence. Plans had to be made to substitute for the deputy head, who would be absent on maternity leave from half term. The head and the finance officer both found that LMS was continuing to demand much effort, and building maintenance also soaked up planning time. The head was able to find some money in the budget to repaint some of the classrooms but the staff also learned that the playground could not be used for formal games because the surface was breaking up and one of the boundary walls was in a dangerous condition.

Information about cuts in Section 11 funding led to responsive planning, as we mentioned in Chapter 7. The headteacher was informed that the staff funded in this way would be reduced from three to two. Any teacher on a temporary contract would not have the contract renewed after April 1992, a measure affecting two of the three teachers concerned. The project on home-school liaison would cease and be handled centrally in future. Like the staff at Central, the headteacher and staff in Town School opposed the cuts vigorously and were ultimately successful in losing only half a teaching post. However, anxiety was considerable for the staff affected and their work as a team was severely disrupted. One of the Section 11 funded teachers obtained another job and left at Easter. A second, who was worried about the continued uncertainty of her contract, left in the summer 1992. Replacement teachers were not easy to find and at the start of the 1992 autumn term the school had one vacancy to fill for work on a Section 11 project. Overall, work on the Section 11 projects was severely disrupted from the middle of the 1992 spring term.

The LEA inspectors had commented on the fact that the staff were not teaching much history and geography, something that the head realized but which she defended because she felt that at Key Stage 1 the main priority should be to teach the children spoken and written English. In the summer term the school celebrated its sixtieth anniversary in a week of plays, displays and parties. Extensive planning and organization was required for this school-based initiative, but it did enable the staff to focus on history. The school had also been involved in a school-based music project which had involved all the children in a particular year group and had been very successful.

The head also became increasingly concerned about the long-term viability of the school and began planning how to achieve a greater degree of security. Her worry was caused by a steady decline in the school roll, which would have implications for the LMS budget, and the fact that the site was large and expensive to run. The intake of white pupils into the school was decreasing. In the event, she and the chair of governors wrote to the LEA chief education officer about their concerns and an LEA working party was set up to explore future options.

## Link with flexible planning

Like Central, Town School staff were able to follow the cyclic planning model and continued to work throughout the year on the priority areas that had been identified. Though school work suffered minor disruptions, such as the breakdown in the heating system, most plans did not have to be altered significantly.

While priorities were identified in the development plan, the pattern of activities in each area was not fully worked out when the plan was compiled. For example, the statement in the plan about the special needs priority implied that the staff would identify and assess the full range of special needs; evaluate and then amend, introduce or continue provision of support; and create a special needs policy for the school. Initiatives within this priority were introduced during the year. They included the short-term intervention project, a paired reading scheme and additional support for able pupils. The development plan was useful in enabling staff to agree certain goals but did not constrain further planning for change within or outside the plan itself.

The most significant spasmodic change in information about external innovations was the unanticipated cut in Section 11 funding, dictating a planned response from staff. The difficulties that the head anticipated the school would face in future were not raised in the 1992/3 development plan, possibly because she perceived that little could be done at school level other than drawing the issue to the attention of LEA staff and seeking assistance.

Planning for change included a continual component. As at Central, the head led the process of seeking information about external innovations, monitoring progress in school, and adjusting plans accordingly.

## Highway Middle School

Planning within the financial- and academic-year cycles was a major feature of the summer term 1991 (Table 8.3). The development planning process was launched with a view to producing a three-(academic)-year plan. Work on history and geography within the National Curriculum directly reflected the central government timetable for their introduction. Although the school did not cater for pupils at Key Stage 1, the head was keen to develop an assessment policy in preparation for meeting legal requirements in future years.

Partial delegation within LMS was a major change dictating planning according to the financial year, but a lack of firm information and spasmodic changes in such information as was received forced the head to adopt an incremental approach to financial planning, meaning that LMS was a more or less permanent focus. For example, the governors had refused to accept the LEA's provisional budget for 1991/2 - the deficit on paper was £11,000. By the middle of term information was received that the LEA had increased the budget by £3,000. The final budget had still not been received by the end of term.

Meanwhile, the prospect of an increase in pupil numbers for the next academic year prompted much negotiation between the head and LEA staff to ensure that the extra pupils would secure an extra tranche of money within the LMS budget. Only when the head was certain could she go ahead with the appointment of an additional teacher.

The crisis of the leaking roof became the top planning priority. The move to temporary sites at the beginning of the autumn term was planned very rapidly in response to the discovery that repairs had not been completed during the summer holidays, as the head had expected, because the LEA procedure of putting the job out to competitive tender took so much time.

**Table 8.3** Flow of plans at Highway Middle School

| Change | Summer 1991 | Autumn 1991 | Spring 1992 | Summer 1992 |
|---|---|---|---|---|
| Development planning | ——————→ | – – – – – – – – – – – – – – – – – – – –→ | | |
| LMS | —————————————————————————————————→ | | | |
| *Assessment | – – → —————→ | – – – – – – – – – – – – –→ —→ – – | | |
| *History and geography | – → ——————→ | – – – – – – – – – – – – – – – – –→ | | |
| Art, music, PE | – – – – – – – – – – – – – – – – – – – – – – – – – –→ | | | |
| *Section 11 | – – – – – – – – – – – – – – – – – – – – – – – – – –→ | | | |
| Reorganization | – – → —————————————→ | – – – – – – –→ | | |
| Move to temporary sites | – – – – → ———————————→ | – – – – – – – – →| | |
| Field trips | | | ——————→ | |
| Fire | | | | ——————→ – – →|
| Increase in pupil numbers | ——————→ | | | ——————→ |
| Staffing for 1992/3 | | | | – – →———→ |
| Registers | | | ——————→ – – – – – – – – – – →| |

Most of the autumn term was dominated by the short-term priority of planning to cope with the temporary situation, plans being adjusted when the original deadline for return to the main site expired while work on the roof had yet to be completed. Planning for implementation of changes based on the academic year, such as assessment, took a back seat. When the head discovered that the LEA had charged the school's LMS budget for services connected with the temporary sites, she responded by negotiating with officials to have these charges removed.

LEA plans for reorganization proceeded apace, the head and her deputy (the teacher governor) being involved in meetings to set up the shadow governing body which would prepare for the proposed amalgamation with the other two schools on the same site. The receipt of the DES circular on recording unauthorized absences led to the deputy's response of collating information from class registers and following up unauthorized absences. At the end of term, the move back to the main site was planned and implemented within a couple of weeks, leaving a planning legacy of settling in and unpacking all the materials which staff had taken away with them.

The break with routine practice concerning residential field trips - making the same offer to all pupils - and the unanticipated high response led to planning being dominated throughout the 1992 spring term by the short-term task of implementing the sequence of trips. At around the middle of term news broke that the LEA reorganization was to be postponed for a year, reducing the external pressure on staff to prepare for amalgamation. The term ended dramatically with a fire started by vandals. Staff had to make plans for finding alternative accommodation, making the building safe, and compiling a list of items to be replaced under the terms of the LEA's insurance policy.

In the summer term staff planning for the implementation of National Curriculum subjects resumed. The 1992/3 LMS budget was received, credited with the money claimed earlier by LEA staff connected with the move to temporary sites. No out-turn figures for 1991/2 had been received shortly before the end of term. Several teachers had applied for posts elsewhere, stimulating senior staff to make contingency plans for their replacement, depending on which staff proved successful. Planning for art, music and physical education within the National Curriculum remained in the background, being scheduled for staff to discuss at the beginning of the 1992 autumn term, the point from which programmes of study had to comply with the new legal requirements. Even here, staffing issues arose which affected plans for subject coordinators to prepare to lead the implementation of changes in practice. The art coordinator was absent through illness for several months. The teacher with expertise in physical education gained a post in another school, leading to another teacher taking on the responsibility. The Section 11 project was small-scale, since there were relatively few pupils from minority ethnic groups. When information was received in the 1992 spring term about the grant allocation, the head proceeded with the appointment of a part-time teacher.

## Link with flexible planning

Planning in this school reflected mainly the more spasmodic and continual components of the flexible planning model. Although much planning for change was framed in terms of annual cycles, the many sources of turbulence meant that stable conditions necessary for cyclic planning were not much in evidence. It proved impossible for plans to be created at one point in the year, followed simply by implementation until the next planning exercise to formulate the following year's plans. Repeated and unpredictable spasmodic changes in information about LMS, influenced by other changes such as the move to temporary sites, dictated frequent updating of plans including how to deal with problems over LMS itself. Routine planning of staffing and classes for the academic year was carried out in response to changes in relevant information received after the beginning of the financial year, so entailing adjustment to the LMS budget.

Spasmodic influences on planning not only affected cyclic changes, including the demise of the development planning exercise itself, but also led to short-term priorities for a planned response. The two major crises and the unexpected take-up of the field trip offer dictated a rapid reaction; postponement of reorganization gave an unexpected breathing space for staff to concentrate on short-term priorities, especially the field trips. The headteacher stuck to her tried and tested procedure for short-term planning, leading staff in working opportunistically towards the realization of broad, unchanging principles. The prospect of amalgamation, even when it was postponed for a year, militated against the formulation of long-term goals. This case conforms with the contingency hypothesis we put forward in Chapter 2 (see Figure 2.2) that very high environmental turbulence (and therefore low stability) forces planning in the direction of continual creation, monitoring and adjustment. It is difficult to see how, even if the development planning consultative exercise had been completed, it could have guided the multiplicity of plans made subsequently in response to unpredictably changing circumstances without both modification to existing plans and the creation of additional ones to address new priorities.

## Heartlands Combined School

Cyclic planning at Heartlands was affected by some of the same factors that led to readjustments at Highway, but to a lesser extent (Table 8.4). We described earlier how problems with the LMS budget during the 1991 summer term were exacerbated by uncertainty over pupil admission numbers in inhibiting planning of staffing and classes for the 1991/2 academic year. The timing of detailed planning for the assessment of pupils at Key Stage 1 was dictated by central government provision of the necessary information. The LEA introduced a new report form after staff had completed their existing record, leading to some extra work. Planning for history and geography was undertaken by the coordinator responsible for humanities, who led staff meetings during the summer and autumn terms to assimilate the various attainment targets within the existing integrated approach to topic work. Similarly, a staff working party developed a handwriting policy in consultation with the rest of the teachers.

The headteacher's development plan for the 1991/2 academic year was not formally devised until the 1992 spring term, although coordinators continued to work on curriculum and assessment priorities in the meantime. Her reticence in consulting senior colleagues was influenced by the issue of antagonism between herself, the deputy and a few other staff, but the tension was eased to some extent when the deputy gained a post elsewhere.

Changes in information about several external innovations stimulated planning activity. When an electricity bill was received which was about twice the estimate based on the previous year's consumption, the head vired money from another heading within the LMS budget to pay for an LEA consultant to look into the matter. The LMS out-turn figures for 1990/91 were received in February and preparations made for full delegation from April. The head was able to consider allocating an A incentive allowance which she had withheld until

**Table 8.4** Flow of plans at Heartlands Combined School

| Change | Summer 1991 | Autumn 1991 | Spring 1992 | Summer 1992 |
|---|---|---|---|---|
| Development planning | →---------------→ | | —→ | ------→ |
| LMS | ------→------- | ---→ | —→ | ----→ |
| Assessment | ---→----------- | | ----→ | —→----→ |
| *History and geography | ---→————— | ——→ | ---------→ | |
| Art, music, PE | ------------- | ------- | ---------- | -------→ |
| Section 11 | -------------- | -------- | ---→—→ | ----→ |
| Reorganization | ------------- | ------- | ---→——→ | —→------→ |
| *English | -----→ | | | |
| Appraisal | | | | ----→—→—→ |
| Increase in pupil numbers | ————— | → | | |
| Arts festival | | | -----→——→ | ------→ |

now. On the other hand, planning for the following year was inhibited because
it was not clear what the LMS budget would be after reorganization, when the
school would lose the year seven pupils.

The LEA postponement of reorganization precipitated adjustment of plans
to make use of the space that staff had anticipated was to have been freed. Planning for staffing and classes for 1992/3 proved difficult because of the number
of pupils, including those now expected to be in year seven, adding to the existing complexities following from the introduction of vertically grouped classes in
1991. The school was given a larger Section 11 project grant than that for which
the head had bid, giving rise to the possibility that a part-time teacher might be
allocated an A incentive allowance by the LEA as team leader for the school. The
head planned to increase the employment of the existing part-time staff responsible for English as a second language, but their contracts were now for three
years and based with the LEA, rather than the school.

Combined schools, none of which faced amalgamation under the LEA
reorganization plans, were the first primary-sector schools in the borough to
begin implementing appraisal. Training for staff was provided in the 1992 spring
term and the head's own appraisal started in the summer. Staff anticipated that
some of them would be appraised the following term. A high priority for the
head was to celebrate the eightieth anniversary of the opening of the school. She
launched the idea of an arts festival, and a committee of teachers planned a play,
a concert, an art exhibition, a book fair and a dance theatre workshop. In this
way, space was created for a one-off school-based initiative despite the heavy
innovation load.

Little work was done to meet the requirements of art, music and physical
education within the National Curriculum. Coordinators for these subjects
attended in-service training provided by LEA staff and awaited the arrival of
the final documents from the National Curriculum Council. Key Stage 1 assessment for 1992 was planned once the documents were received, proving more
straightforward than the previous year. Cover for the year two teachers was
provided by the assessment coordinator and teachers whose classes were being
taken by students on teaching practice. Staff changes led to planning for replacements, culminating in the head being offered a post in another LEA.

## Link with flexible planning

The head's cyclic approach to development planning was curtailed during the
fieldwork period for reasons which were explored in detail in Chapter 6. However, planning to implement assessment and history and geography still followed the academic-year cycle, driven by the externally imposed deadlines for
implementation. The high rate of spasmodic changes in information related
to LMS stimulated incremental adjustment of financial plans and the rapid
increase in pupil numbers caused similar problems to those experienced at
Highway. Although there were no major crises, spasmodic changes in information about other external innovations - most notably the postponement of
reorganization - led to responsive adjustments. We noted earlier, for example,
how the original expectation that the school would be reorganized in 1992

influenced the decision to introduce vertically grouped classes. Postponement meant that new assumptions had to be made in planning staffing and classes for 1992/3.

In this case, the head coped with the situation largely on her own, monitoring progress with changes, making adjustments as the need arose and even creating the new plan of organizing an arts festival. The possibility of outlining long-term plans was restricted by the prospect of reorganization, and most plans were primarily concerned with immediate demands for change. All three components of the flexible planning model were present in this school, with somewhat fewer spasmodic influences than at Highway.

## Southside First School

Work on development planning conformed to the academic-year cycle imposed by LEA staff, the consultation and planning exercise being carried out at the end of the 1991 summer term, after which little reference to the plan was made (Table 8.5). Similarly, partial delegation within LMS went smoothly, the combination of an adequate budget and timely information from LEA staff enabling a budget to be set at the beginning of the financial year, followed by monitoring of spending. Apart from a nagging query over the size of the water bill, the head was not troubled by spasmodic changes in information about the budget itself, in contrast with the borough schools. Assessment of pupils at the end of Key Stage 1 was addressed as soon as the necessary information was received. In 1991 detailed planning for implementation was held up because materials did not arrive until shortly before the central government deadline for assessment to begin. Teachers directly involved decided to hold back from planning for the following year because they expected the form of the tests to be changed.

History and geography were dealt with smoothly by the humanities coordinator, supported by a working party. Changes to integrate the new programmes of study within a two-year cycle of class topics were agreed with staff by the end

**Table 8.5** Flow of plans at Southside First School

| Change | Summer 1991 | Autumn 1991 | Spring 1992 | Summer 1992 |
|---|---|---|---|---|
| Development planning | — — → | ———→ | — — — — — — — — — — — — — — — → | |
| LMS | — — — — — — — — — — — — — — — — — — — — — — — — — — → | | | |
| *Assessment | — — → ———→ | — — — — — → | ——————— → | — — — → |
| *History and geography | — — → ———————— | | → — — — — — — — — → | |
| Art, music, PE | — — — — — — — — — — — — — — — — — — — — — — — — — — → | | | |
| *Section 11 | — — — — — → ——————— | | → — — — — — → | ——————→ |
| Reorganization | — — → ———————————— | | | → |
| Inner-city bid | | ▸———→ | — — — — — — — → | ——————→ |
| Nursery project | — — — — — → | | | |
| *Special needs and induction | | ————————————→ | | |
| *Science | | ————————→ | | |
| Emergency closure | | | ▸ ——→ | |

of the summer term, and the coordinator then arranged for some teachers to attend LEA in-service training courses and proceeded with procuring resources. In a similar way, the consultation and planning exercise within the development planning initiative led to coordinators responsible for special needs, the induction of staff and science responding to priorities identified by their colleagues.

A major difficulty with planning for reorganization was caused by the fact that information about future staff came through spasmodically. The uncertainty over staffing precluded any development work being planned beyond the reorganization date of September 1992. The advent of reorganization began to impinge upon staff during the 1991 summer term when the head and deputy learned that they were to be reappointed. LEA staff decided that the reorganized school would cater for slightly fewer pupils than at present, meaning that fewer posts carrying incentive allowances would be available than were currently occupied by staff. The head worked out which curriculum areas should be covered through incentive allowances and announced that the B allowance for art and craft and the A allowance for music would be removed. The teachers in these posts would have to secure a post elsewhere or lose their incentive allowance.

The LEA's incremental approach to assimilation of staff from the 9-13 middle schools, which were due to close or to become primary schools, created uncertainty over staffing which was to last right up to the reorganization date. For example, all staff on B incentive allowances were invited at the end of the 1991 summer term to apply for their own or equivalent posts in other schools. In the autumn term, A allowance holders were invited to apply for any B allowance posts left over, then in the spring term A allowance posts were advertised. Any staff who had not served in the LEA were on short-term contracts which finished by the reorganization date and could not be guaranteed a post. The final round of posts to be allocated were main-scale teachers, but by this time some staff already allocated a post had moved out of the LEA, creating more opportunities for promotion. One teacher at Southside on an A incentive allowance gained a C post in another school, leaving a gap to be filled at Southside. The head was repeatedly engaged in negotiation with governors and LEA staff over the acceptance of teachers from within the school or redeployed from other schools in the light of LEA allocation decisions.

The head contributed to the uncertainty over staffing when she took the offer of early retirement. When staff learned of her decision, several staff members who had wished to stay at the school as long as they could continue working for her applied elsewhere. The deputy took maternity leave and subsequently resigned. Replacements were appointed for both the head and deputy. Little progress was made with the implementation of changes in art, music and physical education, both because the coordinator for each of these subjects gained a post in another school and because it was impossible to engage with staff in developing these areas of the curriculum until it was clear who the staff of the reorganized school would be. A heavy agenda for development work was stacked up for the new head and staff of the reorganized school.

Against this backdrop, implementation of changes in Section 11 posts began during the 1991 summer term with the allocation by LEA staff of two additional assistants. The head appointed two people with no experience of working in schools, expecting LEA staff to provide induction support. It soon became evident that the new assistants did not know how to work with children and that the LEA had not yet set up any induction arrangements. The head responded by arranging with experienced staff to provide some induction support. In the second half of the term, the head held a meeting with the assistants to express her concern about their lateness and absenteeism.

The invitation at short notice to bid for support under the central government's inner-city initiative caused a brief flurry of activity at the beginning of the autumn term. The head responded, after which nothing was heard until LEA staff contacted her in the second half of term to invite the school to bid to participate in a sustained reading intervention project bearing little relationship to her proposal.

The temporary appointment of an experienced nursery teacher to cover for a maternity leave during the 1991 summer term enabled the head to capitalize on her expertise and enthusiasm in introducing a school-based initiative. The teacher consulted the nursery nurses and, with their full support, implemented a change in the approach to teaching, giving the children greater responsibility for their own learning.

The head was informed that the school would have to be closed for a day just before the end of the autumn term for new electricity cables to be laid to the temporary classrooms. She responded by organizing an extra in-service training day which included a very successful session on individual careers, particularly germane to all staff because of reorganization.

Early in the spring term, material for the 1992 assessment of pupils at the end of Key Stage 1 was received, and the head consulted staff about the possibility of doing the non-statutory tests, which staff agreed to reject. Staff responsible for year-two classes organized the assessment arrangements which went more smoothly this time, although the year-two support teacher found the experience very stressful.

At the end of this term the head was notified that the sustained reading intervention bid had been successful, and she arranged for the two teachers most centrally involved to receive preparatory training. The LEA started providing induction training in the spring term for new Section 11 funded assistants and the existing bilingual assistants and home-school support staff were assimilated into a combined classroom and home support role from the beginning of the 1992 summer term.

By the end of the summer term the head was still unsure whether the sustained reading intervention project would finish at the end of the financial year or whether it would be extended for a further two years. Several posts had still to be allocated under reorganization, and the head was much exercised ensuring that all pupils in the existing school and their parents knew which schools they would attend in September following the change in catchment area.

## Link with flexible planning

Development planning and partial delegation within LMS followed the academic and financial years respectively. Reorganization in September 1992 meant that plans within either cycle could not be taken beyond this date until it was clear what the staffing, the reorganized school roll and the revised LMS budget would be. As we saw earlier, LEA staff decided upon an interregnum of two terms after reorganization when schools would not be expected to have a development plan, so as to give the new staffs time to settle into the reorganized schools. Therefore, no review or extension of the 1991/2 development plan was undertaken. Most priorities within it were related to the National Curriculum whose timetable for phasing in subjects each academic year did not alter. Cyclic planning was therefore a strong element in this school at the start of the fieldwork period, but no cycle could be taken beyond the date of reorganization.

Spasmodic changes in information mainly affected certain innovations planned at LEA level for implementation in schools, most notably the gradual emergence of staff changes under reorganization, with knock-on effects for the roles of coordinators for certain National Curriculum subjects. However, Section 11 and the inner-city initiative were also full of surprises; in the latter case staff implemented a completely different innovation from the initiative proposed in the original bid. There were no major crises or issues unrelated to innovations.

The headteacher monitored the work of staff quite closely and, as in the case of the nursery project, worked opportunistically to realize her educational beliefs and values. She led the process of adjusting plans whenever the need arose, but was increasingly unable to look beyond the short term as reorganization - and the end of her headship - loomed closer. All three components of the flexible planning model were present, with a substantial degree of cyclic planning (cut short by reorganization) and spasmodic changes which affected most external innovations that were not included within the development plan.

## Northedge First School

While there were many similarities among the innovations faced by both city schools, the prospective move back to the refurbished site increasingly dominated planning during the 1991 summer term, to the extent that the head decided to delay the consultation and planning exercise within the development planning initiative until the autumn (Table 8.6). Even then, responding to unexpected difficulties including cramped cloakrooms, disquiet among parents, and high classroom noise levels made it difficult to fit in the exercise, as we saw in Chapter 5. Spasmodic changes in information about the move back inhibited cyclic development planning. Nevertheless, partial delegation within LMS was largely unproblematic and assessment was addressed in compliance with the central government imposed timetable. The deputy coordinated support for the teachers doing the SATs, ensuring that there were always two teachers present.

In the previous year staff had put much energy into improving their work in science but, in the view of the head, needed more time to consolidate the gains

**Table 8.6** Flow of plans at Northedge First School

| Change | Summer 1991 | Autumn 1991 | Spring 1992 | Summer 1992 |
|---|---|---|---|---|
| Development planning | – – – – – – → | —————→ | – – – → | |
| LMS | – – – – – – – – – – – – – – – – – – – – – – → | | | |
| Assessment | – – → ————→ | – – – – – – – → | ————→ | |
| *History and geography | – – – – – – – – – – – – – – – – – – – – – – → | | | |
| *Art, music, PE | – – – – – → —→ | – – – – – – – – – – → | | |
| Section 11 | – – – – → ————→ | – – – – – – – → | ————→ | |
| Reorganization | – – – → | ————————————————→ | | |
| Inner-city bid | ►————→ | – – – – – → | ————————→ | |
| *Move to refurbished site | – – → ————→ | – – – – → | | |
| *Technology | – – – – – – – – – – – – – – → —→ | – – – → —→ – – – → | | |
| Antiracist policy | – – – – – – – – – – – – – – – – – – – – – – → | | | |
| Maths club | ————————→ | – – – – – → | | |

they had made. The imposition of history and geography from autumn 1991 militated against continuing with science, and the head also felt that staff were not ready to take on more changes while they were coping with the aftermath of moving back to the refurbished site. Top priority was given to settling in. Consequently, although humanities was identified as a priority in the 1991/2 development plan, work in this area was in actuality a low priority. Separate responsibilities for Key Stage 1 and Key Stage 2 history and for geography were allocated to staff but they reported increasing diffidence over consulting their colleagues because reorganization meant it was uncertain whether existing staff would remain in the school to implement changes. Physical education was a priority in the 1990/91 development plan and art featured in 1992. Work did not begin on these subjects or music prior to reorganization. The art coordinator learned quite early in the year that her job description would not command a B incentive allowance in the reorganized school and obtained a post elsewhere.

Reorganization had an impact on staffing at Northedge similar to that described above for Southside, the head, deputy and a C incentive allowance holder being appointed in the 1991 summer term and the remaining staff applying for posts and learning of the LEA decision throughout the next year. The head found the experience frustrating and depressing at times, as valued staff she had appointed were allocated to other schools and she found herself receiving a teacher who, she felt, would be unable to cope with the job. The LEA proposal to change the catchment area proved more of a problem than at Southside. We saw earlier how parents from the Afro-Caribbean community, who could not afford to live in the newly designated catchment area, voiced their protest. The head spent time during the autumn term liaising with parents and LEA staff.

Despite the many external pressures, the opportunity was taken during the 1991 summer term to launch the maths club, a small-scale school-based initiative. Development of an antiracist policy proceeded more slowly, the coordinator for equal opportunities completing a draft which was accepted by staff in the 1992 spring term and presented to the governors for approval. One governor expressed concern about the wording and liaised with the coordinator in revising the policy document, which was finally accepted by the governors in the summer term.

The appointment and induction of new assistants funded under Section 11 went more smoothly than at Southside. The first person started work at the beginning of the autumn term. Although she had not worked in schools before, this assistant was willing to take initiatives and was inducted into the role informally by the teachers with whom she worked. The inner-city bid was compiled by the head at short notice and, like Southside, the school was ultimately successful in taking part in the LEA's sustained reading intervention project the following summer.

We noted in Chapter 6 how the head's only copy of the development plan was stolen and not replaced, the document ceasing to guide planning in school. Planning for Key Stage 1 assessment followed the receipt of the necessary information in the 1992 spring term and was implemented without problems except that the computer system for collating results introduced by the LEA failed to work, leaving the deputy with the unexpected task of doing the job manually. The existing bilingual and cultural assistants and home-school liaison officers were assimilated to the same roles within the new LEA Section 11 project. They met with the head at the beginning of the 1992 summer term to agree on their work, and the equal opportunities coordinator took charge of minority ethnic group support staff.

Work on technology took place according to schedule within the 1990/91 development plan, with a training day in the spring term being followed by a 'design and technology week' in the summer. All pupils except those in reception classes were given an opportunity to work in the smaller of the two halls set out with materials and tools. They tackled tasks at different levels connected with the theme 'My Teddy Bear'. The science coordinator was released for the week to work with the teacher of each class, so combining a learning experience for the pupils with professional development support for staff. An open evening for parents was held in which an LEA advisory teacher explained the rationale for technology in the curriculum, pupils' work was displayed, and children talked about what they had done.

There were some ninety-eight appeals from parents whose children would no longer be living within the redefined catchment area under reorganization, but many parents eventually opted for the school in whose catchment area they would be. The head agreed to take the twenty-two pupils whose parents had persisted with their appeal. Staff morale suffered because some individuals failed to gain the post they wanted and others were redeployed to other schools. The head spent much time counselling staff and, by the end of the 1992 summer term, felt ready to take on the challenge of capitalizing on the staff shake-up to regenerate development work towards her vision of good practice. Some of the most competent teachers would remain and a new, dynamic language coordinator was due to join the staff. The head planned to talk about her educational beliefs and values with the new staff at the three training days set aside for reorganized school staffs to begin planning for the future. She intended to set development work on language and physical education in train.

## Link with flexible planning

Cyclic planning operated to some extent, partial delegation within LMS going smoothly, but staff changes under reorganization inhibited work in some areas to implement changes within the National Curriculum. Spasmodic changes in information relating to the return to the refurbished site repeatedly dictated a top-priority response which delayed the consultation and planning exercise within the development planning initiative. The reorganization date marked the end point of planning until it became clear right at the end of the 1992 summer term who the new staff would be.

Spasmodic changes in information about external innovations, from the computerized recording system failure within Key Stage 1 assessment to the protests from parents about the change in the catchment area, led to a planned response through the adjustment of existing plans. An implementation plan had to be created from scratch when the outcome of the inner-city bid was learned and staff were finally informed about the nature of the innovation.

The head was forced to plan reactively as circumstances changed, biding her time until she could take a more proactive stance with new staff of the reorganized school. She monitored the evolving situation continually and adjusted short-term plans as necessary. As with Southside, the possibility of creating medium- to long-term plans was curtailed by the reorganization date but, as the head was expecting to continue after reorganization, she prepared to launch new development initiatives from September 1992. Cyclic, spasmodic and continual components of the flexible planning model were in evidence, although spasmodic changes in information about external innovations, coupled with the advent of reorganization, dictated a strong emphasis on short-term responsive planning.

## FLEXIBLE PLANNING VERSUS DEVELOPMENT PLANNING

Planning in each of the case-study schools reflected a different proportion of the three components of the flexible planning model, many of the factors promoting turbulence discussed in Chapters 3 and 7 being connected with the spasmodic component which demanded a planned response at any point during the year. Although some schools experienced more turbulence than others, even in the county schools - where cyclic planning was most highly developed - not all planning for change could be encompassed within an annual cycle. While the DES advice (see Chapter 1) allows for modification to implementation plans within priorities identified at the audit and plan-construction stages, each school was involved in creating or responding to externally dictated new priorities after the plan had been compiled.

Moreover, the advised restriction on the number of priorities within the county and city LEA development planning initiatives meant that additional priorities, already existing when the development plan was compiled, were dealt with alongside and largely independently of the development plans. While it seems sound advice in principle for school staff to choose to restrict the number of priorities for development at any time so that the capacity of staff for managing change is not overreached, it may not always be possible to fend off external pressures for change and unpredictable crises and issues which may arise at any time, bringing the total number of priorities well beyond the recommended maximum for development planning.

The potentially more comprehensive development plans in the borough schools succumbed to new priorities which halted the cyclic development planning process itself. Even if this process had continued, the spasmodic changes in information about external innovations (including the innovation of LMS, based on an annual cycle), and other crises and issues which subsequently occurred, would have forced new priorities to be created. The findings support our contention that a major limitation of development plans based on annual cycles in turbulent environments lies in the lack of a procedure for occasionally creating new priorities and dropping existing priorities whenever changing circumstances give rise to the need. Put bluntly, development planning based on annual cycles is too inflexible to provide a comprehensive framework for managing planning in highly turbulent times.

## Flexibility versus coherence

Nevertheless, the headteachers in our study exercised some degree of choice in determining how planning for change was carried out. We saw in Chapter 5 how they retained considerable power to orchestrate the management of planning. It seems probable that a cyclic approach to development planning could have been sustained in the borough schools, for example, encompassing assessment and the sub-innovations connected with the National Curriculum which were implemented according to the central government timetable based on the academic year. Yet in all six schools, to the degree that the spasmodic stimuli for responsive planning occurred, the content of plans affected had to be addressed through a more iterative process of creation and adjustment.

The flexible planning model includes contingency planning - considering a range of possibilities and alternative plans - as one way of retaining flexibility which incurs the heavy time and energy cost of planning for various eventualities, not all of which will actually take place. We found only a little evidence of contingency planning, highlighted in the borough schools where both heads considered a range of possibilities when planning the allocation of staffing and classes for the following year.

While the prevalence of spasmodic stimuli points to the need to retain flexibility through the capacity for rapid response to changing circumstances, the contradictory pressure for the formulation of a design setting out a sequence of prespecified changes was also present in all cases. Both development planning and LMS were major innovations based on annual cycles which were part of the planning process itself, the introduction of National Curriculum subjects and assessment followed the academic year, and Section 11 projects were based on three to five financial years. Since cyclic innovations were built into the policy context for schools, the cyclic component of flexible planning (which is almost the exclusive focus of development planning) was bound to be present. No staff abandoned cyclic planning altogether.

It seems likely that planning according to two overlapping cycles is here to stay in so far as LMS becomes institutionalized and the financial information necessary for cyclic operation of the budgeting cycle is made available, and the academic year continues to be the basis for organizing staffing, classes, the curriculum and assessment. Overlap with the academic year imposed spasmodic changes affecting existing priorities and the budget which were largely addressed, as the DES advice allows, by adjustment within the grand design set at the beginning of the financial year.

In Chapter 2 we hypothesized that the relationship between cyclic planning and rapid response to changing circumstances is dialectical, a heavy emphasis on the one tending to give rise to the other. The clearest evidence of such a dialectic was where spasmodic changes in information about external innovations based on annual cycles occurred and where changes in other innovations, crises or issues had implications for plans within the financial and academic year, leading to responsive adjustments.

There was little evidence of the converse: a surfeit of rapid-response planning leading to a greater emphasis on annual cycles. We speculate that this effect would be most likely to happen where the environment was stable enough for a heavy reliance on cyclic planning to be feasible and where heads chose to plan on a day-to-day basis, without restricting the range of priorities. None of our case-study schools was in such a position. The only hint of such an effect was reported at Northedge, where several teachers commented how in the past the head had repeatedly stimulated new school-based initiatives and earlier ones were not always followed through. These respondents felt that ideally fewer changes should be addressed over a longer period of time.

The flexible planning model implies that, at any time, plans will exist along a dimension from the short to the long term, becoming broader and less operational the further into the future they are made. We described in Chapter 5 how the heads each worked towards realizing their 'philosophy', a set of educational and managerial beliefs and values which were long-term in the sense that they were both at the level of broad principle and unchanging. A set of aims for each school had been agreed with staff, often some years in the past, to which heads expected staff to give allegiance. Of the three LEA development planning initiatives, only the county one required staff to specify outline priorities as far ahead as three years, although this idea was also encouraged in the borough scheme. There was evidence in the county schools' development plans that such medium- to long-term priorities were being selected.

As we noted above, staff in the borough and city schools were unable to formulate priorities beyond the anticipated reorganization date which, as it drew closer, restricted plans to the ever shorter term. The postponement of reorganization in the borough pushed this limitation back somewhat, but staff were aware that any changes prior to the new reorganization date would be temporary. At the point where fieldwork ended, of the four borough and city schools only the head at Northedge was expecting to be in a position to begin engaging with staff and governors in developing a long-term vision for the reorganized school. The flexible planning model does not allow for extreme circumstances where the prospect of radical change entailing massive staff turnover and a shift in the pupil age range at a known date blocks the possibility of longer-term planning. Headteachers' beliefs and values and agreed school aims are likely to remain in the run-up to such a change, but not any substantive long-term plans.

We conclude that the flexible planning model did encompass the practice of planning for change in all six schools, but that the balance between its components differed according to the prevalence of factors promoting turbulence which produced changes in information requiring a more or less immediate planned response. Cyclic development planning helped to stabilize the situation in each school, but only in respect of the innovations forming priorities and only where they were not subject to radical alteration.

How effective were the approaches to planning for change adopted in the schools? Moving from a conceptual framework for describing the practice of planning for change in a turbulent environment within six schools, which the flexible planning model provides, to a prescription for practice elsewhere is another story which we take up in the final chapter.

# Chapter 9

# Towards Effective Planning for Turbulent Times

Planning for change in the rapidly evolving context we have described is a complex phenomenon whose understanding requires complex analysis. Teasing out what works best and under what conditions is an even more complex task for a qualitative study of medium size, and much of what can be stated is tentative. So what have we learned?

Innovations and other changes requiring a planned response drove the process of planning for change. A network of factors embracing the school, local and national levels of the education system was shown to affect the balance of internal and external environmental turbulence and stability in the schools we studied. This shifting balance, ever tilted towards the turbulent, dictated that planning for change consisted of *all three* components encompassed by the model of flexible planning: continual, spasmodic and cyclic. Highly significant were the factors leading to spasmodic changes in information about external innovations and, to a lesser extent, crises and issues that forced the process of planning for change to include more or less continual creation, monitoring and adjustment of plans.

One important influence on how planning for change was carried out was the framework offered by development planning. This innovation was designed to bring greater stability into a potentially very turbulent environment by fostering collective work on a limited number of agreed priorities. It was endorsed by central government as a framework for coping with the implementation of multiple changes which encompassed government requirements for plans based on annual cycles related to its national reform agenda. The form which development planning was to take was shaped by LEA staff as a means, in part, of fulfilling their duties to support the introduction of national reforms and to monitor the quality of education provision in their schools, leading in two out of three LEAs to the annual completion of a development plan document which was submitted to LEA staff.

Development planning was based upon sequential annual cycles, according to the implicit assumption that the environment was stable enough to permit development priorities to be identified and updated but once a year. This assumption proved true where innovations were introduced according to a prearranged cyclic timetable. In the county and city schools the process did guide planning for such innovations, and at Highway the priorities identified continued to be a prompt for senior staff long after the process had been abandoned. The question was raised by some senior school staff over how far development planning was necessary, however desirable, given that they were already aware of the agenda and timetable for national reforms that largely constituted their priorities in the plans, and would have planned for their implementation anyway.

Development planning was palliative, but no panacea for dealing with multiple changes. The assumption of relative environmental stability proved false in so far as factors promoting turbulence led to spasmodically shifting circumstances which, in turn, forced other priorities to be addressed, with consequent adjustment of priorities within the development plan. In this respect, the cyclic model of development planning was, perhaps, hyperrational: it did not allow for the evolutionary nature of some changes driving the planning process, in contrast with the more comprehensive flexible planning model which allowed for nonrational interruptions to cyclic planning and alternative, more flexible procedures. On the other hand, the latter model did not allow for the extreme situation of preparing for school reorganization where there was a cut-off date beyond which it was impossible to plan until the new staff had been assembled.

A second assumption underpinning development planning was that sufficient control over whether to adopt changes existed at the school level for the number of priorities to be limited (in two LEAs to a prespecified number). This innovation promised more than it could deliver in a turbulent environment: staff in all the case-study schools were forced to modify the annual procedure or to plan for other changes independently of the development plan in response to these spasmodic factors. Control over development at school level did not extend to choice over externally imposed innovations and, realistically, to those which were technically optional but offered much needed resources. Nor did it cover the need to respond to the few major crises and issues that beset a few schools. The external change agenda effectively limited choice over school-based innovations because it was so considerable as to overreach staff capacity for managing change: of the case-study schools only Highway engaged in a major school-based initiative, and that was completed within a term.

LEA development planning initiatives constituted a major, complex, interrelated (and in two LEAs compulsory) innovation at both LEA and school levels. As such, their implementation in schools was a component of the network of factors giving rise to environmental turbulence as staff learned how to integrate the process and document into their practice. The consultative review and planning process and completion of the document constituted a priority for which staff time had to be provided, in two LEAs at a particular point in the year. Although LEA staff had to operate within parameters set by central government policies for both LEAs and schools, they did exercise choice, as both change agents and users, over the scope of the initiatives. Opting for school development planning (rather than a more restricted National Curriculum development plan) and deciding upon the scope of the initiatives were both LEA decisions. Discretion extended to design features, such as whether to have a document, to restrict the number of priorities, or to specify a particular annual cycle; and to implementation strategies, including whether to make the initiative compulsory, when to introduce or to modify it, and whether to consult school staff about the design or to give feedback on completed documents. The form and timing of the initiatives led to differential impact in the schools, evidence of institutionalization being confined to the county.

Discretion was also exercised at school level within the varied parameters set by LEAs and central government policies. Headteachers were the most influential figures, with greatest - though not exclusive - power to orchestrate the management of planning, including planning for change. They were both change agents for and users of innovations which were part of the planning process, including development planning and LMS. They found room to manoeuvre in shaping the process of planning within these parameters, and finding a place for development planning within it, according to their managerial beliefs and values. Their potency was assisted by a generally large measure of acceptance and support among other constituencies, especially governors and other staff. Heads' choices included how far to commit the school to development planning or to other ways of managing planning; whom to consult over what and whether to bound any consultation; the structure of meetings and working parties; arrangements for disseminating information and internal monitoring; and the implementation strategy for development planning.

Equally, they were influential in shaping the content of plans within externally imposed parameters, and the effort to implement them, according to their managerial and educational beliefs and values. The co-opting of National Curriculum subjects into the existing approach to topic work, the emphasis on multicultural and antiracist initiatives, whether to accede to the views of parents on teaching methods and pupil discipline, how far to adopt the spirit or the letter of the law on religious education and collective worship - all were pivotally dependent upon the headteachers' philosophy and pragmatic concerns.

The power of headteachers was enhanced to the extent that they had successfully orchestrated the development of a mutually supportive staff subculture with widely shared managerial and educational beliefs and values which included the acceptance of change as a normal part of professional life. Conversely, staff who supported the head were empowered to participate in the management of planning for change and so influence the content of plans within the head's parameters. Staff empowered the head where they accepted and contributed fully to the planning process, made a sustained effort to implement agreed changes, and took initiatives that were acceptable to the head.

## EFFECTIVE PLANNING FOR CHANGE

Defining - let alone identifying - effectiveness is less straightforward than it may at first appear. A useful starting point is provided by Hopkins (1987), who suggests that effective schools accomplish the best possible learning and social outcomes for pupils, with least wastage of pupil talent possible, and with the most efficient use of means. Within a context of multiple, largely externally imposed changes we may expect that effective schools implement the required innovations successfully which, if the promise of their design is realized in practice, leads to improved learning and social outcomes.

Given the multiplicity of demands upon a limited staff capacity to manage change, we may also assume that *effective planning for change leads to the most focused effort possible to implement the most important innovations, with the least possible wastage of staff talent, and with the most efficient use of resources*. In other words, effectiveness refers both to the process and the content of plans. The logic behind this definition is that effective planning for change leads to effective implementation of innovations, leading to better management, better teaching and, ultimately, better pupil learning. In short, effective planning for change leads to school improvement - the argument of many advocates of development planning. The causal chain is depicted in Figure 9.1.

At least four problems arise for research which attempts to track the connections between cause and effect. First, the multiplicity of demands for change reflect contradictory educational and managerial values, and effectiveness is therefore a value-laden concept. Effective planning for change implies that the content and process are valued. It is not simply a technical matter which changes are selected, how far they are implemented in accordance with the configuration of their designers, or the degree to which affected parties contribute to decision-making. We saw how headteachers led staff in assimilating National Curriculum subjects within their existing approach to topic work. According to HMI (Office for Standards in Education, 1993), an 'over-reliance on topic work', as opposed to single-subject teaching, is bad news. Whose values are to count - those of staff or HMI?

The possible value positions connected with the content and process of planning for change are illustrated in Figure 9.2. To an HMI, the above example might constitute Position 2: a valued planning process for a content which was not valued. Position 1 would be more in accord with the view of heads in our case-study schools. In so far as our consideration of effective planning for change may have practical implications for planners at school level, the critical variable is the effectiveness of the planning *process*. Possible value divergences affecting judgements of effectiveness include which constituencies should be enabled to contribute to the process or how far consultation should be open or bounded.

Second, it is difficult to prove that an effect was caused by the previous link in the chain, let alone a putative cause several links away. Brilliant planning may fall foul of ineffective teaching; ineffective planning may be compensated for by brilliant teaching.

Third, values apply to the quantity, quality, degree of imposition and strategy for the introduction of planning inputs and their accompanying resources. We cited two schools in our survey where it appeared to be impossible to plan coherently because of the lack of control at school level over the inputs. It is a matter of judgement whether planning for change could be expected to be more effective under such conditions of overloading and under-resourcing. Was the external agenda for change unreasonable for even the most effective planning process?

Fourth, the planning process was itself subject to externally imposed changes, especially development planning and LMS. In the county and the city, compulsory development planning led to the identification of priorities which were dominated by the national reforms. Heads in both LEAs pointed out that they were aware of this agenda and the development plan was not necessary - though more or less desirable - for planning to implement them. The borough schools worked on similar priorities whether or not they had a development

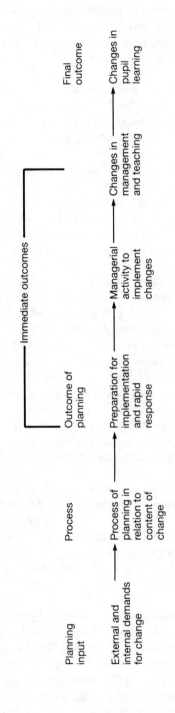

**Figure 9.1** *Planning for change: the causal chain of effectiveness*

| Planning input | Process | Immediate outcomes | | Final outcome |
|---|---|---|---|---|
| External and internal demands for change | Process of planning in relation to content of change | Outcome of planning | Preparation for implementation and rapid response → Managerial activity to implement changes | Changes in pupil learning |

Planning process

|  | Valued | Not valued |
|---|---|---|

|  | Valued | 1 | 3 |
|---|---|---|---|
| Planning content | | | |
| Not valued | 2 | 4 |

Figure 9.2 *Values and effectiveness in planning for change*

plan. For many of the schools in our study this procedure for managing planning was employed because external agents had promoted it or insisted upon the development plan being completed. It may not have been the approach for which staff would have opted, given choice over what might be most effective in their circumstances. The head at Highway had not been constrained from returning to her existing flexible, short- to medium-term approach when the turbulence became too much.

We are therefore wary of being over-ambitious in considering effectiveness and have confined our inferences to the relationship between the inputs and outputs of planning for change, as Figure 9.1 highlights. Demands for new practices arise from outside and inside the school, forming the input to planning for change. The planning process leads to planning outcomes which amount to preparedness for various activities connected with managing change. These intermediate outcomes are directed towards the processes of making most efficient use of resources and implementing better teaching of a better curriculum, in the hope of leading to the final outcome of improved pupil learning.

## Performance indicators

Given these caveats, it is possible to draw inferences about approaches to planning for change that work in a turbulent environment. The views of headteachers and a small number of their staff were sought on whether each case-study school had improved in recent years and on the effectiveness of the school and the approach to planning. There was consensus that the schools had improved, that they were generally effective and that planning was reasonably effective within difficult circumstances.

The evidence on which these judgements were based was largely impressionistic, matching the light-touch approach to monitoring reported in

Chapter 5. At Highway and Heartlands an indicator of improvement was that the schools were becoming more popular with parents. Five of the schools had been inspected in some way (see Table 5.2) within the last three years, and reports had generally been favourable. However, only two inspections were on a large enough scale to make it possible to go into great depth. The Key Stage 1 SAT scores were reviewed in the five case-study schools where SATs were carried out, but at this time school-by-school results were not published so staff did not have this means of comparing outcomes with other institutions. Some harder evidence of pupil learning outcomes was available in the city schools, where the LEA administered an annual reading test for 7-year-olds. Both schools were reported to have achieved quite high scores when the characteristics of the intake were taken into account, and the scores were rising each year.

In making judgements on the effectiveness of their approach to planning, staff commented favourably on several features, such as the system at Southside for keeping staff informed about externally initiated changes. We developed a set of performance indicators for aspects of the process and outcomes of planning for change, in the light of these comments and other interim findings. We tried them out in some of the schools within interviews held towards the end of our fieldwork. These performance indicators are listed in Table 9.1. Some apply also to planning for maintenance which, as we highlighted in Chapter 7, was much affected by planning for change. The responses from staff, not surprisingly, were consistent with the data we had gathered by other means. Examples included satisfaction with procedures for managing planning (process indicator 5) at Southside, tempered by the fact that the separate weekly staff meetings for the lower and upper school staff meant that one group of staff was often uncertain what members of the other group thought about a particular issue; and contrasting perceptions at Heartlands over the balance the head provided between setting a direction and consulting staff (process indicator 3).

The list has the status of hypotheses emerging from our analysis, but it tallies well with the themes associated with successful implementation of innovations in North American schools discussed in Chapter 2. Process indicator 3, for example, implies that heads have a *vision* against which demands for change are assessed which is *shared* and open to question, so assuming the *empowerment* of other constituencies. Numbers 7 and 10 imply *monitoring and problem-coping* through responsive, evolutionary planning. Number 9 indicates serious consideration being given to the *staff development and resource assistance* required to implement planned changes.

These performance indicators may be used as a checklist for school staff reviewing their approach to planning for change, with one proviso. A danger with performance indicators as a practical guide is that they can be interpreted in an atomistic and mechanistic manner, as if a valid assessment could be made by, say, adding up the number of indicators judged to be in place. These indicators must be taken together, since some are checks and balances for others. For example, process indicators 3 and 4 relate to each other. If heads do too much filtering of external demands for change, other staff and governors

**Table 9.1** Performance indicators for planning for change

---

*The planning process*

1 There are efficient arrangements for sorting and disseminating documentary information coming into the school.

2 There are efficient arrangements for disseminating information picked up by staff responsible for particular innovations.

3 In making major decisions about changes the head provides a balance between setting a direction and taking into account the views of staff and governors.

4 The head filters external demands for change in order to protect staff from innovation overload.

5 There is a clear set of structures, roles and procedures for managing planning, including delegation of planning tasks and provision of time.

6 The effectiveness of these structures, roles and procedures is monitored.

7 Staff respond quickly by reviewing and modifying priorities whenever the need arises and communicating with those who need to know.

8 Plans for change lead to sustained action to implement them.

9 Plans for change take into account staff development needs and the resources required.

10 The implementation of plans is monitored.

*Outcomes of planning*

11 Staff are clear about current aims of the school, policies, priorities, arrangements for implementing changes, and their role in contributing to planning.

12 Staff and governors feel adequately consulted while not overburdened with planning activity.

13 Staff are protected from innovation overload.

14 Staff are not taken by surprise by new demands that are within the school's capacity to avoid.

15 Responsive action is taken when monitoring of planning indicates that it is required.

16 Staff receive support when they identify a need in relation to managing planning and to the implementation of particular changes.

17 Where there are consultative groups such as working parties they complete their tasks on time.

---

may not be satisfied that heads have struck a good balance between setting a direction and taking into account their views. They also link directly with outcome indicators 12-14: whether staff and governors feel adequately consulted, are protected from overload as far as is feasible in a context of high external compulsion, and avoid receiving unnecessary nasty surprises depends on how far the head keeps them informed, consults them and demonstrably takes their views into account.

Used holistically, these indicators enable the judgements of people at different levels within a school to be checked against each other, and direct attention towards particular sources of evidence for these judgements. Process indicator 3 invites questions to be asked of each constituency about who is involved in setting the direction for change; indicators 8 and 10 invite the search for evidence of the existence of procedures for monitoring both the effectiveness of planning arrangements and progress with the implementation of planned changes.

The performance indicators are not associated with particular practices, whether development planning procedures or flipchart lists. It would be presumptive to assume that any of the detailed practices in our case-study schools could be the one best way of doing the job in the varying contexts of other schools. The approaches reported in this book are, however, a source of practical ideas to try or to avoid, depending on local circumstances.

## A necessary condition for effectiveness?

Our findings provided abundant evidence that one overriding necessity was a planned response to spasmodic changes in circumstances caused by factors giving rise to internal and external environmental turbulence which, quite often, could not be predicted at school level. It seems inconceivable that, where the operation of such factors compels a planned response to be made, effective planning for change would not include rapid-response procedures. Even our schools most wedded to the most comprehensive form of development planning were not exempt from the *ad hoc* addition of priorities and updating of existing plans. Chapter 8 illustrated how the number of compulsory and technically optional external innovations ensured that staff in those schools whose development plans put a prespecified limit on the number of priorities had to work on other priorities for change outside the plan. Development planning, as currently conceived, seems limited in its potential as a framework for managing planning in schools facing a high level of turbulence because it pays insufficient attention to the factors which dictate a flexible response.

On the other hand, development planning is strong on planning according to sequential annual cycles which are likely to be a feature of any school context, not least because of planning for maintenance requirements connected with the academic and calendar years. In the United Kingdom, LMS looks as if it is here to stay and planning according to the financial year will be equally necessary wherever LMS initiatives are institutionalized. Effective planning for change, even where the environment remains as turbulent as it was for our study schools, will have to work within at least two overlapping annual cycles.

Therefore, we conclude that structures and procedures which offer a working reconciliation of the tension between cyclic planning for long-term coherence and continual, responsive planning for short-term flexibility are a necessary condition for effectiveness in planning for change in turbulent times. We suggested the possibility in Chapter 2 that schools may accord with the finding of Burns and Stalker that an organizational response to an increase in environmental turbulence may result in separate structures and procedures for dealing with maintenance and development activity. Development planning in our case-study schools may be interpreted as offering a 'mechanistic' framework, dealing admirably with demands that fitted within the annual cycle. Alternative 'organic' means of dealing with demands that did not comply with the development planning framework were dealt with alongside and compartmented off from it except, to some extent, at Central. Here the half-yearly review and updating provided an opportunity to integrate the two procedures.

A key challenge for schools, as long as external pressure for reform continues to create such turbulence, is to orchestrate the management of planning so as more fully to integrate cyclic and rapid-response planning. Our assumption that the influences of coherence and flexibility are contradictory implies that any attempt to create a simple blueprint for managing planning would be hyperrational pie in the sky.

Conversely, should the context of schooling become more stable, the hypothesis put forward in Chapter 2 (and not tested in this study) is that both cyclic and more incremental approaches may be effective. If this assumption proves correct, the practical implication is that greater reliance on cyclic planning would be both feasible and advisable where parameters for planning are based on such cycles. Cyclic development planning linked with LMS seems to have greater potential as a comprehensive framework guiding planning for change in more tranquil times.

## IMPLICATIONS OF THE RESEARCH

How far is it possible to generalize from our findings to support the implications for various audiences that we wish to highlight? As outlined in Chapter 1, the project was not designed to provide a representative picture of the national situation, even in respect of multiracial primary schools. Its findings cannot, in themselves, be taken as representative of a general case. Two considerations suggest that we did not select a unique set of LEAs and schools.

First, the national policy context determined to a large extent the external demands for change, heavily influencing LEA interventions. Many demands including the National Curriculum were shared among all schools, although multiracial primary schools were faced with additional changes, most notably the Section 11 bidding process. The demands of reorganization were not restricted to such schools, nor did they affect all schools across the country. While we sought the most turbulent contexts likely to be found among schools in England at the time, other schools and LEAs were dealing with many similar factors giving rise to turbulence and stability. Second, as we have indicated throughout this book, other research and inspection evidence is available which enables some of our findings to be located within trends established by other researchers. Although it was not a generalizable study, supporting evidence suggests that it is legitimate to highlight implications of the findings for others.

### Implications for researchers

The study linked one type of environment with planning for change. We did not find a school where high turbulence was unaccompanied by responsive planning between consultative review and planning exercises with development planning initiatives. Nor did we examine the range of approaches in reasonably stable environments. Work in other types of organization, say secondary schools, in the United Kingdom and in other national policy contexts, would enable a more sophisticated understanding to be achieved of the factors influencing the balance of turbulence and stability and their effect on planning for change.

The flexible planning model is based upon a theoretical assumption that the social world is nonrational in many respects, but still ordered enough to be subject to a form of rational planning which lives with a contradiction, rather than attempting to rationalize a way round it. There seems scope for much further theory-building within the paradigm for which Wise (1983) so cogently argued.

Much is known, mainly from extensive North American research, about the process of implementing single innovations, but the impact of multiple innovations on the change process has been insufficiently studied. Fullan notes how:

> This single innovation perspective largely reflects the lessons learned from the 1970s and early 1980s, and can be very useful for examining individual innovations. The broader reality is, of course, that schools are in the business of contending with *multiple innovations*.
>
> (1991, p. 49)

Little work has yet been done either on the ways innovations, other changes and the rest of ongoing work in schools interact, or on how an evolving innovation profile is managed. The dimensions defined in Chapter 2 and explored in Chapter 7 demonstrate how pervasive an influence on planning for change multiple innovations, together with responses to unplanned crises or issues, can be. This seems a promising line of enquiry, not least because few schools have the luxury of addressing one innovation at a time, and even individual innovations are likely to impinge on other work.

Another area worthy of further exploration is the causal link between development planning and school culture. Our evidence, along with that of others (Constable *et al.*, 1991), raises a chicken and egg question over how far a culture with norms of collaboration and continuous improvement (Fullan, 1991) is necessary for full engagement in development planning or whether development planning is the paradigm case of a school improvement strategy which transforms the staff professional subculture, as Hopkins (1992) contends. We suspect that there is a two-way connection and, if so, the practical problem remains in many schools over how simultaneously to transform this culture and to plan and implement changes effectively. A major study of development planning in primary schools currently under way (Mortimore *et al.*, forthcoming), which includes a focus on school culture, seems likely to shed light on this issue.

## Implications for school-level practitioners

Headteachers (as key orchestrators of the management of planning) and governors will find food for thought in many of our findings. Among the most significant practical questions are:

- How far may structures and procedures for rapid response planning be incorporated as an integral and routine part of the framework for managing planning?
- Could development planning be adapted so that a feasible review and updating procedure is put in place whenever changing circumstances give rise to the need to reconsider current priorities or to adopt new ones?

- What updating information about changes - and changes in the changes - needs to be communicated to whom and by what means?
- How far should headteachers adopt a consultative management style which extends to the management of planning and when is it not appropriate to consult?
- What part should governors play in the planning process and what are the advisable limits to their involvement, given constraints of time and lack of professional knowledge?
- Over what changes should each parent be consulted rather than relying upon their representatives on the governing body?
- How far should efforts be made to develop and sustain an emphasis on equal opportunities, multicultural and antiracist education in a context of declining external support, especially from central government?
- How much account should be taken of wishes expressed by parents when they conflict with professional beliefs and values of staff?

In addition, the practical relevance of the rules of thumb for flexible planning listed in Table 9.2 and developed as an outcome of the earlier multiple-innovations project (Wallace, 1991d) is confirmed by our present study. They suggest that a healthy cynicism about the policies and implementation strategies of external agencies should be cultivated, and that living with ambiguity and the tension between coherence and flexibility is a normal way of life in primary-sector schools.

## Implications for LEA policymakers

At the time of writing it is unclear whether LEAs will continue to exist, at least in some areas of the United Kingdom, for much longer. It is already evident that their role is becoming one of providing services at the behest of schools, rather than being the policymakers that so many were at the time of our fieldwork. Where such a role continues, a key consideration for staff in many LEAs is whether to carry on using development planning for schools to fulfil accountability purposes. Freeing up the process from the annual round of information-gathering that completion of documents represents may improve the potential of development planning as a framework for managing planning for change. Only the information needed for planning at school level need be collected, it may be gathered whenever it is required by school staff, and much of it need not be written down.

Designers of development planning initiatives for schools may usefully consider whether it is worth prespecifying a limit to the number of priorities being addressed in any year while external compulsion to implement multiple changes remains high. Equally, it seems worth holding on to the notion of prioritizing and avoiding, where possible, taking on too many changes. HMI (1992b) noted the tendency of some school development plans to be over-ambitious. The advocated process could be supplemented by adding regular and

**Table 9.2** Rules of thumb for flexible planning

---

**Do**

- articulate a long-term vision as a focus for development in school;
- periodically consult widely and seek consensus on priorities for change;
- expect to alter priorities, associated targets and plans for action;
- arrange a flexible procedure which is economic of time for regular review of plans for change and for responding whenever necessary to changing circumstances;
- frequently update and extend the period covered by detailed plans;
- keep those who need to know informed about detailed changes in plans and avoid telling those who don't need to know;
- actively seek information about externally initiated changes from as wide a range of sources as possible;
- take into account the capacity of staff to cope with more changes or modifications to existing plans;
- consider the risk of wasted work if the decision is taken to make changes to existing practice before the final details are known about external innovations;
- make contingency plans (without going into great detail) where it seems possible that existing plans may require modification;
- consider the likelihood of being held to account for external innovations which are not implemented as their instigators intended: much legislation is not realistically enforcible and the adaptation of innovations may become accepted as normal practice.

**Don't**

- plan in detail further ahead at any time than seems feasible, given the possibility of unpredictable changes;
- generate more written plans than are needed for coherence: much may be kept in the head and communicated orally;
- worry about living with confusion and ambiguity: most issues will be clarified in time;
- let immediate responses to crises take the place of attempting to retain a coherent direction for development;
- take any policy statement or information about it for granted.

---

Based on Wallace (1991d, pp. 45–6).

*ad hoc* rapid-response review and updating procedures to build in greater flexibility.

## Implications for national policymakers

We come finally to those whose reform agenda and strategy for implementation have caused so much turbulence in our case-study schools and LEAs. Our study showed how professional staff at school level still managed to find some room to manoeuvre to adapt external innovations according to beliefs and values which did not tally with those of policymakers, as in the retention of topic work and a multicultural orientation within the ethnocentric National Curriculum. HMI noted that 'despite the fact that primary schools are responding to an unprecedented degree of curriculum and other reforms, the culture of primary teaching has not changed overnight' (Office for Standards in Education, 1993).

The question arises over how far a government which has pledged to increase school autonomy (DFE, 1992) will have to accept that with autonomy may come diversity of a type that runs counter to the spirit of ministers' reforms. Between the passing of the 1988 Education Reform Act and the 1993 Education Act, the secretary of state will have taken a multitude of new powers to the centre of the education system. Even though the 1992 White Paper was entitled *Choice and Diversity*, the effect of many central government reforms has been to centralize control and foster diversity of a limited kind within centrally defined parameters. It is not clear whether central government will tolerate primary schools which express diversity of a type that would not meet with ministerial approval, such as a topic approach to the curriculum. At what point will tighter limits be imposed on school autonomy and diversity of schooling?

Political issues connected with the cultural diversity of multiracial schools and their community included the under-representation of people from minority ethnic groups on governing bodies and among teaching staff compared with the proportion of pupils. To what extent is the government prepared to facilitate greater involvement of people from minority ethnic groups in their children's education as governors and staff in schools? While we found little evidence of direct racism in our study schools, the continuing restriction under Section 11 funding of support to pupils from the New Commonwealth seems both anachronistic and institutionally racist within the definition offered in the Swann Report. Pupils from outside the New Commonwealth, principally refugees and children of students from overseas, who needed specialist help with learning English to give them access to their entitlement to the National Curriculum (guaranteed by the 1988 Education Reform Act) were ineligible for Section 11 funded support. Staff were faced with a Catch-22 situation: denying access to the National Curriculum or using Section 11 staff - their sole source of ESL expertise. Either way they were technically breaking the law. There seems to be a strong case for overhaul of this legislation. Since the research was completed a new factor has arisen which may result in increased institutional racism. It originates with central government but may be expressed through curtailment of local authority efforts funded through Section 11. In the light of its public expenditure survey of November 1992, central government announced that it could not afford the level of financial help with the Section 11 projects that had been agreed just a few months before (Yaseen, 1992). Accordingly, the Home Office contribution to Section 11 funded projects was reduced from April 1993, and is set to be cut further over the next two financial years. Given the other spending restrictions imposed upon local authorities by central government, it seems unlikely that local authorities will be able to increase their share of Section 11 support by the 72 per cent that Yaseen estimates will be necessary from 1995 to sustain projects at the level agreed in 1992. Tinkering with central government public expenditure policy may produce the side-effect of an even bleaker future for minority ethnic group support staff and their pupils: more than a thousand jobs in primary schools are likely to be under threat.

Although social disadvantage is not necessarily associated with people from minority ethnic groups, our fieldwork took us mainly to urban schools catering for pupils from both minority and majority ethnic groups - and in some cases parents - with urgent social and educational needs. Is it justifiable for central government to impose the greatest innovation load upon schools whose pupils and parents have the most pressing educational needs, so threatening their education and hence potential for social mobility? Will continuing such a practice favour the prime minister's (John Major's) vision of a 'classless society' or the perpetuation of an underclass?

There is evidence that implementation of the central government reforms during the period of our fieldwork had yet to bring the promised higher standards: 'There is little evidence yet of LMS having any substantial impact on educational standards, although specific initiatives have led to improvements in the targeting of resources and staff, and so to improvements in the quality of educational experience' (HMI, 1992a, p. 11). Office for Standards in Education (Ofsted) reports on the teaching of English, mathematics, science and technology during 1991/2 indicated a patchy picture of small increases and decreases in standards in Key Stages 1 and 2 (*Times Educational Supplement*, 1993). The study by Weston *et al.* (1992) revealed how the way in which the National Curriculum was divided into subjects and phased in year by year made it extremely difficult to plan for coherent curriculum provision at school level. Could more have been achieved?

The testimony of teachers at invitation seminars within a review of the National Curriculum suggests that implementation was hindered by the central government strategy for introducing this policy:

> Some of the concerns expressed at the seminars can reasonably be interpreted as teething problems inevitable in a period of curriculum reform. Teachers talked, for example, of the speed of implementation, the lack of teaching resources and the inadequacy of their own subject knowledge ... a systematic and focused programme of support would make a difference to the speed with which the situation improves.
>
> (NCC, 1993, p. 7)

Need such 'teething problems' be inevitable? Is it reasonable and, ultimately, effective to subject school staff to the teething problems connected with addressing simultaneously such a range of innovations as were reported in our study schools, with limited time to prepare or respond to spasmodic changes and with very limited resources? A period of greater stability would enable the innovation overload to be reduced to more manageable proportions, yet recent legislation, heralded in the White Paper as detailing 'the final stages of a great transformation of education', bears all the hallmarks of adding to the existing level of turbulence. Not least is the projected drive to remove surplus pupil places, which promises more reorganizations of the kind that confronted our borough and city schools. It remains to be seen whether (as the evidence of research suggests) the teething problems caused by the scale and pace of central government reforms will result in an education system for the twenty-first century which is without teeth.

# References

Alexander, R. (1992). *Policy and Practice in Primary Education*. London: Routledge.

Alexander, R., Rose, J. and Woodhead, C. (1992). *Curriculum Organisation and Classroom Practice in Primary Schools*. London: Department of Education and Science.

Arnott, M., Bullock, A. and Thomas, H. (1992). *The Impact of Local Management on Schools: A Source Book*. First Report of the 'Impact' Project. Birmingham: University of Birmingham School of Education for the National Association of Headteachers.

Audit Commission for Local Authorities and the National Health Service in England and Wales (1991). *Management within Primary Schools*. London: Her Majesty's Stationery Office.

Bacharach, S. and Lawler, E. (1980). *Power and Politics in Organizations*. San Francisco: Jossey-Bass.

Baginsky, M., Baker, L. and Cleave, S. (1991). *Towards Effective Partnerships in School Governance*. Slough: National Foundation for Educational Research.

Bagley, C. (1992). *Back to the Future*. Slough: National Foundation for Educational Research.

Berman, P. and McLaughlin, M. (1978). *Federal Programs Supporting Educational Change*, Vol. VIII: *Implementing and Sustaining Innovations*. Santa Monica, Calif.: Rand Corporation.

Bolam, R. (1975). 'The management of educational change: towards a conceptual framework', in Houghton, V., McHugh, R. and Morgan, C. (eds) *Management in Education*. London: Ward Lock.

Bolam, R. (1982). *Strategies for School Improvement*. Report for the Organisation for Economic Co-operation and Development. Bristol: University of Bristol School of Education.

Boyd, W. (1988). 'Policy analysis, educational policy and management: through a glass darkly?', in Boyan, N. (ed.) *Handbook of Research on Educational Administration*. New York: Longman.

Bradford Education (1992). *School Development Planning Handbook*. Bradford: Bradford Education Committee.

Brown, S. and Baker, L. (1991). *About Change - Schools' and LEAs' Perspectives on LEA Reorganisation*. Slough: National Foundation for Educational Research.

Burns, T. and Stalker, G.M. (1961). *The Management of Innovation*. London: Tavistock.

Caldwell, B. and Spinks, J. (1988). *The Self Managing School*. London: Falmer.

Caldwell, B. and Spinks, J. (1992). *Leading the Self Managing School*. London: Falmer.

Commission for Racial Equality (1988). *Ethnic Minority School Teachers: A Survey in Eight Local Education Authorities*. London: CRE.

Constable, H., Norton, J. and Abbott, I. (1991). *Case Studies in School Development Planning*. Sunderland: Centre for Post Experience and Research, Sunderland Polytechnic School of Education.

Conway, J. (1984). 'The myth, mystery, and mastery of participative decision making in education'. *Educational Administration Quarterly*, **20** (3), 11-40.

Cope, R. (1981). *Strategic Planning, Management and Decision Making*. Washington: Association for Higher Education.

Counselling and Career Development Unit (1992). *Coordination of Strategic and School Development Planning*. University of Leeds: CCDU.

Cunningham, W. (1982). *Systematic Planning for Educational Change*. Palo Alto, Calif.: Mayfield.

Davies, B. and Ellison, L. (1992). *School Development Planning*. Harlow: Longman.

Deal, T. (1985). 'The symbolism of effective schools'. *Elementary School Journal*, **85** (3), 601-20.

Department for Education (1992). *Choice and Diversity: A New Framework for Schools*. Cm 2021. London: Her Majesty's Stationery Office.

Department of Education and Science (1987). *Report by Her Majesty's Inspectors on LEA Provision for Education and the Quality of Response in Schools and Colleges in England 1986*. London: DES.

Department of Education and Science (1988a). *Education Support Grant*. Draft circular. London: DES.

Department of Education and Science (1988b). *Local Management of Schools*. Circular 7/88. London: DES.

Department of Education and Science (1988c). *School Governors: A Guide to the Law. County and Controlled Schools*. London: DES.

Department of Education and Science (1989a). *Planning for School Improvement*. London: DES.

Department of Education and Science (1989b). *Discipline in Schools*. Report of the Committee of Inquiry chaired by Lord Elton. London: Her Majesty's Stationery Office.

Department of Education and Science (1989c). *School Teachers' Pay and Conditions Document 1989*. London: Her Majesty's Stationery Office.

Department of Education and Science (1990). *Grants for Education Support and Training 1991-92*. Draft Circular. London: DES.

Department of Education and Science (1991a). *Development Planning: A Practical Guide*. London: DES.

Department of Education and Science (1991b). *The Education (Pupils' Attendance Records) Regulations 1991*. Circular 11/91. London: DES.

Department of Education and Science (1992). *Statistics of Schools 1991*. London: DES.

Enfield (1985). *Curriculum Initiatives Group: Supporting Institutional Development*. Mimeo. Enfield: London Borough of Enfield.

Flew, A. (ed.) (1979). *A Dictionary of Philosophy*. London: Pan.

Fullan, M. with Stiegelbauer, S. (1991). *The New Meaning of Educational Change*. London: Cassell.

Galton, M., Fogelman, K., Hargreaves, L. and Cavendish, S. (1991). *The Rural Schools Curriculum Enhancement National Evaluation (SCENE) Project: Final Report*. London: Department of Education and Science.

Gronn, P. (1986). 'Politics, power and the management of schools', in Hoyle, E. and McMahon, A. (eds). *The Management of Schools*. London: Kogan Page.

Hall, G. and Hord, S. (1987). *Change in Schools: Facilitating the Process*. Albany, NY: State University of New York Press.

Hanson, M. (1979). 'School management and contingency theory: an emerging perspective'. *Educational Administration Quarterly*, **15** (2), 98-116.

Hargreaves, D. and Hopkins, D. (1991). *The Empowered School*. London: Cassell.

Havelock, R.G. (1969). *Planning for Innovation through Dissemination and Utilization of Knowledge*. Ann Arbor, Mich.: Center for Research on Utilization of Scientific Knowledge, Institute for Social Research.

Her Majesty's Inspectorate (1992a). *The Implementation of Local Management of Schools*. London: Her Majesty's Stationery Office.

Her Majesty's Inspectorate (1992b). *Education Observed: The implementation of the Curricular Requirements of ERA. An Overview by HM Inspectorate on the Second Year*. London: Department for Education.

Home Office (1989). *A Scrutiny of Grants under Section 11 of the Local Government Act 1966*. London: Home Office.

Home Office (1990a). *Section 11 of the Local Government Act 1966*. Circular 78/1990. London: Home Office.

Home Office (1990b). *Section 11 of the Local Government Act 1966 Grant Administration Proposals*. Draft Circular. London: Home Office.

Home Office (1990c). *Section 11 of the Local Government Act 1966 Grant Administration: Policy Criteria*. London: Home Office.

Hopkins, D. (ed.) (1987). *Improving the Quality of Schooling*. Lewes: Falmer.

Hopkins, D. (1992). 'Self evaluation and development planning as strategies for school improvement'. Paper presented at the fourth research conference of the British Educational Management and Administration Society, University of Nottingham.

House of Commons (1985). *Education for All*. Report of the Committee of Inquiry into the Education of Children from Ethnic Minority Groups (The Swann Report). London: Her Majesty's Stationery Office.

House of Commons Education, Science and Arts Committee (1986). *Achievement in Primary Schools*. London: Her Majesty's Stationery Office.

Hutchinson, B. (1993). 'The effective reflective school: visions and pipedreams in development planning'. *Educational Management and Administration*, **21** (1), 4-18.

Inner London Education Authority (1977). *Keeping the School under Review*. London: ILEA.

Inner London Education Authority (1985). *Improving Primary Schools*. Report of the Committee of Enquiry chaired by Norman Thomas. London: ILEA.

Johnson, G. and Scholes, K. (1988). *Exploring Corporate Strategy* (2nd edn). London: Prentice-Hall.

Kast, F. and Rosenzweig, J. (eds) (1973). *Contingency Views of Organization and Management*. Chicago: Science Research Associates.

Katz, D. and Kahn, R.L. (1978). *The Social Psychology of Organizations* (2nd edn). New York: John Wiley.

Kaufman, R. and Herman, J. (1991). *Strategic Planning in Education*. Lancaster, Penn.: Technomic.

Keys, W. and Fernandes, C. (1990). *A Survey of School Governing Bodies* (2 vols). Slough: National Foundation for Educational Research.

Keys, W. and Fernandes, C. (1993). *What Do Students Think about School?* Report for the National Commission on Education. Slough: National Foundation for Educational Research.

Kogan, M. (1975). *Educational Policy Making*. London: Allen & Unwin.

Levine, D. and Liebert, R.E. (1987). 'Improving school improvement plans'. *Elementary School Journal*, **87** (4), 397-412.

Lewis, J. (1983). *Long Range and Short Range Planning for Educational Administrators*. Newton, Mass.: Allyn & Bacon.

Lindblom, C.E. (1959). 'The science of muddling through'. *Public Administration Review*, **19**, (2), 79-88.

Lindblom, C.E. (1979). 'Still muddling, not yet through'. *Public Administration Review*, **39**, 517-26.

Louis, K.S. and Miles, M. (1990). *Improving the Urban High School: What Works and Why*. New York: Teachers College Press.

Luffman, G., Sanderson, S., Lea, E. and Kenny, B. (1987). *Business Policy: An Analytical Introduction*. Oxford: Blackwell.

March, J. and Olsen, J. (eds) (1976). *Ambiguity and Choice in Organizations*. Bergen: Universitetsforlaget.

March, J. and Simon, H. (1958). *Organizations*. New York: John Wiley.

McMahon, A., Bolam, R., Holly, P. and Abbott, R. (1984). *Guidelines for Review and Internal Development in Schools*. Primary and Secondary School Handbooks. York: Longman for Schools Council.

Merriam, S. (1988). *Case Study Research in Education*. London: Jossey-Bass.

Miles, M. and Huberman, M. (1984). *Qualitative Data Analysis*. London: Sage.

Mortimore, P., MacGilchrist, B., Savage, J. and Beresford, C. (forthcoming). 'School development planning in primary schools: does it make a difference?', in Hargreaves, D. and Hopkins, D. (eds) *School Development Planning: A Progress Report*. London: Cassell.

National Audit Office (1991). *Repair and Maintenance of School Buildings*. London: Her Majesty's Stationery Office.

National Curriculum Council (1989). *The National Curriculum*. Mimeo. York: NCC.

National Curriculum Council (1993). *The National Curriculum at Key Stages 1 and 2*. York: NCC.

Nias, J., Southworth, G. and Yeomans, R. (1989). *Staff Relationships in the Primary School.* London: Cassell.

Nias, J., Southworth, G. and Campbell, P. (1992). *Whole School Curriculum Development in the Primary School.* London: Falmer.

Odden, R. (ed.) (1991). *Education Policy Implementation.* Albany, NY: State University of New York Press.

Office for Standards in Education (1993). *Curriculum Organisation and Classroom Practice in Primary Schools.* London: Ofsted.

Owen, D. (1992). *Ethnic Minorities in Great Britain: Settlement Patterns.* 1991 Census Statistical Paper No. 1. Warwick: Centre for Research in Ethnic Relations.

Patterson, J., Purkey, S. and Parker, J. (1986). *Productive School Systems for a Non-rational World.* Alexandria, Va: Association for Supervision and Curriculum Development.

Poulter, S. (1990). 'The religious education provisions of the Education Reform Act 1988'. *Education and the Law,* **2** (1), 1-11.

Rogers, E.M. and Shoemaker, F.F. (1971). *Communication of Innovations: A Cross-Cultural Approach.* New York: Free Press.

Sarason, S. (1971). *The Culture of the School and the Problem of Change.* Boston, Mass.: Allyn & Bacon.

Sarwar, G. (1991). *Proposals for Progress: British Muslims and Schools.* London: Muslim Educational Trust.

Sheffield Education Department (1991). *School Development Planning under LMS: A Guide for Schools.* Sheffield: Sheffield City Council.

Simon, H. (1947). *Administrative Behavior.* New York: Macmillan.

Simon, H. (1989). 'Making management decisions: the role of intuition and emotion', in Agor, W.H. (ed.) *Intuition in Organizations.* London: Sage.

Skelton, M., Reeves, G. and Playfoot, D. (1991). *Development Planning for Primary Schools.* Windsor: NFER-Nelson.

Steiner, G. (1979). *Strategic Planning: What Every Manager Must Know.* New York: Free Press.

Tansley, P. and Croft, A. (1984). 'Mother tongue teaching and support: a Schools Council Enquiry'. *Journal of Multilingual and Multicultural Development,* **5**, 368-84.

Taylor, M. (1991). *SACREs: Their Formation, Composition, Operation and Role on RE and Worship.* Slough: National Foundation for Educational Research.

Taylor, M. (1992). *Equality after ERA.* Slough: National Foundation for Educational Research.

*Times Educational Supplement* (1990). 'Science plans "best of a bad job" '. 14 December, 3.

*Times Educational Supplement* (1991a). 'Backlog of repairs "will get worse" '. 16 August, 4.

*Times Educational Supplement* (1991b). 'Ever smaller and more manageable'. 27 September, 10.

*Times Educational Supplement* (1993). 'New curriculum paying dividends'. 19 March, 4.

Wallace, M. (1991a). 'Coping with multiple innovations in schools'. *School Organization*, **11** (2), 187-209.

Wallace, M. (1991b). 'Contradictory interests in policy implementation: the case of LEA development plans for schools'. *Journal of Education Policy*, **6** (4), 385-99.

Wallace, M. (1991c). 'Flexible planning: a key to the management of multiple innovations'. *Educational Management and Administration*, **19** (3), 180-92.

Wallace, M. (1991d). 'Development plans: an LEA solution causing a primary school problem?'. *Education 3-13*, **19** (2), 39-46.

Wallace, M. and McMahon, A (1993). 'Ethnic minority support staff in primary schools: a deprofessionalised semi-profession?'. *School Organization*, **13** (3), 303-17.

Wallace, M. and Hall, V. (1994). *Inside the SMT: Teamwork in Secondary School Management*. London: Paul Chapman.

Warwickshire County Council (1991). *PRIDE (Process for the Review and Internal Development of Education) in Our Schools: An Aid to Development Planning*. Warwick: WCC.

Weindling, D. and Earley, P. (1987). *Secondary Headship: The First Years*. Windsor: NFER-Nelson.

Weiner, S. (1976). 'Participation, deadlines and choice', in March, J. and Olsen, J. (eds) *Ambiguity and Choice in Organisations*. Bergen: Universitetsforlaget.

Weston, P., Barrett, E. and Jamison, J. (1992). *The Quest for Coherence: Managing the Whole Curriculum 5-16*. Slough: National Foundation for Educational Research.

Wise, A. (1983). 'Why education policies often fail: the Hyperrationalization hypothesis', in Baldridge, V. and Deal, T. (eds) *The Dynamics of Organizational Change in Education*. Berkeley, Calif.: McCutchan.

Yaseen, M. (1993). 'Tears and fears for Section 11'. *Education*, 9 July, 30-1.

Young, K. and Connelly, N. (1981). *Policy and Practice in the Multiracial City*. London: Policy Studies Institute.

# Index

Index